THE BLACK MIGRANT ATHLETE

THE BLACK MIGRANT ATHLETE

Media, Race, and the Diaspora in Sports

MUNENE FRANJO MWANIKI

University of Nebraska Press

LINCOLN AND LONDON

Portions of chapters 2–4 previously appeared in "Reading
the Career of a Kenyan Runner: The Case of Tegla Loroupe,"
International Review for the Sociology of Sport 47, no. 4 (August
2012): 446–60, http://irs.sagepub.com/content/47/4/446.full.
pdf+html. Final, definitive version of this paper published by
SAGE Publications Ltd. All rights reserved. © Munene Franjo
Mwaniki.

Manufactured in the United States of America

∞

Library of Congress Control Number: 2017944082

Set in Minion Pro by John Klopping.

For Sarah

CONTENTS

Preface   ix

Acknowledgments   xv

Introduction: Black African Immigration to the West   1

1. Race and Sport: Situating the Black African Athlete   27

2. Everyday Othering: Boundary Making and Maintenance   48

3. Model Minorities: Origin Stories, Hard Workers, and
Humanitarians   72

4. "Bad" Blacks: Contingent Acceptance and Essentialized
Blackness   97

5. Immigrant Reception: Nationalism, Identity, Politics, and
Resistance   124

6. The Diasporic Athlete: Blackness and Meaning in the African
Diaspora   155

7. The Sporting Migrant: Antiblack Racism and the Foreign
Other   182

Appendix A: Methodology and Data-Gathering Procedures   191

Appendix B: Individuals in the Study   201

Notes   211

Bibliography   227

Index   239

PREFACE

This project was born out of my personal experiences in trying to make sense of the world and my place in it. I grew up, second-generation Kenyan on my father's side and fourth-generation Croatian on my mother's, in a small rural town in North Carolina. According to the 2015 census the county I grew up in is around 85 percent white and 2.5 percent black/African American. The county is named after Andrew Jackson and borders the Eastern Band of the Cherokee Reservation. In 2010 the black population was around 2 percent, rounding up, and things were not any more diverse decades earlier when I was a child. All of this to say that in the early nineties the only other black person, let alone African/Kenyan, I knew was my father. My father's family lived and still lives in Kenya, and while we visited when we had the money, I did not have consistent interaction with them until those who were my age came to the United States for college. My mother's big Croatian American family all lived and still live in and around Pittsburgh, Pennsylvania, which was at least a ten-hour drive away, so I saw them only once or twice a year.

Needless to say, I was rather racially and ethnically isolated from my extended family and within my rural town—both from anything African or Kenyan and from the very small local African American population. There were ten black students among the one thousand students in my high school. To escape this isolation—to see and feel like I was interacting with people who looked like me—I often turned to sport. I played sports, watched them, and even loved the early video games on my Nintendo and Super Nintendo. Sport and the explosion of hip-hop and rap culture offered ways of living, however constrained and forced by limited options, my blackness and masculinity. They offered something cool and youthful that I could build an identity on. It might not have been an identity fully accepted by my town or classmates, but it was one that helped me navigate my difference and buffer experiences against my exclusion.

It was during the early nineties that I first became aware of Africans playing in the National Basketball Association (NBA). I had known that "Africans" played soccer and ran marathons, but those were sports either not widely available to watch (soccer) or boring to me (distance running). I first learned about Hakeem Olajuwon and rooted for him—along with my father—to win those back-to-back championships with the Rockets in the midnineties. At the same time we took note of Dikembe Mutombo, then Manute Bol, and it seemed as though we would be seeing a rapid influx of talent from African countries to U.S. basketball. If an African was playing, then we were watching and rooting for him or her to succeed. My youth was instilled with a pan-African outlook that I could draw meaning and identity from given my locality. We pulled for Nigeria during their Olympic gold medal win in Atlanta, and later, during the 1998 World Cup final, I would cheer for France while my father rooted for Brazil. Looking back, the split shows a somewhat predictable generational divide. For my father, Brazil will always be the team that first took it to the colonial powers with African players, while for me the French team by then "looked" more African and diverse. Still today my father will root for the African teams, then the Latin American teams with Afro-Latino players, then the "European African" teams (whose numbers have been growing), and then anyone but the United States (England never enters the conversation).

And then everything seemed to die down. The explosion of African talent into the NBA never happened on the scale it seemed it was going to, African national teams either fell apart or continued to scuffle, and eventually I forgot about how many Africans were or were not in American sport. There always seemed to be one or two Africans in the NBA, but no one like Olajuwon. I was too young to keep up with foreign soccer leagues, and the games were certainly not on television. You might hear about a great African soccer player, but our media in the United States made soccer a difficult sport to follow. It was not until I reached university and began to invest more time into (American) football that I began to once again see names similar to mine. Specifically, as I paid more attention to the collegiate ranks of both football and basketball, I saw that I had been missing a great influx of players with African backgrounds. However, you would never know, because relatively little attention was being paid to the roots of these athletes—or, as many were and are second generation, the roots of their parents. I became curious about this omission. I wanted to know more about these players and their backgrounds. I wanted to know what sort of stereotypical information about "Africa" was, or was not, being created around or through them by the media.

The research in this book sought to satisfy that curiosity. At first I wanted to simply know how different African athletes were represented by the media. It became apparent quickly that such an approach was going to be insufficient, because those representations are tied up in how the "West" thinks about race. For my data I poured through archival news sources on the careers of ten athletes: Hakeem Olajuwon, Dikembe Mutombo, Tegla Loroupe, Mwadi Mabika, Catherine Ndereba, Tirunesh Dibaba, Christian Okoye, Tamba Hali, Didier Drogba, and Mario Balotelli. This list is obviously not exhaustive, and it is not a "best of," either. These athletes and the flow of their careers allowed me an entry point into a larger conversation about being foreign and black in sport. This larger conversation—what I like to think of as a "web" of related discourses, intersecting with other (non)celebrity, (non)minority, (non)migrant athletes as well—also allowed me to develop analytical tools with which to think about the transnational activities of migrant African athletes. So, while this book is "about" the ten individuals listed above, it is in some ways not really about them at all. The end result is an examination of how the "innocent" world of (sport) media works to keep blackness—individuals, cultures, identities, communities, and nations—marginalized.

To enter this larger conversation concerning foreign black Otherness in sport I use a methodology that conceptualizes the celebrity athlete and spectacle event as a nexus of power relations that we can "read," or make intelligible. By using an approach borrowing from different aspects of discourse analysis, cultural studies, and social learning theory, we come closer to understanding the representations and experiences of migrant athletes on pertinent topics such as immigrant reception, experiences with racism, identity, and nationalism. Further, in taking a transnational approach toward African sport labor migration, we can explore how the movements, experiences, and activities of these athletes across two or more borders challenge the imagined coherency of the nation-state. A concern for the different modes of alterity placed on the Other, including the how/when/where/why "they" are represented as such, is a strong focus to my work here. Hence the focus on black Africans is a means to discuss some of the broader social implications of representing the "Other." I have included a more complete discussion on my methodology and brief descriptions of the individuals included in my research in the appendices.

The structure of the book is as follows. The introduction discusses the history of African immigration to the West both in general and for sport. It introduces the topic and grounds it in the relevant work on immigration from African countries circa 1965 to today while also weaving in the concurrent history of immigration to the West for sport purposes. The exploration of this history, the racism of Western immigration policies, and the development of African sport labor migration to the West make clear the broader implications for the representation of the black African athlete.

The first chapter delves into the development, construction, and representation of "the black athlete" throughout the twentieth century. The historical racial project resulting in the creation of "the black athlete" has its roots in slavery and segregation, Western imperialism and colonialism, and the transnational development of white supremacy. This chapter helps us know and historically trace the stereotypical and often contradictory representations of black African athletes that I examine in the next three chapters.

In chapter 2 I begin by talking about the mundane and everyday processes of Othering and boundary making. I examine how the black African migrant athletes in my study are casually kept foreign and separate from the nation-states within which they live, compete, and often naturalize. These representations would be more harmless if they were not often linked to the more stereotypical representations of African countries (and at times Africa itself) as corrupt, diseased, dangerous, backward, and so on. Hence Africa and its many peoples are continually stereotyped through the African athlete performing in the West.

In the third chapter I examine discourses about the backgrounds of black migrant athletes and times when they are held up as exceptional individuals for their humanitarian and charitable efforts. Hegemonic discourses on the backgrounds, or "origin stories," of these athletes often rely on stereotypes of Africa, while the humanitarian efforts of black African athletes often lead to them being problematically positioned as saviors of Africa. These discursive processes ultimately reinscribe the West as Africa's benefactor while simultaneously locating the African athlete in Africa (as foreign) instead of the West and remarginalizing native black communities for failing where Africans have "succeeded."

The acceptance of the foreign black Other is always contingent, however, and in chapter 4 I interrogate the "acceptance" of black African athletes that I demonstrate in chapter 3. Though they are often represented as exceptional individuals, the athletes in my study were still at times represented along stereotypical notions of blackness as they regard competence, demeanor, deservedness, and respectability. In this chapter I seek to emphasize the often tenuous position of the black immigrant in Western societies and the salient reinscription of native black communities as deviant. When black African athletes fail to adhere to white Western norms, they are derided not only for their blackness but for their foreignness as well.

Having considered the representation of black African athletes, the next two chapters take a slightly different approach. In the fifth chapter I begin to include in an explicit manner other sources of data (autobiographies and web content, particularly interviews and presentations) and read against the dominant discourse, exposing its inconsistencies, in order to discuss issues of immigrant reception, nationalism, citizenship, politics, and resistance. In this chapter I attempt to tease out how the experiences of the athletes in my study upon immigrating to the West may have informed their political outlook and sentiments toward the West and attaining citizenship. I stress that these athletes are indeed active in negotiating their host societies but remain constrained in their actions due to the nature of celebrity and the media.

In my sixth and final substantive chapter I look more closely at issues of diaspora and transnational blackness. This chapter looks at three aspects of black African migrant athletes: (1) their diasporic presence in the West and their meaning to native black communities, (2) their meaning to diasporic black immigrant communities, and (3) their meaning on the African continent and/or in their home country. It is often assumed that the black African athlete in the West is a huge celebrity in his or her native country, while almost nothing is said about foreign and native black communities in the West and how these athletes are consumed by them. This chapter challenges these media assumptions and oversights, focusing on moments when we can "see" the black diaspora, in a broader sense, engaging with black African athletes to form positive identities and fight white supremacy.

Chapter 7 concludes the book, and in it I address some of the lingering issues I believe my research poses. A great deal has happened since I collected the data and continues to happen, and I use this opportunity to speak on a range of issues and to tentatively offer suggestions for ways forward. The rise of extreme right-wing political movements in Western societies, societies that had been congratulating themselves on ending racism, means that there are deep and persistent issues that will not be easy to change or perhaps even meaningfully address at the moment.

ACKNOWLEDGMENTS

A number of people made this book possible. First, to my wife, Sarah, who (through her hatred of Illinois winters) pushed me to finish my dissertation and find a "real" job: It's great not to be a graduate student anymore and steadily accomplishing everything I want in life with you. To my parents, who have showered me with love and support throughout the years; they have probably read this so many times that they won't read the final copy: I understand. To the educators throughout the years who have encouraged my work and given thoughtful feedback: I now realize that professors have no time, and so I'm grateful for every minute you've spent on me. To my departmental colleagues at Western Carolina University, who couldn't have been more welcoming and supportive: I doubt I could have found a better work environment. Finally, to the University of Nebraska Press, everyone there who has helped make this a reality, and the anonymous reviewers who have made this process as simple as possible: Thank you.

Introduction

Black African Immigration to the West

Popular sport often serves as one of the first cultural spaces in which recent immigrants can gain widespread social recognition within their host countries. As sport globalizes a rising number of athletes are migrating to fill the talent needs of various sports around the world. However, this labor migration is currently dominated by black and brown bodies moving primarily from the global South to the West. Given current global trends toward rising inequality this movement is unsurprising and, despite increasing rules and regulations on immigration, shows no signs of slowing down. We are often told that sport exists as a social good, that it develops moral character, brings people together, and ameliorates social boundaries. Yet this apolitical ideology is a utopian ideal perpetuating only the "right" kind of politics. Our commonsense understandings of sport mask its existence as a contested terrain for both maintaining and challenging sociocultural norms and boundaries. That most individuals in the West access sport through globalized corporate media entities consistently shown to actively reinforce cultural norms means that most of us are exposed to a single repetitive discourse concerning race, class, gender, and sexuality.

This book explores discursive practices of racism in Western sport media as they concern black African migrant athletes. It deploys discourse analysis and a cultural studies approach in an attempt to understand how black African athletes are represented (re-presented to the West), how they navigate their lives, and what they mean to black African diasporic communities in the West. While the body of liter-

1

ature on race and racism in sport is extensive, less has been done in studies of sport to explore the relationship between not only Western and African countries but also Western societies and their growing African immigrant populations. By focusing on the West as a (not uncomplicated) whole, we can more easily apprehend global processes and logics of antiblack racism—global white supremacy—in sport. In my work here I explain how discursive representations of black African migrant athletes are indicative of global white supremacy but also how global white supremacy in sport impacts black communities by saliently discouraging the development of what is often called the "black diaspora."

I take this line of study because previous researchers in the West have tended to lump, or homogenize, the black populations they study in order to discuss blackness, or whiteness, as a whole. While there is merit to this approach, I believe there are insights to be gained by looking a little more closely at black African migrant athletes—certainly not a homogeneous group themselves—and the complexity of their representations and experiences. I do not intend to privilege black African athletes through this research, and their experiences with oppression and representation are not held to be above others'. Rather, I seek to add to the scholarly conversation on blackness and antiblack racism as a common (forced) experience among all those considered "black" (the association of darkness, the dark Other, with inferiority)—particularly as it applies to (im)migration and (im) migrant communities.[1] Indeed, my research complements previous research concerning patterns of migration, issues of national identity, racist representations, and antiblack policies in many other geographies of sport, such as player transfers and emigration from Latin America, Africa, and Asia to European soccer leagues; Indigenous Australians competing in Western/Australian sport; Pacific Islanders participating in New Zealand sport; West Indians and Asians playing cricket within, for, and against England; and in the United States, Latinos in baseball and Asians in basketball.[2] The list goes on and on, but we can begin to see the globally contested terrain of sport in the maintenance of white supremacy and the simultaneous adoption and contestation of sport by nonwhites around the globe. In each of these bodies of literature we see contestation and struggle over access to and the meanings of sport locally and globally, between "blacks" and "whites," and within "blackness" itself. As noted, it is not my intent here to privilege "black Africans" but rather to use their experiences as foreign Others to demonstrate the workings of white supremacy at a global level—an approach that I think has been missing in the intersection of sociology and sport.

That said, throughout my work I use the term *native black* to refer to the established black communities in various countries that have a political history of racial struggle within those countries. I remain vague here because the ever-increasing movement of people across borders makes an obvious and clear division between, or definition of, "native" or "foreign" difficult, particularly in Europe. Thus I am well aware that terms such as *Black European, African American, American African, Afro-French, Afro-German, Afro-Italian,* and *Black Briton* are dynamic, complex, and under ongoing contention. What is more important to me is that black African immigrants often arrive in their destination country with different political outlooks and personal goals than, for example, African Americans. These differences have often led to conflict, or intraethnic Othering, between "foreigner" and "native." For a variety of reasons these differences have sometimes led to different—seemingly preferential—treatment of black immigrants by whites in terms of attitudes, representation, and employment.[3]

In order to understand the representation of migrant African athletes it is important to understand the larger context and history of immigration. The rest of this chapter covers two important aspects of immigration: a history of African immigration to the United States and Europe and a history of black African athletic labor migration to the West. My aim here is to give the reader relevant information on black African immigration with which to understand my later analysis. By no means is it possible to provide an exhaustive review of the history or experiences of black immigrants here. Instead I would like readers to gain an appreciation of the different yet similar contexts awaiting black African migrants upon their arrival in the West. The strategies used to create and maintain barriers to black immigration continue to play an important role in racism and discrimination against all blacks, as well as other people of color.[4]

Black African Immigration to the West

No contemporary history of African immigration would be complete without acknowledgement of the Atlantic slave trade. The slave trade and concurrent processes of colonialism created and gave importance to the idea of race as we know it today. While the idea of race and practices of racism have mutated over time, the history of the slave trade is no less important. As Paul Gilroy explains, the slave trade was central in creating the "Black Atlantic," or the dispersal of African peoples around the Atlantic via the Middle Passage. The Atlantic slave trade gained in significance and intensity around 1650, and from that time through the eighteenth century, millions of Africans crossed the Atlantic to the Americas, where they became the majority of new settlers. The slave trade grew from around thirty-six thousand slaves being imported each year at the beginning to the eighteenth century to a high of eighty thousand a year in the century's last few decades. The rapid and sustained demand for slaves driven by plantations in the Caribbean, Brazil, and the fledgling American colonies inflated prices and created a greater supply of slaves. At the same time, African participation in the slave trade was at least partially fueled by numerous civil conflicts and wars along the western and central coasts of Africa. With the sale of slaves being one of the few ways to quickly attain weapons in a period of great turmoil, many leaders seem to have been willing to sacrifice their populations for power. While African involvement in the slave trade is seen by some as redeeming European involvement, we must remember that the kind of slavery that came to exist in the Americas—chattel slavery—was unlike anything that existed on the African continent. Nonetheless, it was this interplay between African political agency and the greed of European shippers and plantation owners that sent millions overseas, eventually leading to demographic exhaustion in some areas of western Africa.[5]

In the American states the struggle for freedom and civil rights throughout the nineteenth and twentieth centuries helped consolidate a distinct African American cultural identity. This presence of black-ness in the very heart of the United States and in its development as an imperialist power has yet to be reconciled. It is also this presence that has served to conflate "African American" with "black" in the American imagination, whereas in the European context blackness is seen as foreign rather than internal. There are many details and par-ticularities here that I will address later. During the struggles of Afri-can Americans in the nineteenth and twentieth centuries there was very little African immigration to the United States. There was some immigration from the West Indies—which played a significant role in the struggle for civil rights in terms of leadership—but black African immigration lagged due to the obvious reasons of racist immigration control, European colonialism, and black African poverty. As April Gordon notes, the early twentieth century saw around six thousand immigrants from Africa come to the United States *each decade*, and further, many of those were from (white) South Africa and Egypt, not (black) sub-Saharan Africa. The majority of black Africans who did migrate to the United States were men from wealthy or privileged families who studied at European or U.S. colleges and universities and later returned home. It was not until the colonized African states began to gain their independence that the number of black African immigrants to the United States began to rise.[6]

The rise of black African immigration coincided with the gains of the civil rights movement in the 1960s. More inclusive immigration laws and scholarship opportunities made America a more attrac-tive place to study and work. This change occurred while European countries—particularly England and France—were simultaneously closing their doors to black postcolonial migrants. Many of these changes in the United States began with the oft-noted 1965 Hart-Celler Immigration Act, a kind of extension of the civil rights legislation of the era that began easing and phasing out racist national quota sys-tems that were biased toward European immigrants. For example, the previous immigration law—the 1952 Walter-McCarran Immigra-tion Act—set the African quota, the total number of visas allowed per year, at 1,400. Europe's limit was 149,667. The 1965 law made it eas-ier for highly skilled and educated Africans to immigrate, facilitated family reunions (primarily by allowing women and children to immigrate), and aided undocumented Africans in attaining citizenship.[7]

Though the Hart-Celler Immigration Act offered a great improvement over the quota system, the law essentially made black immigrants from newly independent African countries compete with white European immigrants on the basis of skills. This means that the law not only was racially biased against black Africans from intentionally underdeveloped postcolonial nations but tended to privilege those black Africans who had already benefitted from the colonial system—the colonial elites. Later, under pressure from the United Nations, the Refugee Act of 1980 redefined the U.S. definition of refugees. This redefinition meant that the number of immigrants from Ethiopia, Somalia, Eritrea, Ghana, and Liberia was greatly increased due to their ability to claim status as refugees and asylum seekers. Later laws, such as the Immigration Reform and Control Act and the Immigration Act, passed in 1986 and 1990 respectively, further helped undocumented Africans adjust their immigration status and allowed for increases in immigration diversity, especially for those Africans migrating with employable skills.[8]

Throughout the 1970s and 1980s the collapse of many African states led to push and pull factors for emigration, where those who had the means to leave those countries and seek better opportunities elsewhere often did so. Pertinent factors include economic globalization (the pressures of neoliberal policies and structural adjustment programs), civil wars, natural disasters (drought and famine), political instability, and corruption. Because of these factors the foreign black population in the United States grew by 134,000 in the 1980s, 323,000 in the 1990s, and 759,742 in the 2000s. In 2009 more sub-Saharan Africans had migrated to the United States annually since 1990 than in any year during the Atlantic slave trade. From 1990 to 2000 African immigrants were the fastest-growing immigrant population in the United States, growing nearly three times faster than the Latino immigrant population and four times faster than the Asian immigrant population. Yet according to John Logan, the available census tabulations force us to count as African only those born in African countries, meaning that only the first generation counts as African.

Logan estimates that the "true" population of African immigrants, especially in metropolitan areas, including second and third generations, may be up to 20 percent higher than official census figures.[9]

While the United States was relaxing immigration controls, Britain and other European countries were simultaneously beginning to close their doors on former colonial subjects. For example, the 1971 Immigration Act in the United Kingdom effectively stopped primary immigration. When the law took effect in 1973 it essentially limited immigration solely to family reunification. Black African immigration to Europe differs from that of the United States both currently and historically, yet many of the same issues of racism that impact the U.S. immigration system exist. There is, of course, a long history of black communities and populations all over Europe, some existing since the fifteenth century. However, because European countries, in contrast to the United States, desired to keep slavery and the slave trade an "external" issue, black communities in Europe remained small and dispersed given the limited possibilities for immigration. Many black populations began within towns and cities known for shipping, such as Liverpool, which has one of the oldest black communities in England. Being a sailor was one early occupation into which blacks could gain entry. In some cases these small communities may have "benefitted" by being able to go unnoticed in European society, and by extension to avoid white racism, a situation that would change with the "end" of colonialism, African independence, and increasing black African immigration to Europe.[10]

Yet the process of racial awareness in black Europe has been slow precisely because of the wide dispersal of black communities, language and territorial barriers, and political crackdowns by different countries to prohibit the development of anything like the U.S. civil rights movement. The further absence of legal apartheid, as in South Africa or the Jim Crow United States, has made the fight for equality in European countries difficult as well, especially when countries cling to ideologies of color blindness and multiculturalism. Though France is perhaps best known for such a stance, during Germany's brief stint as a colonial power miscegenation was outlawed in its colonies but remained legal in Germany itself. Despite being heavily debated and contested, those marriages within Germany were allowed to stand and the offspring of those unions were, however minimally, considered German "citizens." This history has allowed Germany to claim a measure of color blindness in its approach to racial discourse, while ignoring the often brutal and oppressive lives of children of mixed parentage, which, under Hitler, extended into the realm of forced castration and death.[11]

By the early twentieth century and into World War II black populations in various European countries had grown large enough to begin fighting against the discrimination and racial terror they faced on a daily basis. For example, politically active black communities were evident early on in France (circa 1920s) and later in England (circa 1950s—although in 1919 blacks organized and protested against their racist treatment in different cities). This development of racial consciousness and political protest goes hand-in-hand with colonial countries bringing in large numbers of Africans and Afro-Caribbeans to help fight the two world wars. It is also reflected in African American World War II veterans returning to America and among those African soldiers forced to return to African colonies. Even though black communities had been in Europe for centuries, the immigrant influx after World War II gave the appearance that blacks had just "appeared." Unsurprisingly, immigration from former colonial countries eventually spurned a conservative, ethnocentric backlash.[12]

For instance, the British Nationality Act of 1948 established the right of colonial and commonwealth subjects to work and live in the United Kingdom. But with the help of conservative and nationalist political voices such as Enoch Powell, the Conservative Monday Club, and, later, Margaret Thatcher, those rights began to be eroded, beginning with the Commonwealth Immigrants Act of 1962 and the 1968 Immigration Act. The 1962 act, through a voucher system, essentially allowed black immigration only when labor was needed, and the 1968 act further limited right of entry to former colonials by requiring that the immigrant, a parent, or a grandparent to have been born in the United Kingdom. The previously mentioned Immigration Act of 1971 essentially ended primary immigration to the United Kingdom by amending and adding to the previous two immigration acts with the purpose of further distancing the United Kingdom from its past empire. Fears of immigration, driven by political actors and mass media across Europe, have rendered the long histories of black communities invisible. More to the point, the conceptual merging of the term *immigrant* with *black* has made every black an immigrant and all immigrants black in the popular white national imagination, an issue that remains problematic both academically and politically.[13]

Today the largest black European communities can be found, predictably, in England, Germany, France, and Spain. More recently, black African migrants have been moving toward the Netherlands, Italy, Portugal, and, increasingly, Greece. Each of the these countries has its own history of interactions with racist media imagery, the slave trade, and (neo)colonialism, in some cases longer than that of the United States. The recent and ongoing tragedies of desperate black migrants trying to cross the Mediterranean or navigate the western coast of Africa to reach Europe betrays the global economic inequality perpetuated by Western countries. The brief but telling 2015 European policy of "let them die"—based on the idea that saving migrants would encourage others, similar to the logic that welfare makes (black) people "lazy"—demonstrates the ongoing lack of black humanity and has contributed to the global spread of the #BlackLivesMatter movement. Established black communities in Europe (including the United Kingdom) have long gone unnoticed and unrecognized, thereby allowing them to be marginalized politically and economically for many decades. This invisibility has meant that blacks in Europe face problems similar to those of blacks in the United States: undereducation, unemployment, and imprisonment, combined with an overrepresentation in the cultural spheres of sports and entertainment.[14]

Yet despite relatively recent increases in immigration, African immigrant communities in Europe remain small. In fact, the overall black population makes up only about 2 percent of Europe's total population. As in the United States, this small population size has led to problems of invisibility and racialization within society. Black African immigrants immediately find themselves at the bottom of the social order upon arrival in Europe. They are racialized into local understandings of blackness—which may vary in detail between different countries but achieves similar outcomes—and face the harsh realities of racial discrimination as a result. Currently, concerns are also mounting about the level of racial violence in Europe, particularly as it concerns the ongoing migration of refugees from North African countries. Given the small size of black communities, this racialization also means that white violence against black African communities often fails to face justice, especially in former Soviet Bloc (Eastern European) countries. Further, Europe's preoccupation with Islamophobia means that blacks are often not the primary target of racism and discrimination or violence, which to some extent adds to their invisibility and marginalization. And again, the ideology of color blindness to which European governments cling, despite the ongoing rise of nationalist parties, only exacerbates the problems of racism and discrimination for native as well as foreign blacks, Arabs, and Muslims.[15]

There are other factors working against black Europe as well. As in the United States, there are issues of stereotyping and interethnic Othering among different black populations in Europe. For example, recent immigrants to Britain often hold feelings that native blacks are lazy and failed to take advantage of the opportunities "given" to them. In France the postcolonial African immigration resulted in what has been called an "exteriorization of the interior." As the black postcolonial immigrant population grew—the "interiorization of the exterior"—there was a simultaneous process of ghettoization (exteriorization) of blacks, both immigrant and native, most visibly into what are called the *banlieues* (metropolitan suburbs).[16] Historically and into today, this process has set black populations (usually Afro-Caribbeans and Africans, but Arabs as well) into socioeconomic conflict against other black populations, thus giving lie to and making difficult any notion of black unity.[17]

As in the United States, whites may at times receive black immigrants better than native blacks due to their linguistic accents or manner of dress, further fueling the desire of black immigrants to differentiate themselves from native black Europeans. The struggle over scarce resources and jobs has hindered the development of black consciousness and the community development needed to build social movements that reach past the local or national level. Despite the economic consolidation of the European Union, citizenship remains a state project that continues to have a negative impact on the civil rights of minorities and their ability to (im)migrate to and travel within Europe. The lack of a *European* citizenship has made a coherent notion of "Black Europe" difficult to formulate, as black communities in each state are embroiled in their own political struggles.[18]

In bringing together these two broad histories, the only similarities we can draw between black African immigration to Europe and to the United States are the similar racial logics they encounter and the ambivalent (at best) receptions they receive in their host countries, from both native blacks and whites. Native blacks, whether in Britain, Germany, the Netherlands, France, Belgium, or other countries, struggle daily against institutionalized forms of racism and, increasingly, more overt forms of racial terror from neofascist organizations. Within the long history of black communities and populations in Europe, the two world wars were particularly important for bringing a permanent black population into being. It is this racist and racialized historical context that black African immigrants experience when they migrate to European countries. Their experiences are not easily captured in broad terms because of the complexities of migration and identity (including class, gender, nationality, etc.). As with black African immigrants to the United States, black African immigrants to Europe fail to fit neatly into European (homogeneous racial) national identities, as their activities and experiences are inherently transnational and diasporic, going beyond and continually crossing the boundaries of the nation-state.[19]

Athletic Labor Migration

The history of black African athletic labor migration is inevitably linked to and resonates with nonsport migration. The histories of black African athletic labor migration to the United States and Europe have many similarities yet also differ in numerous ways. Some of these differences include the sports being played, recruitment practices, reasons for migration, the process of migration, and so on. My aim here is to briefly demonstrate the progression of sport labor migration as it concerns black African athletes in the last thirty to forty years. Throughout, I draw attention to the fact that sport, though it tends to privilege athletes, does not make the black migrant immune to racial hostilities, discrimination, or stereotypes.

The Globalization of Sport

The migration of athletes would not be possible without the globalization of sport itself. According to John Bale and Joseph Maguire, the globalization of sport is tied in a relationship with the continued professionalization, or rationalization, of sport, which in turn propels its further globalization. This self-propelled process is evident through the manifestation of international sports organizations, the global standardization of rules, increased competition between nations, and the establishment of global competitions—such as the Olympics and the World Cup. Concurrently, sports clubs (such as Manchester United and Real Madrid) and associations (most notably the International Federation of Association Football [FIFA] and the NBA) are basing their business models on those of transnational corporations (TNCs) in order to market themselves as global entities and take advantage of an increasingly transient athletic labor population. Because globalization is driven by a capitalist impulse, the "globalization of sport" is not an even or unbiased process. It is those (predominantly Western) leagues with wealth and corporate media backing that have been able to "globalize" their sport. As with non-sport processes of globalization, the spread of popular Western sport forms across the globe has at times entailed the (colonial) destruction of native sport or movement forms and has increasingly led to the exploitation of black and brown (post)colonial bodies. It is the latter phenomenon that Bale describes as a "brawn drain" from developing countries.[20]

Despite this unevenness, as sport continues to globalize it engages a greater number of individual actors working in various capacities. An awareness of these individual actors keeps us from losing sight of local understandings of sport within the sometimes homogenizing ideal of global sport. It is within this environment of increased—if uneven—interdependency between the global and local that highly skilled elite athletes now exist. Though migration for sport purposes seems unproblematic, the migration and life of the athlete are caught in a web of power relations. Transnational athletes confront political, cultural, economic, and geographical issues that intersect with other actors in sport, such as owners, administrators, coaches, agents, and media personnel—all of whom are faced with similar circumstances. These athletic laborers are expected to adapt and culturally perform at the local, national, and global levels simultaneously the minute they enter a stadium. As Joseph Maguire and Mark Falcous note, highly skilled migrant athletes are similar to other, nonsport, highly skilled migrants in that they are subject to "local, national, [and] global technological, political and economic state, transnational and TNC policies" that reflect and reinforce the more recent changes realigning the nation-state. The assumption that these athletes can, will, and want to adapt and perform adequately has implications for their treatment by fans, their organization, and the media.[21]

Migration to Europe

The history of African athletic migration to Europe begins with colonialism in the early twentieth century. It was within the "civilizing missions" of European powers—Britain, Germany, Portugal, the Netherlands, Belgium, and France—that European sport forms were first introduced to the colonized Africans, simultaneously replacing and destroying many indigenous sport and movement forms. These European sport forms, primarily soccer and athletics (running and field events) but also cricket in Asia and the West Indies, were sometimes introduced before formal colonialism and only later imbued with colonial ideology. As part of their civilizing missions, particularly in British and French Africa, these sport forms received limited resources in the form of equipment and facilities and were disseminated through cultural institutions such as schools. The value placed on sport also made it possible for individuals who excelled athletically to receive some limited amount of social acknowledgement or standing from the white colonists.[22]

Soccer leagues and national teams in France, Portugal, and Belgium began playing African players, primarily from their colonies, in the 1930s, 1950s, and 1970s, respectively. In Britain, black immigrants of African and West Indian ancestry, often of mixed parentage, played at the amateur and professional levels beginning in the early twentieth century, though it took until 1978 for the English national team to select a black player. In fact, in 1889 the "Kaffirs" of the Basuto tribe in Lesotho (Southern Africa) became the first soccer team to visit and play in Britain. Throughout the 1900s African teams from Nigeria (1949), Ghana (then Gold Coast, 1951), and Uganda (1956) would tour the United Kingdom, in part for sport and in part as a political diplomatic mission, as it was becoming evident that African independence was close at hand. Aside from the players being patronized and stereotyped—both athletically and sexually—in the media, these African tours were used by the colonial powers to show their white citizens that the imperial project had not been completely in vain and that Africans were capable of acquitting themselves as "civilized sportsmen." Yet in many respects black soccer players were allowed to play professionally so "early" only because the sport itself was not yet tied to the national imagination in the way that tennis was in France or cricket in England, for example. Black players were strictly excluded from both of the latter sports.[23]

Similarly, the performances of Kenyan distance runners like Nyandika Maiyoro, in the 1950s, and Kipchoge Keino, in the 1960s, were significant in their transformation of what British whites thought was possible by the "African" athlete. Though it was thought that African runners would never dominate distance running because of their supposedly inadequate training, lack of technical skill, and "front-running" style of competition, it had to be acknowledged that African runners were not completely without merit. After Kenyan runners won multiple medals at the 1968 Mexico Olympics new stereotypes emerged to explain their success, perhaps the most longstanding being the supposed altitude advantage Kenyans have over other runners because of where they grow up. The success of Kenyan runners in the 1960s and 1970s resulted in their intense recruitment by U.S. universities, often those that could not afford to recruit or entice top domestic talent. I will return to African distance running more fully in the next section, but for now it is just important to note that the "sudden" emergence of African distance running in the latter twentieth century is not without its colonial roots.[24]

In the case of international soccer, it would be almost unthinkable in the modern era to see the French national team without an African from one of the former colonies. Today France is no longer exceptional in that regard—for example, see Belgium, Germany, the Netherlands, and Portugal. Aside from the implications concerning race, migration is also important because of the money involved in European soccer leagues. It has led researchers to explore the growth and the complexities of the relationships between African countries and players on the one hand and European soccer clubs and the International Federation of Association Football (FIFA) on the other, among a host of other actors.[25] According to Raffaele Poli, the number of foreign players in European clubs on average increased from 4.8 to 9.8 from 1995 to 2004. In the same time frame, the absolute number of African players in top-level clubs increased from 160 to 316, so that they made up 17 percent of all foreign players in top-level clubs and 20 percent in all clubs throughout Europe. By 2010 the latter figure had risen to 23.1 percent. For reference, Latin Americans made up 13.9 percent of all foreign players in European clubs, Eastern Europeans constituted 27.7 percent, Western Europeans 31.5 percent, and other athletes 3.8 percent. These numbers gain in significance when we consider that "foreign" players also include European expatriates (immigrants) who, presumably, have an easier time migrating within the European Union.[26]

Just as the West has been criticized for neocolonial economic practices in its approach to African countries after their independence, the recruiting practices undertaken by European soccer clubs have often been equated with neocolonialism at best and neoslavery, or a second "scramble for Africa," at worst. Indeed, the main receivers of African soccer talent are very often former colonial powers such as Belgium, France, and Portugal; Britain is an exception because rules make it difficult to immigrate directly and play for an English club. The recruitment of African players, concentrated in Western Africa, has historically been predatory, speculative, and without sufficient regulation or oversight. Too often African players have been brought to European countries under the auspice of playing professional soccer only to be cut or dumped by teams and left on the street with no money, contacts, or way to get home when they fail to live up to expectations. The combined lack of worker protections and the difficulties involved in attaining work permits leave very young players vulnerable to exploitation and corrupt intermediaries. Though FIFA has instituted new rules recently to curb such practices, new loopholes have emerged and the rise of soccer "academies" for youths in African countries continues the exploitation of African athletic talent under a new name.[27]

Research on these academies has shown their great diversity, ranging from the professional to the illegal. As Paul Darby and Eirik Solberg explain in the case of Ghana, while professional academies in Ghana are run by clubs in Europe, which does not set them above critique, the illegal academies are often run by local businessmen. Both the existence of European clubs in Africa and the rise of local businessmen to fill a need are indicative of the confluence of global and local actors. The academies also point toward a recent focus of anthropologists of sport migration: the dense network of actors that are involved in and impacted by athletic labor migration. The proliferation of illegal academies is in some ways indicative of the immense popularity and success of Ghanaian soccer players who have secured lucrative contracts overseas and raised the profile of the national team in recent years. However, the prevalence of illegal academies is also an indicator of the degree to which poverty, lack of opportunities, and the inability to make a living playing soccer locally are prevalent not only in Ghana but in other African countries as well. Often these academies, professional and illegal, are questioned on their merits in providing soccer knowledge and the degree to which they stress academic achievement. In a sport where very few youths will make it to Europe or the professional ranks, oversight and regulation are needed to make sure these athletes have a skill set to fall back on if their dreams of professional soccer never materialize.[28]

Yet a number of intricacies make the case of African soccer migration more complex than straightforward European domination. Much like distance running in Kenya, soccer across Africa is the product of colonialism and an effort to civilize the "African" through sport. After independence, many African leaders continued to see sport as a way to build national identities and pride among the youth, and to that effect they invested, to varying degrees, in the establishment of national teams and professional soccer clubs.[29] Unfortunately, the histories of economic and political instability across the African continent have meant that many of these leagues have fallen under, as they were largely supported by governments and did not receive enough commercial endorsements, if any, to function independently. As Frantz Fanon predicted, a capitalist concept of sport in developing countries would be ruined by professionalization and commercialism.[30] We can read these "failures" as further casualties of the underdevelopment of the African state throughout (neo)colonialism. The lack of income by professional clubs means that they were and are not able to invest in equipment or facilities, pay their players appropriately, or prevent them from leaving the country to pursue better opportunities in Europe, the Middle East, and North and South Africa. It is in the pursuit of better economic opportunities that there is a history of corruption, as African club officials and European sports agents exploit young talent for income. In part, the focus on the success of a few celebrity players—like Didier Drogba—masks the failings of most by making success seem more likely than it really is. With education in African countries often failing to lead to a fulfilling occupation, a career in sport is becoming more acceptable than it once was among parents of youthful players. Desperate youths have been talked into signing contracts that give away up to 50 percent of their pay or have been given the impression that their contract meant they had a spot on the team only to be cut weeks later and lose their living arrangements. It is not known how many African youths have thus become street children in Europe.[31]

All of these negative factors constitute a significant push factor inducing African soccer players to migrate overseas. However, we must guard against simple understandings of migrant push factors, as doing so eliminates players' agency and context. Pierre Lanfranchi and Matthew Taylor explain that there are many individual motivations in the decision to migrate, and indeed, there is some difficulty in conceptualizing what a migrant "footballer" should be. In the history of African players in European leagues, some Africans used their ability to play soccer to gain access to education, some started playing after they already were getting an education, and some migrated strictly to play professionally. Today we see similar patterns of migration along with additional complexities of reverse migration, European "expertise" taking important coaching and management jobs with African national teams, and second-generation immigrants who have the ability to play internationally for the African country of their parent(s) but have no direct link with that country.[32]

For African women who migrate to play soccer abroad, a number of the same motivational factors are involved. Though soccer is an extremely popular sport for women, especially in the United States, the number of African women being recruited to play abroad is low (there is minimal recruitment of African women to U.S. universities) and there has been little research in general on the migration of women for sport.[33] As Sine Agergaard and Vera Botelho point out, the motivation for European clubs to recruit foreign players does not likely rest on economic gain or publicity because profits in women's soccer tend to be modest. More likely, clubs are looking abroad in order to improve and stay near the top of their league. For the women themselves, sporting ambition and validation of a career in sport become strong motivating factors because, again, salaries are modest. African women in particular, who share the migrant ambitions of African men, may be coming from leagues that are run poorly or societies that do not recognize their efforts as athletes.[34] Still, it appears that women are spared the exploitation men face regarding athletic labor migration to Europe, at least in part because of the marginalization of women's sport, both socially and economically.

Migration to the United States

Concurrent with developments in Europe, black African sport labor migration to the United States has developed along a slightly different path and, given the relatively small numbers of Africans in U.S. sport, does not attract the same level of attention in academia. The first African athletes to emerge in the States were located on college campuses. Primarily they were among the early migrants from recently independent African countries or from wealthier families who were seeking higher education. Once in the United States and at universities, many were recruited by coaches on campus for various reasons and were lured to participate because of the scholarship money available. The scholarship money in particular led a small population of African student athletes to participate in track and field, basketball, and football.[35]

It was not long, however, before the international success of African athletes in track and field would lead to their heavy recruitment by U.S. universities. Often these programs would offer scholarships without ever having seen the athlete perform. According to Bale, the low cost of African recruitment relative to recruiting a domestic American athlete, combined with low oversight of international recruitment, led to abuses similar to those in European soccer today. In particular, schools with little desirability for local (American) athletes were drawn to international recruitment. Hence, when we look at the patterns of migration of African runners, primarily Kenyans and Nigerians, to U.S. universities we see distinct concentrations—talent pipelines—to specific schools throughout the 1970s and 1980s. For Kenyans, the University of Richmond, Iowa State University, Washington State University, and the University of Texas–El Paso were significant destinations, while for Nigerians the University of Missouri and Mississippi State University were dominant recruiters.[36]

With a large influx of international black African talent arriving at U.S. universities beginning in the late 1960s and increasing in the 1970s and 1980s, the National Collegiate Athletic Association (NCAA) took measures to curtail the immigration of foreign athletes. In particular, the association instituted a set of age restrictions that hindered African participation in universities because Africans tended to enter university at a later age, in their early twenties. Though not explicitly stated, the new rules addressed concerns over having "too many" (black) foreigners on college athletic teams. Such a concern links with the discourse on antiblack immigration broadly but also resonates within the sport of distance running itself, as it has historically been conceived as a "white man's" domain. Further, during the period of heavy migration it was often thought that African athletes benefitted from the "higher levels" of competition they received from white American athletes. Yet none of the early Kenyan runners we may think of as "world class" trained at U.S. universities, and even later, U.S. universities essentially exploited existing mature talent. The heavy recruitment of Kenyan runners to the United States during this time period led to the underdevelopment—the aforementioned brawn drain—of athletes within Kenya and hurt their performances on the global stage. Such an occurrence challenges the assumed rationality and technological supremacy of Western training regimes. Regardless, following the implementation of the NCAA rules, the number of African recruits to American universities declined in the late 1980s and then leveled off through the 1990s. Unfortunately, more current research has not been conducted to gauge where recruitment numbers currently stand.[37]

In the last ten to twenty years there has been an observable increase in the number of African players on collegiate basketball and football teams. While the football players appear to be predominantly second-generation immigrants, there is a greater mix of first- and second-generation immigrants playing basketball. Examples of recent NBA recruits from NCAA college basketball include Joel Embiid and Gorgui Dieng, while examples of those who have been drafted from European leagues include Bismack Biyombo, Serge Ibaka, and Giannis Antetokounmpo (second generation). Festus Ezeli and Emmanuel Mudiay immigrated to the United States before they were established athletes, Ezeli through a family member and Mudiay as an asylum seeker. The extent of this migration has yet to receive adequate academic attention. Whereas previously athletes would be directly recruited to a university, and in track and field they often still are, now athletes are coming in at the high school or community college level and then transferring or being recruited to college programs. Another difference is that African athletes are now primarily scattered throughout the United States and, to a lesser extent, Europe (including the United Kingdom) and Canada. Talent is usually identified in Africa through a player's presence on a national team or the ever-increasing number of basketball camps on the continent—often backed by the NBA, which has an interest in finding cheap labor like baseball has in Latin America. The young athletes—usually in their mid- to late teens—are then helped to come the United States by individuals (or nonprofits) who house them and work with a school—whether a public high school, junior or community college, or Christian or private academy—to get them a visa so they can legally stay. If everything goes smoothly the players will improve their skills and receive a scholarship to play NCAA college basketball. In the European context things operate similarly to soccer, as a young athlete is identified by a coach or scout, offered an opportunity to train or try out with a team or club, and then ideally debuts for that team and begins making his way up the ranks.

Current NBA center Joel Embiid would be a good example of this process in the United States. After beginning to play basketball locally in Yaoundé, Cameroon, the sixteen-year-old Embiid was invited by Luc Mbah a Moute—former UCLA and current NBA player, also from Cameroon—to attend the well-known Basketball without Borders camp in South Africa. From there Embiid was enrolled in Montverde Academy in Florida (where Mbah a Moute went to school). He then attended the Rock School (also in Florida) before being recruited to the University of Kansas and then drafted by the Philadelphia Seventy-Sixers of the NBA. Embiid is a contemporary example of the kind of networks that have arisen and multiplied to get African players an opportunity to play in the United States. Of course, not every player can or will succeed, and the dark side to this kind of player recruitment is more appropriately termed human trafficking. As Alexandra Starr has reported, when young immigrant athletes fail in the United States the resources available to them are few and often unknown to the athlete. They may find themselves homeless with little or no money for food and liminal legal status because their official entry papers (visa) identify them as "students" at schools in which they were never enrolled. Those responsible for trafficking the athletes (scouts, coaches, and host parents)—often betting on some sort of payday if the players succeed, such as money to steer a player toward certain universities or programs—tend to evade any sort of repercussions.[38]

At the same time, there are no centralized ways to count or report how many youths migrate to the United States in the hope of playing basketball, so it becomes difficult to track them over time unless they are actively playing. These underreported outcomes contradict the stated missions of the basketball camps in various African countries that many players are eager to attend. Though the camps stress education and not professional athletic competition as an end goal, Michael Ralph's work on a basketball academy in Senegal indicates a convergence toward a professional focus. With few options for the economic advancement of youths, basketball, second only to soccer, has become lodged in the imaginations of children and young adults who dream of better lives, as well as their parents. Ralph articulates the processes of globalization, specifically the role of Michael Jordan and diasporic community "imagining," that have translated into beliefs among Senegalese players of their ability to play basketball because they share a "style" or "rhythm" with African Americans. While the notions of hope and success through sport demonstrate certain process of diasporic communication, it remains frustrating that sport is seen as a legitimate way out of poverty.[39] I will return to these topics in later chapters.

As mentioned above, it is difficult to track immigrant players unless they are actively playing. For those who are playing, one source of information on the international scope of basketball migration is the websites run by Eurobasket (Eurobasket.com, USbasket.com, Afrobasket.com, Latinbasket.com, etc.). Their data for five recent years (2012–16) show 569 men and 84 women from African countries having played basketball in the United States at the high school, community or junior college, university, or professional levels. Nigeria easily dominates the sample with 251 men and 29 women, Senegal is next with 88 men and 13 women, and Cameroon rounds out the top three with 52 men and 10 women. Eurobasket claims that a total of 3,428 foreign players have played basketball in the United States in the last five years; African women and men together account for nearly 20 percent of all foreign players in the United States—whereas Africans made up only 4.4 percent of the total U.S. immigrant population in 2013. Eurobasket's data likely underestimates the share of Africans because it only counts citizenship, thereby eliminating many second-generation players who do not have dual citizenship in an African country, which would be of interest for countries like France (124 players in the United States), Germany (86), the United Kingdom (173), and Canada (309), all of which have players of African descent among their expat ranks.[40]

Further, the Eurobasket website shows see how many players each African country currently has playing abroad. As an example, for Nigerian women we see that in 2016 twenty-eight were playing in the United States (although the data appear to count players for the years 2012–16, as "current" players), but an additional twenty-one were playing overseas in places such as Spain, Australia, and Portugal. Similarly, 122 Nigerian men have played in countries other than the United States; Spain, Italy, Germany, and the United Kingdom dominate, but they also play in countries like China, Bahrain, Chile, Finland, Iran, and Qatar. Problems with the data aside, we can at least glimpse how the rising popularity of basketball and the NBA over the past three decades has created a transnational sport labor migrant class that draws from African countries in a significant and increasing way. While the process of recruiting players may still be similar to the kind of rudimentary scouting that led Hakeem Olajuwon to Houston, the networks have greatly expanded and intensified and have begun trying to find labor at younger and younger ages.[41]

This increase in transnational sport labor migration, as indicated above, has also meant increased participation for women. Though African men have dominated the focus of immigration studies, the athletic labor migration of women has been developing as well. In *The Brawn Drain*, written in 1991, Bale explains his bias toward men as not being purposeful but rather due to issues of patriarchy in African countries that have barred women from entry into competition. The experiences of Jepkorir Chepyator-Tomson, who ran for the University of Wisconsin in the early 1980s, reveal of the complexity facing African women in sport, even though she competed at a time when women in general were still struggling to gain a foothold in sport. Chepyator-Tomson explains how she faced criticism in both Kenya and the United States because by participating in sport she failed to live up to expectations of her as a mother of two children. Yet what is often lost in this discussion that tends to center on "African" patriarchy is the support role that men often play in the lives of female athletes. For Chepyator-Tomson, both her father and her husband played important roles in supporting her athletics and her education. Hence Kenyan (African) men were important in helping her navigate sexism in Kenya *and* the United States (the West). As I will discuss in later chapters, we must recover the humanity of African men in relation to women in order to avoid (1) remarginalizing African men and (2) privileging Western (post)feminism—and Western exceptionalism more broadly. At the time of Bale's writing African women were just beginning to become prominent athletes on the global stage. In 1989 Kenyan women took four of five top places at the World Junior Cross Country Championships, and Bale projected that such a showing would increase their recruitment into sport. Indeed, the years since have seen African women from different countries maintain a presence in track and field events on the global stage. Though women participating in high-level sport still face challenges, younger generations are more accepting and unmoved by the presence of women in athletics. As in the West generally, this cultural change is taking place because of what women have been able to accomplish and the minds they have been able to change over time.[42]

Conclusion

It is clear that the West's recruitment of African talent is a poorly regulated complex of networks that lend themselves to abusive exploitation. Too much money and power at the top, too many middle*men* struggling to get by, and too many youths rapidly losing hope in a meaningful and stable future are not only features of contemporary sport but reflective of the current global economic structure in general. While many might not know of the nature of sport recruitment, there are plenty who do, and we have seen some attempts to lessen the possibility of exploitation. One example is article 19 of FIFA's "Regulations on the Status and Transfer of Players," which specifically prohibits the international transfer of players under the age of eighteen. While there are exceptions to the rule, established in 2001, it seems unlikely that even strict enforcement, started in 2015, will fully address the problem. This is because many African soccer players migrate when they are just a little over nineteen years of age (19.4) on average, which is younger than players from all other points of origin: Latin America (22), Western Europe (22.4), Eastern Europe (22.7), and "Other origins" (21.1). As just discussed in the U.S. context, some are arriving as early as age fifteen or sixteen. These relatively early ages of migration make it all the more difficult to navigate and adjust to a new country.[43]

Another effort aimed toward helping trafficked players are organizations like Foot Solidaire, located in Paris, France. This organization is dedicated to stopping the trafficking of young players and assisting those who have already been brought to Europe. It claims to have helped more than 1,400 young players from its founding in 2006 to 2014. More often than not, however, individuals must find help from organizations unrelated to sport. In her report on trafficked players in the United States, Alexandra Starr noted that one individual received support from the African Services Committee—which aims to provide housing, health, legal, educational, and social services to immigrants, refugees, and asylees from Africa—after he made his way to New York when Amateur Athletic Union (AAU) basketball did not work out. In the end, the general public tends to be uninterested in stories about corruption and exploitation in sport, essentially seeing them as necessary evils to "develop talent" and "give opportunity" to young players. In an environment where the successes and riches are easily seen it is difficult to mount a response, or counternarrative, for and by those who are rendered invisible through their "failures."[44] It is also important not to look past the fact that these are predominantly black and brown athletes whose lives are often rendered meaningless in Western media. In such a media landscape their presence in the West is more likely to be constructed as their welcome and lucky shot at success rather than as a result of ongoing political, economic, and racial violence.

1

Race and Sport

Situating the Black African Athlete

The representation of black athletes has its roots in how blackness itself has been constructed over time. Indeed, we can go back to the formation of our modern conceptions of race—their development through the intensification of the Atlantic slave trade—and find similar tropes existing today. I cannot possibly give a full overview of the entire body of research here, but it is worthwhile to sketch a few important points of departure and mention some of the work that has been done on black African athletes and black (im)migrant athletes in particular. To those ends this chapter will first examine what Ben Carrington describes as the racial project of "the black athlete." Carrington's work is important not only as a framework in demonstrating the development of the notion of "the black athlete" as a departure, or change, from previously held notions of white *physical* supremacy but also in its discussions of why the black athlete is so important to the study of race, sport, and sociology—as a racial spectacle for the masses.[1] Following this, with an eye toward my own analysis, I will examine some of the previous research that has been done on the representation of black African and black (im)migrant athletes. We will begin to see that there are very clear similarities with how early diasporic black—African American and Black British—athletes were constructed in the West.

Formation of the "Black Athlete"

My research is founded on the premise that sport represents the main cultural field within which black (African) immigrants can first make their presence known to their host society. The first exposure of recent immigrants to members of the dominant society is more likely to be through sport than any other means, especially for those who have little contact with members of racial minority groups. The implication here being that studying sport can give us insight into how Western media is making sense of foreign blacks for its white middle-class target audience. This offers insights that are, of course, different from those provided by other forms of textual analysis that have tended to privilege, for example, works of literature or music. While the analysis of different cultural forms has offered immense insight and contributions to social theory, the often marginalized study of sport offers an analysis of culture that gets at the heart of the masses, including the working class and semiliterate.[2] Sport saturates our everyday, impacting us whether we follow it closely or despise it thoroughly, and hence it is an aspect of society that is difficult to ignore completely—particularly in Western societies. Sport is a populist cultural form that covers a wider swath of the population—especially when we consider race, gender, and class—than any specific form of literature, film, fashion, or music can. While other cultural forms lend themselves to being "read" along the lines of conventional literary criticism, Carrington notes that sport's "very physicality, the emphatically embodied nature of its performance, the sheer diversity of sporting forms and sites, and its assumed 'non-art' instrumental rationality, make[s] it a distinct cultural type that cannot easily be 'read' in the same way as these other cultural practices."[3] In the following pages I hope to adequately address the cultural form that is sport at some of these different levels of significance.

In *Race, Sport and Politics: The Sporting Black Diaspora*, Carrington expertly traces the development of what we consider "modern sport" to the logics of rationality and modernity that allowed Europe to brutally conquer, colonize, and exploit the resources of the world. As European expansion after 1492 led to increasing growth through the influx of wealth found elsewhere in the world, Europeans began to see the complexity of their societies as an indication of higher human development. European countries believed that they dominated the far reaches of the globe because of their natural and inherent traits of rationality, ingenuity, and strength (masculinity). Non-Europeans lagged behind the "development" of Europeans because they lacked the rational traits of civilization and could only hope to learn them—when such a thing was even given a thought—through a disciplined, or colonial, "schooling." This relationship between the colonizer and the colonized or enslaved was built on the assumption of the inherent nonpersonhood of the non-European Other. Non-Europeans were consistently infantilized, made childlike, in historical texts, speaking to their lack of full personhood that allowed Europeans to think of themselves as beneficent adults. Any form of resistance by the enslaved or colonized only further confirmed their innate irrationality (emotion) as the Other by rejecting the "gracious" gift of the colonizer. Hence the rise of Europe and the industrial revolution were seen to result from European society's own internal qualities and not the mass plundering and enslavement of non-European peoples. These kind of beliefs and shared benefit from participating in the colonial and slave economies over time helped crystallize a transnational identity among Europeans that distinguished them from non-Europeans. This identity has revolved around slightly different dichotomies—civilized versus savage, Christian versus heathen, European versus non-European—but, as Charles Mills comments, "they all eventually coalesced into the *basic* opposition of white versus nonwhite."[4]

In his body of work on the creation of white masculinity, James Mangan explains that the rapid social and economic changes in Europe around 1850 (modernization) led to an obsession with personal fitness and the rise of specific forms of leisure that had not previously existed. Around the end of the nineteenth century and the beginning of the twentieth sport began to be emphasized in schools throughout Europe (particularly in the United Kingdom) and "professional" leagues in baseball, football (American and European), and rugby were organized. Sport also began to take on an important role as an agent of militarism, imperialism, and morality for the nation-state at this time. We see the popularization of ideas such as "Muscular Christianity," which held that a well-trained body was a moral one, and social Darwinism, which saw war as necessary for the vitality and protection of society and the white race. As Mangan discusses, a militant masculinity was established in Europe over time that was developed and proven on the playing field and through the concept of "athleticism." Militarism and imperialism became valued concepts integral to patriotism and necessary for self-defense, wars and violence became rites of passage for boys, a militant masculinity was designed to expel all that was feminine and intellectual, and imperialism itself became seen as a moral endeavor tied to civilizing savage heathens.[5]

All of these concepts became interdependent. By the 1880s sport was successfully being used as a means to socially control young men in European public schools as well as colonial natives. The establishment of schools in sub-Saharan Africa was centered not on building well-educated subjects but rather on "building character" (submissiveness) and converting the native to Christianity. Sport thus became a defining feature of colonial "education" because it was thought to promote a morality and manliness that could then be controlled by colonial administrators. Though colonized subjects around the world would resist these colonial discourses in different ways, sport nonetheless became an important colonial technology that significantly remade "traditional" cultures while simultaneously driving the impulse among the colonized to further organize and resist through colonial sport forms—soccer and cricket in particular.[6]

It is within this context that the notion of "modern sport" is still rooted. More recent versions of modernization theories hold that the "traditional mentality" of the non-European precludes the scientific and progressive ways of thinking that spurred Europe's rise. In these formulations, Europe is the natural creator and disseminator of culture, progress, morality, and everything else that is "good" in the world. Europe naturalized the myth of its self-propelled progress, morality, and rationality so that it came to validate classical colonial practices and ongoing practices of economic neocolonialism. "Modern sport" betrays its Eurocentric creation through its positioning against "traditional" movement forms that go unacknowledged as "sport." We are often told that the (colonial) primitive, lacking in mental and social complexity, had little to no notion of rule-bound (complex) sport forms. It was thus the rational European mind and colonial project that extended our notion of modern sport to the rest of the non-European world. Again, this was a process whereby any involvement or notion of addition by non-Europeans to European sport tended to be marginalized or ignored. That we are now geared toward seeing sport as the outcome of a rational and "civilized" process belies the often irrational and brutal aspects of both its expansion throughout the colonial world and its ongoing contemporary reliance on exploiting violence—on predominantly black and brown bodies— for profit.[7] Hence it has always been a myth that modern sport has achieved some sort of temporal or moral distance from primitive or traditional sport forms. Sport "[embodies] not so much modernity and its self-declared properties—secularization, rationality, meritocracy, and so on—but rather the *incomplete, partial and paradoxical* elements of competing modernities that refuse to be disavowed."[8] As with most dichotomies, we are given and made to assume complete separation, yet we can see that "modernity" and "tradition" are always intertwined. This means that modernity's obsession with tradition ensures that tradition is always internal to (within) modernity and necessary for its continued existence. Yet the myth of modernity as having left tradition behind allows, in this case, modern sport to appear separated from its history of white supremacy, colonialism, and sexism.[9] In short, sport acts as if it is apolitical.

Carrington argues that the formation of "the black athlete" in history is the result of an ongoing racial project—"sporting racial projects"— rooted in sport as a mass commodity spectacle.[10] Michael Omi and Howard Winant, in their theory of racial formation—"the sociohistorical process by which racial categories are created, inhabited, transformed, and destroyed"—describe racial projects as the ideological links between social structure and cultural representation. As they explain, "Racial projects connect what race *means* in a particular discursive practice and the ways in which both social structures and everyday experiences are racially *organized*, based on that meaning."[11] The black athlete conceptualized as a racial project thus carries important meaning for our everyday discursive practices, but also for how those practices are translated into or maintained in our social structures. Drawing on the work of Anne McClintock and her ideas on how scientific racism was most effectively disseminated to the masses through everyday commodities (commodity racism as consumer spectacle), Carrington similarly sees sport as a form of racial spectacle through which popular racism is "lived, embodied and challenged."[12] As the black athlete emerged throughout the twentieth century our "categories of 'blackness,' 'whiteness,' and even of 'race' and 'sport' have changed over time and *changed as a result of their co-articulations with each other*."[13] So not only have our racial categories—particularly the assumed natural advantages and disadvantages of different races—been changed by sport, but sport itself—who it is for and who is excluded—has been influenced by black athletes gradually pushing the boundaries of "blackness." Sport becomes productive of racial discourses, shaping and shaped by race, that then have an impact on our other social institutions.

These changes over time in our categories of race and sport due to the emergence of the black athlete can likely begin with many individuals, but at the level of global significance there is no better starting point than the African American boxer Jack Johnson. When Johnson beat Tommy Burns in 1908 to become the first black heavyweight champion of the world it marked the beginning of a shift in conventional thinking about race. Until then white supremacy was based on the notion of both mental and physical superiority over nonwhite populations. It was "well-known" that blacks lacked stamina and courage and were weak in the midsection but not the head—because of their thick skulls. Not only did Johnson physically dominate Burns and later challengers, notably Jim Jeffries in 1910, he also displayed superior technique and the ability to out think white competitors during fights. His success was an inherent critique of the main pillars of white supremacy that maintained racial oppression around the world and paid the "wages of whiteness" for poor and working-class whites, but it is important to remember that his impact on racial ideologies was not limited to the United States.[14]

Theresa Runstedtler explains that during the early twentieth century many black American men and women traveled to Europe and worked on ships or as porters, performers, and athletes, seeking ways to make a living that were denied them under Jim Crow. Runstedtler's work is important for understanding how a "global color line" was coming into being at this time. As Jack Johnson traveled around Europe, Australia, and Latin America, his routes mimicked those of other black Americans attempting to find a place for black political freedom. Like those other black Americans, what Johnson found was that white supremacy and the Jim Crow color line inevitably followed him wherever he went. His victories did not bring him true freedom or acceptance in European societies; instead he found it more and more difficult to find white opponents to fight in countries that had previously enjoyed the spectacle of interracial boxing. As Runstedtler points out, commercial spectacles of race at this time were used to reach semiliterate and working-class audiences and foster national identities around "white control." Such spectacles—including fairs, exhibitions, images, and commodities focused on the display black- ness and black peoples—occurred throughout the United States and Europe. While often fostering jingoism and a contempt for anything foreign or Other, such spectacles bolstered notions white supremacy (especially in Europe) while folding black Americans, black Europe- ans, and black Africans into the same (colonial) subject position. In the sport of boxing in particular, it was easy for advertisements and reporters to lean on the "uncivilized" nature of the sport and specu- late as to how or why the ever "primal/primitive/savage" black boxer might have an advantage over white men.[15]

The late nineteenth and early twentieth centuries were also a time when science was being used to provide a legitimate basis for white male supremacy. The ideas of eugenics and social Darwinism in par- ticular were compelling and created concern that the white race was in decline. This concern was often explicitly gendered, as it was thought that modernity had made white men physically soft and morally vul- nerable to the nonwhite Other. The maintenance of white supremacy not only required segregation from nonwhites but also led to poli- cies that essentially criminalized disease and deformity, leading to the forced sterilization of unwanted populations in many instances. Sport was important because it was thought that sports such as box- ing, football, and rugby could "make men out of boys," instill moral character, and prepare males for their rightful place as leaders in the world, whether as soldiers or colonial administrators. "Muscular Christianity" became an important ideology that made physical activity, games, and recreation more religiously acceptable and led to the development of sport programs within public school systems and independent organizations—such as the Young Men's Christian Association (YMCA) and the Boy Scouts. Additionally, the popular transnational figure of the "great white hope" fit a discourse that allowed everyday white and working-class men (often newly arrived immigrants in the U.S. context) to play a role and imagine themselves as making a contribution to the "white man's burden" of imperial rule over the nonwhite world.[16]

After World War I, with its heavy death tolls, white supremacy found itself pressed more vociferously by the populations it had oppressed for so long. The movements and ideas of nonwhite peoples still flowed across the migratory routes of working-class black transnationals, carrying information and ideas from one location to another. As Runstedtler tells us, a black counterculture began to organize in a more urgent way than ever before. Militant black masculinities, racial pride, black radicalism, and diasporic coalition building found their expression in various movements such as the Harlem Renaissance, Negritude, and El Negrismo and in the continued work of black intellectuals like W. E. B. Du Bois. The contributions of black athletes to this greater awareness among black peoples cannot be overlooked. Runstedtler explains how Johnson's victories over Burns and Jeffries helped colonized people around the world—Afro-Cubans, Filipinos, Asian Indians, and so on—further develop their own notion of self-determination. The victories against white male physical supremacy by black and nonwhite athletes during this time not only showed that white physical superiority was a myth but also brought into question white geopolitical supremacy and the idea that whites were the best or most capable rulers. Though it would be some time still before many of these places gained any notion of formal independence or saw the legal end of segregation, the seeds of resistance and the inherent political nature of black athletes saw rapid development during this time. In the displays of Johnson as well as other early black athletes Carrington sees the development of "the black athlete" as a racial trope. Despite significant efforts, the ideology of white supremacy simply could not account for the athletic displays people were now routinely seeing, primarily among black fighters in the boxing ring. Throughout the twentieth century, as the black athlete became a mainstay on the sporting landscape, the idea of white physical advantage eroded even further and an emphasis on trying to find the black "advantage" emerged.[17]

The success of the individual black athlete could not, of course, be due to hard work and dedication. Racial science of the 1930s became engrossed in trying to account for the "problem" of black success. To those ends, the black athlete was poked and prodded, measured and quantified in an attempt to ascertain the underlying physiological mechanisms that allowed for athletic success. Despite the fact that most studies were fundamentally flawed by taking "race" as an onto-logical reality and not a social construction, the latent functions of the studies successfully reduced black athleticism to the body. Hence we begin to see the development of conceptions of the black ath-lete as "natural," "innate," unthinking, and reactive. Any notion that black athleticism might have larger implications for colonial beliefs about the intellectual or mental capabilities of blacks was patently ignored. Quite the opposite, we begin to see the "natural" athleticism of blacks being used to further entrench white intellectual superiority through the establishment of the mind/body dichotomy. Since blacks were "gifted" in physical endeavors, they must be deficient in cog-nitive ones. More than ever the supposed character-building bene-fits of modern sport and explanations for athletic success applied to whites only. Thus when white athletes succeeded it was attributed to hard work, dedication and perseverance, but for the black athlete it was and often still is considered "natural" advantage.[18]

As Carrington explains, the scientific search for "black athleti-cism" was not necessarily the problem; rather, "the *belief* that there was such a thing as 'the black athlete' helped *constitute the object itself*."[19] Hence the notion that "the black athlete" exists as a coherent subject is what is so problematic. The discourses of the various fields contributing to sport science did not discover "the black athlete" but rather created it by assuming its existence and coherence in the first place. Carrington adds that "the 'black athlete' does not exist in any meaningful ontological sense outside of the discourse of white sports science and popular imaginings. The 'black athlete' is a construction made from the repertoire of colonial fantasies about blackness that find their fullest expression in the shape of *sporting negritude*."[20] We can think of sporting negritude as generally referring to the angry, uncontrolled, and ungrateful black body that succeeds only through natural (animalistic) ability and oversight from white (intellectual and rational) coaches and trainers. The "black athlete" is thus superhuman and hypermasculine (also hypersexualized) but remains (politically) controllable by white patriarchy through complex processes of objectification and commodification. It is also through these discourses that whiteness comes to know and define itself, as it always has, as the absence of that which is blackness. By defining blackness as natural, animalistic, and unchanging, whites could maintain their beliefs in supremacy by knowing themselves to be intellectually, technologically, and morally superior.[21]

Through his physical feats, Jack Johnson not only brought about the formation of "the black athlete" as a racial trope but also largely contributed to the construction of the black athlete as angry, brash, uncontrolled, uncivilized, arrogant, and flashy. He embodied a vehement rejection of the passive and deferential black man that white supremacy expected, instead embracing a working-class black masculine identity. By dating and marrying multiple white women during the Jim Crow era, driving (and crashing) expensive cars when few could drive, wearing gold and diamond jewelry (including gold-capped teeth), and actively taunting his white competitors in the ring, Johnson went far beyond what the black bourgeoisie thought proper or tasteful at the time. It is at this point in the early twentieth century that we see white disdain for "the black athlete" emerge. The "black athlete" was seen as ungrateful, unprofessional, and dishonorable, and it is this image that has stuck in the white imagination ever since. Johnson's effrontery was not forgotten when Joe Louis rose to be heavyweight champion of the world, as his management's efforts to ensure that Louis would be "respectable" only reinforced the notion of "the black athlete" in the public imagination through its absence. It is important to remember also that black women during this time faced the color bar (Ora Washington) and discrimination (Althea Gibson) or were held to standards of middle-class white femininity if they wanted "acceptance" in sport (Wilma Rudolph). Black women were able to achieve great things in sport in the latter half of the twentieth century but they were and still are artificially constrained by both race and gender stereotypes. Hence "the black athlete" (male and female) has served as an object of both fear and admiration in the white imaginary, but always has represented something inherently primitive and in need of control, discipline, and training—ultimately trapped in the colonial dichotomy of good/bad subject. That working-class black masculinity is (still) seen as "authentic" or "real" blackness, a naturalized deviance that blacks can correct only through submission to white male supremacy, continues to muddle our conversations on race.[22]

Toward Constructing the Foreign Black Other

If "the black athlete" is important in actively forming our conceptions of race in the West in a broad manner, then "the foreign black athlete" must present some particularities in the processes of racial formation. Being "foreign" certainly indicates some outsider status, and thus the representation of the foreign black Other is likely to reflect, at least, the intersections of race, nation, and culture. Representations of the foreign black Other will indicate how the West thinks about itself and how it thinks about its "elsewhere"—"Africa" in this case. As mentioned previously, my divide here between "foreign" and "native" is not uncomplicated, especially when we consider that blackness is in many ways kept "foreign" (external) to the concept of the nation-state (culture) even when it is putatively and fundamentally internal—as with African Americans. The contemporary "foreign black athlete," however, gives us a subject that is "novel" to the Western nation-state and, importantly, differs from the "native" black community within Western societies. As we will see later, the foreign/native separation is important only insofar as it is useful for interrogating the manipulations of blackness by the West. It is not my intention here to construct "the foreign black athlete" (or "the black African athlete") as separate from "the black athlete." The concept of

"the black athlete," as discussed above, is always already tied to colonial notions of "African" athletic (in)ability in the explanations for the
successes and failures of both "native" and "foreign" black athletes.
As John Hoberman explains, the success of black athletes early on
was popularly thought to be due to a Darwinian drama on the "Dark
Continent" that forged muscular endurance and fortitude through
environmental hardships—in other words, running away from big
cats and poisonous bugs.[23]

These faux evolutionary beginnings—with the additional explanations of slavery and "selective breeding" in the United States—
have been a central and deeply rooted aspect of the formation of "the
black athlete." They willfully ignore the long history of complex civilizations on the African continent that were destroyed by the slave
trade and colonialism in a fashion similar to the fates of other native
peoples around the globe. The consistent reduction of black athleticism to natural or savage origins has its origins in the European
colonial mentality and its links to white masculinity. In the colonial
setting, the need to distinguish between black and white masculinities in part rested on the notion of "courage" as an integral part of
male dignity. Throughout the colonial "adventure" white men had
access to, gained prestige from, and validated their conquests through
a discourse of courage. Meanwhile, those natives who would inevitably resist colonial rule were denied such access to masculine courage; instead their displays in conflict (or sport) were seen as reckless
or animalistic. Because blackness was seen as the cultural antithesis of whiteness, black athletes' physical aptitude could at times be
admired yet remained far from threatening white male supremacy.
Little has changed in our contemporary moment, as white men frequently cheer and root for black male athletes while supporting political viewpoints that hurt black communities. White colonial anxiety
about the supposed athletic advantages of black athletes has been reconciled through the aforementioned reinscription of athleticism itself
as primitive and unintellectual. What threat black athleticism posed
to white masculinity was further nullified through the racial pseu-
doscience of the twentieth century that was designed to find physical differences separating black from white.[24]

As global economic structures grew and intensified throughout the twentieth century, the valorization of technological advancement and rational efficiency has continued to exclude blacks from modernity. The inability of African peoples to "progress" since colonialism "ended" has only reinforced the colonial imagery of the "lazy" subject. Thus Africans, and non-Europeans more broadly, are not seen as competent or able workers for the global economy.[25] While athletic dominance may have meant something with regard to masculine courage and survival during colonialism proper, it is now something that continues to link black athletes to premodern savagery. As Hoberman explains, "In the age of the global cognitive elite, athletic superiority is, in a Darwinian sense, a vestigial trait that possesses ornamental rather than strategic value for nations whose stereotyped racial identities bar their membership in what [Hugh] O'Donnell calls the 'entrepreneurial capitalism' of the Center."[26] Hence the very meaning of athleticism to the nation-state at the global level has changed, without improving the fortunes of those in developing countries who have invested in it. The only labor those from African countries are able to provide (invest in) is exploitative physical labor for international and national sports bodies centered in the West. Needless to say, the Eurocentric nature of global sport and its abuses in developing countries concerning athletic development and recruitment are rarely explored in the media.

It is no surprise, then, to look at the construction of "the black African athlete" over the last forty to sixty years and find the same stereotypical descriptors I have been discussing. Runstedtler, for example, discusses the early twentieth-century (circa 1920s) boxer Amadou M'Barick, who was seen as the "Jack Johnson of Europe" for his flashy style and relationships with white women. M'Barick, born in French Senegal and nicknamed "Battling Siki," was a decorated soldier who fought for France—along with 134,000 other Africans—during World War I. An example of the increasingly blurred boundaries between Europe/Africa and citizen/subject, M'Barick was frequently framed in the media as an uncivilized and untrained jungle savage and often compared to gorillas and chimpanzees. All of this despite M'Barick's own narrative that he had grown up in a city and had never even seen a jungle. By surrounding interracial boxing spectacles with these discourses, promoters not only realized profits but also revealed the basic white supremacy at the heart of French colonialism at a time when race and racism were thought to be something imported from the United States.[27]

We can see the persistence of these stereotypes if we jump to the latter part of the century, as John Hoberman describes how Ghanaian soccer player Anthony Yeboah was compared to gazelles and seals and was described as being "sensitive" while playing in Germany during the early 1990s. Hoberman also brings attention to stereotypes about black Africans being unable to play in the cold, to fit into a system of (rational) play, to play in central (thinking) positions, and generally to lack in stamina and determination. When we look at other research that has focused specifically on black Africans we find similar things through the years. "Scientific journalism" has historically focused on the bodies of African runners (bone structure, lung capacity, running posture, etc.), their cultures (physical labor during childhood), and their environment (hot, dangerous, and at high altitude). The "African athlete" has long been seen as raw material for Western "processing" into athletic glory, while simultaneously denying "the black athlete" full inclusion into the Western category of "hero" or "legend"—not to mention the nation-state.[28] Themes of genetic and physical superiority or cultural and geographical determinism persist to this day through media discourse as a way to explain the successes and failures of black African athletes in sport.

In his rhetorical examination of the neocolonial discourse surrounding Nyandika Maiyoro and Kipchoge Keino, John Bale discusses how the two Kenyan distance runners challenged the white colonial frame of what was possible for "the foreign black athlete." Because the successes of Maiyoro and Keino throughout the 1950s and 1960s and beyond intruded on what was thought to be a white sport (space), Bale sees them as postcolonial transgressors in that they forced a revision of the colonial stereotype that black distance runners did not have the stamina to win races. Due to these transgressions into white spaces—by virtue of being black and foreign—media coverage of these two runners presents a range of contradictions in what Bale describes as neocolonial discourses. These discourses consist of surveillance, appropriation, idealization, and negation. Briefly, discourses of surveillance refer to colonial and neocolonial practices of measuring the bodies of black Africans—the colonial subject. In the sport of distance running this shifts to include the measuring of time, speed, and distance in order to compare black African athletes—by Western standards—against those in the West and around the world in a simple and straightforward manner, lacking any context. Discourses of appropriation deploy what Bale calls the "conversionist fantasy," such as the notion that the success of Maiyoro are indicative of "a stage" of African development toward Western norms. Such fantasies indicate that if "the foreign black athlete" has the "right" training and adapts to Western norms then he or she will become a "civilized" athlete. Of course, the discourses of idealization and negation ensure that "the black athlete" is never allowed to be civilized. Idealization refers to the attribution of black African athletic success to aforementioned "natural" factors (environmental determinism) but also, at times, to the notion of a distinctive black "style" that promotes winning. Meanwhile, negation explains black success as the result of an unfair advantage—whether through physical, environmental, or tactical means (e.g., cheating). Both idealization and negation narratives fail to consider black athletic success as the result of numerous factors, including dedication, culture (popularity of the sport), and history.[29]

Similarly, J. Nauright and T. Magdalinski's discursive analysis of swimmer Eric Moussambani at the 2000 Sydney Olympics sheds light on how Western media blames black athletic failure on cultural (traditional) backwardness. After the other two swimmers in his 100M heat were disqualified, Moussambani was forced to swim the race alone. His solitary swim and the relatively poor time he achieved made for a provocative image and garnered a disproportionate amount of media attention. As the authors argue, the discourses surrounding Moussambani's performance are notable in that they revive colonial modes of thinking and talking about the black foreign Other. Through their analysis the authors identify three prominent frameworks within which Moussambani was situated by the media: (1) Moussambani as the embodiment of the Olympic spirit, (2) Moussambani as the exotic African, and (3) Moussambani as a representative of the need of athletic civilizing. Each of these relates to the larger picture of the West being portrayed as the authority in all things and Africa being situated as the Other in need of civilizing.[30]

Within the first framework, the authors discuss how the media continually described Moussambani's performance as "heroic," but not in a way befitting heroes in the West. At a time when the Olympics are increasingly subject to critiques from various sides concerning doping, corruption, and overcommercialization, Moussambani was quickly turned into the "noble savage" who could regain the lost innocence of the Olympics—and by association, the West. This discourse is paternalistic for a number of reasons. It posits that there were no expectations for Moussambani to be competitive and that his "simple" nature and naïveté made his presence valid only because "we" (the West) can learn something about ourselves—what Western societies have lost through modernity—from him. The second framework refers to how media framed Moussambani's upbringing and training in Equatorial Guinea. Moussambani was portrayed as uncultured and primitive, creating a culture/nature, West/Africa dichotomy that further validates the West's cultural and technological superiority. Moussambani's upbringing in Equatorial Guinea was described in pastoralist terms, often bringing attention to a childhood spent swimming in waters populated by crocodiles, thus further linking him with nature. His Olympic training was seen as insufficient because it occurred without the use of Olympic-size swimming pools, appropriate coaching, or "sophisticated" training regiments. The third framework, "Moussambani as a representative for athletic civilizing," situates the advanced swimwear worn by the elite athletes (Speedo FastSkin) against Moussambani's simple one-piece Speedo briefs. The authors focus on technology as another sign of the civilized/uncivilized divide. Moussambani's near-naked black skin (state of nature) represents the technological shortcomings of his training and country. Even when Moussambani tried on one of the newer swimsuits, he was viewed simply as an imitator of Western cultural norms.[31]

While Moussambani was discursively kept "outside" of both the (predominantly white) sport of swimming and the Olympics more generally (because his presence was aided by a program to help internationalize the sport of swimming), his construction as a noble savage was otherwise quite typical—as we will later see. Comparably, former Major League Soccer (MLS) star Freddy Adu was represented through the tropes of noble savagery but he was also considered an "American" and part of the "American Dream" immigrant story. As Kyle Kusz explains, Adu's fame and celebrity in 2004—when he made his MLS debut at the age of fourteen—were deeply tied to the logics of neoliberal racism. These logics—of hard work, individualism, obedience to authority, assimilation, nationalism, and color-blindness—created a space for Adu in (white) American culture, media, and marketing as long as he adhered to them. Importantly, neoliberal racism also performs a dual function of contrasting Adu's immigrant status and success with the successes of African Americans, while simultaneously displacing (temporarily) Adu's blackness as meaningless to his achievements. So the discourse around Adu celebrated him and his single mother as the success story that "everyone," but especially African Americans, should follow. By characterizing him as working hard, being humble, and sacrificing, discourses about Adu and his mother saliently critique the African American community, which, within neoliberal racism, is seen as failing to take advantage of the opportunities America provides—relying too much on the "race card" as an explanation for its failures. In short, these discourses of neoliberal racism allow white American society to think that it is a postracial society when it is not. Kusz goes on to tell us that when Adu's career began to falter—at one point he inferred that he would like to play for the Ghanaian national team—his blackness and foreign alterity came back to the fore. Not only was Adu compared to the "problem" black athletes of the time (most notably Terrell Owens), but online message board posters advocated for his deportation.[32] These ideas are important to the research I discuss throughout this book, and we will return to them in later chapters.

In a different research approach, Jim Denison and Pirrko Markula look at the ubiquitous press conference as an important part of sport and a space where the black athlete is in direct communication with an overwhelmingly white press corps. The authors focus on legendary distance runner Haile Gebrselassie and the social aspects at work due to his status as an Ethiopian and the international (European) nature of the reporters at one of his press conferences, all of whom have been exposed to stereotypical images of Africa throughout their lives. Many social forces are at work in the press conference. For example, it is one arena where athletes have a chance to portray and construct themselves as athletes and as individuals. These constructions are then interpreted by the media, which will disperse the information that most people will end up consuming because they themselves do not have access to elite athletes. The authors are interested in how Gebrselassie presents himself and Ethiopia while being questioned by reporters who are simultaneously looking to construct meaning around him. Much of the discursive action Denison and Markula explore centers on a European preoccupation with the African body as athletic, its opposition to white athletic bodies, and the oversimplification of the cultures African runners are presumed to be from.[33]

Contrary to their expectations of finding individual agency, Denison and Markula find that Gebrselassie's performance at the press conference was a spectacle for Westerners by Westerners. They describe how the political questions Gebrselassie was asked regarding the problems of Ethiopia ultimately served to take pressure off of Western societies in terms of aid to Africa. His efforts to explain the problems of his country and describe his humanitarian goals show how the press conference was carefully directed by the Western media to satisfy their curiosity about Ethiopia without allowing Gebrselassie to fully articulate his being and intent. We learn little to nothing about what Gebrselassie thinks about the West—especially as it concerns larger political questions of inequality the West has a hand in—while he and his various "solutions" to the problems Ethiopia and Africa face are constructed to represent all of Ethiopia or Africa. The end result is a new stereotype, the African "humanitarian businessman" or the "good" businessperson who has gotten rich (in the West) and intends to wisely help her or his people with his or her millions. This stereotype allows for the continuation of unequal status among African countries and the West. Gebrselassie is posited as a kind of "savior" of "Africa," which serves to reinforce neoliberal notions of African self-help (Africa for Africans). The West is thus able again to congratulate itself for the "opportunities" it has given to otherwise poverty-stricken black Africans to succeed through hard work and then help others become less dependent on Western aid (welfare).[34] This is another important concept that we will return to in later chapters.

Conclusion

In this chapter I have tried to establish the importance of "the black athlete" as a racial trope and to begin carving out a conceptual space for "the foreign black athlete" as the same. The importance of the way in which, over the course of the twentieth century, "the black athlete" became a significant and primary driver of our understanding of race and sport cannot be understated. Much as "the black athlete" becomes the popular image of blackness, so too does "the foreign black athlete" represent not only an athletic form of blackness but also the "good" immigrant—insofar as the individual adheres to the expectations of white supremacy. The persistence of colonial stereotypes of the black subject in general ensure that blackness does not threaten white supremacy, and there is much to be learned about how white supremacist discourses make this happen via the foreign black Other.

These foundational beliefs about the colonial subject are deeply tied to the development of Western nation-states and their imperial practices. That the racism inherent within Western conquest of the globe has been present for over five hundred years is a testament to its durability as an organizing principle. Moon-Kie Jung describes three deep "schemas" of racism that have provided its durability over time and necessarily linked it with other deep and durable social structures. For our purposes, we can think of a schema as society's fundamental tools of thought and the various principles of action and habits of speech and gesture that are built with these fundamental tools. Schemas make up the meaningful and cultural parts of social life in informal, unconscious, and often assumed ways. What gives a schema "depth" is the degree to which it is conscious or unconscious within society, with deeper schemas being more resistant to change and transformation (but never static).[35]

Jung's first schema of racism is the concept of race as a partitioning of human beings based on some notion of inherited traits. There is always historical specificity concerning how and how many racial categories exist, and these schemas have the potential to articulate with other deep schemas, as "the race schema insistently combines with heteropatriarchy, producing and rationalizing racialized categorical boundaries through the regulation of sexuality, gender, reproduction, and kinship." The second schema concerns the suitability or unsuitability for social inclusion on the basis of race and "conjoins easily with nationalism, producing and rationalizing racialized inclusions and exclusions by the state and others." And the final schema concerns the belief of superiority and inferiority as it pertains to race and "readily articulates with capitalism, producing and rationalizing racialized material inequalities."[36]

Because of the depth of these schemas and their fundamental role in the rise of Euro-America, they are "subconsciously enacted in practice and cannot be simply 'unthought.'"[37] It is also important to recognize that these schemas of racism operate at and intersect with multiple levels simultaneously—the individual, local, regional, national, and global. For my interests here in particular, the interplay of racism at and between different nation-states and globally is what makes this project feasible. It is the aggregation of different racisms throughout all levels, utilizing and accumulating immense resources and power, that Charles Mills has called "global white supremacy," "the unnamed political system that has made the modern world what it is today."[38] Jung is worth quoting at length here:

> The nation is just one scale at which structures exist and analyses can be carried out. This is not to say that nation-states, or states more generally, do not matter. Given the past and continuing salience of states, we could reasonably expect to find denser webs of structures within them than across them. But even the most isolated state is not hermetically sealed. Furthermore, among structures, racism has been so "transnational," or transtatal, as to require little argument: its "trans-

nationalism" is, if not axiomatic, historically incontrovertible. From its genesis to the present, even before the advent of "nations," racism has been part and parcel of globally momentous "transnational" structures, including slavery, colonialism, imperialism, and migration.[39]

Studies looking specifically at African athletes and issues of race and racism have tended to be concentrated in the format of journal articles and book chapters. The most significant limitation of these formats is, of course, space. So we have ended up with a number—not a large number—of articles and book chapters that are saying something about one specific athlete (usually) but without the space to make a larger argument about transnational or global forms of racism(s). In much of the research done on African American, Black British, or variously "diasporic" black athletes we actually begin to lose sight of how colonial stereotypes about the African subject remain prevalent in how blackness as a whole is constructed. In some ways it is almost as if the research in sport has itself forgotten that Africa and African athletes are still around and playing a very significant contemporary role in the production and formation of race and racism—not to mention diaspora. It is my aim in the following chapters to bring the black African athlete back into the conversation.

2

Everyday Othering

Boundary Making and Maintenance

Casual discourse and conversation can often tell us a great deal about the values of society and how that society views minorities and foreigners. Hence I begin here with what can be called the mundane practices of Othering in Western media. These everyday discursive practices rely on seemingly harmless descriptors yet serve to reinforce racial and national boundaries, including commonsense understandings of black athleticism. Edward Said, in a theoretical engagement with Michel Foucault, states that while all discourses are composed of signs, they do more with these signs than just designate things. This "more" is what we must uncover and describe. In the discourse of Orientalism (for Said), "more" refers to the power and institutional force to make statements and evaluative distinctions about the Orient (the Other).[1] In addition, I argue that the mundane is linked with more explicit, often stereotypical, understandings of blackness, immigration, nationality, and the African continent. In keeping foreign black Others distinct and separate from their host countries and native black Others, the experiences and existence of foreign black communities are ignored and any resistive political potential with native black communities (or native Others) is muted. It is this movement from the mundane to the specific with which I am concerned in this chapter and my analysis.

I have divided this chapter into three parts. In the first I focus on the everyday labeling of black African athletes as "African" in some way. Second, I examine the nicknames of some of the athletes in this study and discuss how they reflect Western opinion and attitudes toward black African immigrants. Third, I explore the role of gender in the representation of black African immigrants through mundane representations of black African female athletes.

Mundane and Everyday Labeling Processes

Beginning with the mundane, we can discern some salient processes of Othering. For example, the athletes in my study are often innocently referenced, or labeled, by their point of origin or nationality. This labeling process is a common feature in media throughout my study, regardless of origin and regardless of whether the athlete in question is white or black or brown. Yet we can also read these consistent tendencies as reproducing and maintaining hegemonic sociopolitical geographies. Richard Iton explains that part of the struggle of native blacks in the United States after the civil rights movement has been trying to find the space within language to effectively go beyond the nation-state as an imposed limit to political imagination. The normalization of black politics in the United States and the coerced withdrawal from communist and anticolonial movements during the Cold War still influence political discourse today. These same limitations on national political imagination are hurting black communities in European countries as well.[2] Perhaps if the geographies of Africa and African countries were not already defined in the negative things would be different, but, as we will see, mundane references to nationality quickly link to more explicit kinds of Othering, such as reference to names, languages spoken, poverty, family structure, and other stereotypes of Africa in general. These more explicit processes are similar to yet different from the simpler forms of labeling but make a needed link to broader representations of the African continent.

Everything about Mutombo—beginning with the fact that he's come a long way to play in the league, from Kinshasa, Zaire—appears to be outstretched. His full name in itself is a *paragraph*, Dikembe Mutombo Mpolondo Mukamba Jean Jacque Wamutombo. He speaks the following languages: English, French, Italian, Portuguese plus *several tribal tongues* from his native land. He tells tall tales.[3]

On Sunday in Kansas City, the Jets will meet one of the more interesting new players in the National Football League, Christian Okoye of Enugu, Nigeria. Okoye is a 253-pound, 6-foot-11/2-inch running back who has been timed in 4.46 seconds over 40 yards and is the league's top rookie runner this season. He has gained 344 yards and is 11th in the N.F.L. in rushing, which is commendable for someone who first played football four years ago at the age of 22.[4]

These examples demonstrate that references to nationality, foreign names, and "tribal" languages or "dialects" are extremely common in everyday reports about African athletes. In particular, the shortcut used in referring to African languages with millions of speakers, such as Swahili, as tribal or a dialect is a salient feature across a number of the representations in this study. Zdenek Salzmann explains that the term *dialect* "refers to a form of language or speech used by members of a regional, ethnic, or social group. Dialects that are mutually intelligible belong to the same language." Though mutual intelligibility varies, clouding the distinction between language and dialect, Salzmann goes on to argue, "All languages spoken by more than one small homogeneous community are found to consist of two or more dialects." Because of its large dispersal, English is actually one of the most dialectally diversified languages, yet it would be nonsensical to say that an individual knows "three American dialects" to opaquely refer to the U.S. Midwest, South, and Northeast.[5] Hence the use of the term *dialect* by Western media renders the languages of Africa as *extremely* local, "tribal," insignificant and without name, unknown and unknowable.

Relatedly, the focus on accent or subtle surprise that these athletes can speak English, French, Italian, and Portuguese demonstrates the quickly forgotten history of Western colonialism and its role in spreading European language forms throughout Africa. Repeated references to national belonging are often seen, even when such information is unnecessary or extraneous, as we see with Okoye, and at times draw attention to or devalue certain aspects of their Otherness, as we can see with Mutombo's name being labeled a paragraph. Since discourse involves a certain way of thinking about and acting upon our social world, these hegemonic discourses serve to promote our thinking in Western-centric nationalist terms. These athletes are foreign, even if citizens of Western countries, their cultures do certain things differently (that may or may not amuse us), and their respective countries have properties (racialized geographies) different than "ours" in the West.[6] As I discuss in the next chapter, these descriptors are also part of constructing these athletes as "model minorities" insofar as they are differentiated from native blacks, allied with middle-class values (hard work, education, multilingual skills), and naïve (noble savages).

Second-generation athletes like Mario Balotelli face a unique situation. Born in Italy of Ghanaian parentage, Balotelli is described as "Italian" throughout most mentions in my analysis, although early in his career frequent explanations of his Ghanaian roots appear. We can interpret these media efforts as trying to reconcile Balotelli's national belonging to Italy as a "white" nation with his racialized status as a black African. The inconsistent and contradictory nature of media attempts to "fix" Balotelli to a certain location betray the importance of and persistent links between race and nation.

> Inter ran no further risks and secured their win on 61 minutes through the young Balotelli, whose low drive from a tight angle rolled past Rubinho as Marco Rossi fumbled a goal-line clearance. The Italian-born with Ghanaian origins confirmed his great form after the brace that last weekend helped Inter salvage a 3-3 home draw with Roma.[7]

> The young talent, who was born in Italy to Ghana parents and adopted by an Italian family, has at times angered his coach by displaying lack of tactical discipline on the pitch. He has also overreacted to fouls from opponents and racial taunts from the stands. There were never, however, doubts about his class, which made him a mainstay in Italy's national youth team and a candidate to the senior squad.[8]

The establishment of Balotelli's Otherness thus qualifies his being Italian, and it is worth noting the confusion in the media regarding what to call Balotelli. Early on he is called a Palermo-born Ghanaian, Ghanaian, Italian-born Ghanaian, Ghanaian-Italian, and Italo-

Ghanaian before being more consistently called Italian. Balotelli's parentage is a contradiction that requires explanation only because he is not Italian in the commonsense understandings of what it is to be Italian. Balotelli is quite obviously black, and because blackness is not associated with "being" Italian, his parents serve as a way to discredit his Italian birth. In other words, he is Italian but he is really Ghanaian. Notably, his birth parents are often discredited through a discourse of abandonment via the reporting that they casually left Balotelli in the street due to his early childhood health concerns. What actually happened is difficult to discern through media accounts, as the abandonment discourse dominates accounts by Balotelli's birth parents, who claim to have tried to legally get Mario back from his adoptive parents. That Balotelli's birth parents are acting from an economically and racially marginalized position goes unacknowledged and unexplored. Regardless, such discourse reinscribes broad stereotypical notions in the West of "bad" immigrants as it concerns responsibility, national burden, and reproduction. That Balotelli was "rescued" by a white Italian family and essentially became Italian through them, the mother specifically, constructs Balotelli more as an acceptable exception than a welcomed insider or "real" Italian. That Balotelli's adoptive family are framed as "saviors" who rescued him from an otherwise undesirable (black) family situation resonates with the larger problematics of the "white man's burden" or the "white savior industrial complex." A discourse of white/Western saviordom is a constant and predictable feature in representations of black African athletes.

Beyond the Labels

In terms of mundane or everyday issues of labeling, it is not necessarily the mentioning of nationality that is problematic, as global sport media tends to include such information regardless of country of origin. Rather, it is how nations are represented through the representation of their athletes. Ivory Coast (Drogba), Nigeria (Olajuwon and Okoye), the Democratic Republic of Congo (Mutombo and Mabika), Liberia (Hali), and Kenya (Loroupe) are consistently represented in stereotypical ways, through their respective celebrity

athletes, as war-torn, stuck in poverty, diseased, and culturally backward. Though the athletes themselves have "escaped" Africa, they still
embody or are linked with the stereotypical descriptors of Africa, the
"problems" of African countries and cultures, and the many peoples
who live in Africa.

> Lagos . . . is urban Africa at its most horrendous. Three-fourths of the
> city's residents live in rooming houses in which the average occupancy
> is more than five people per room. Almost 40% of the work force is
> unemployed or underemployed. In the early 1970s Lagos became an
> oilrich boomtown, but now, along with the world petroleum market,
> it has gone fairly bust. The place is a symbol of capitalism run amok.
> Skyscrapers hard by open sewers. Emaciated livestock pitifully nos-
> ing into a jam-up of cars, trucks, taxis and "mammy wagons"—half-
> van, half-bus, all-rattletrap. Horrid junkyards, firetrap shantytowns,
> broken-down marketplaces and inactive construction sites domi-
> nate the landscape. Smoke and grime and foul odors are staples of
> the atmosphere. Bribery and hyperinflation are staples of the econ-
> omy, DO NOT URINATE HERE signs are plastered all over the exte-
> rior walls of the bus station.[9]

Discourses on urban Africa, or any specific African city, are rare
in my data, as media tends to focus more on the African country as
a whole. The above example, from a lengthy *Sports Illustrated* piece,
tries to provide some background on where Olajuwon came from
but ultimately fails to provide us with anything we do not already
know or could not guess about African squalor. In many ways we
learn that the on-the-ground conditions are perhaps worse than we
may have imagined. Despite the author's culture shock and his obvious fear, upon arriving in Lagos he interviews a couple of people
close to Olajuwon who confirm to us the decrepit nature of Lagos
and assure us that Olajuwon is more a product of his family than
of Nigeria.[10] This discourse positions Olajuwon, then (in the early
1980s) still a charming media novelty, as outside and above the "normal" corrupting influences of even his home country and city. He
is thus "worthy" of his success in the United States because he is
"above" other Nigerians, with their uncleanliness and, ironically, their

rampant capitalism. Elsewhere we will see examples where Lagos is described as a cosmopolitan city, but I have highlighted this article because it appears that the author actually traveled to Lagos and Olajuwon's home, because it was published in *Sports Illustrated* (still a prominent sports magazine in the United States), and because it goes into quite a bit of detail about Olajuwon's background. That Lagos can be either horrendous or cosmopolitan is indicative of the kind of discursive maneuvering deployed to construct Olajuwon as a model minority against either the backdrop of Africa(ns) or African Americans. In each instance Olajuwon "benefits" but blackness as a whole is restigmatized.

For many of the other athletes in my study, discourses of African poverty, political conflict (war), disease, and death are consistently brought into their representations. While such problems do objectively exist on the continent, my concern is with the routinization of such information. The normalization of African conflict and misery is treated in a shallow, and at times casual, manner. Repeated images of black death and suffering—as in the seemingly unending showings of the deaths of Eric Garner, Walter Scott, and Tamir Rice (among others) on American news programs and social media—numb society to the pain of death, naturalize antiblack racism, and foreclose any possibility of meaningful reform. In the African context, the constant detailing of death, disease, and poverty creates a one-dimensional image of life on the continent and avoids any serious engagement with Western responsibility for the ongoing underdevelopment of Africa.

Meanwhile Congo native Mabika . . . sat alone wrapping ice on her knees. . . . This is a stark contrast to what her life could have been had the Sparks not taken her in tryouts in 1997. Her home, Congo (formerly Zaire), remains racked by economic and social problems. This season her mother, Helen, received a temporary visa to come to the USA at the request of the WNBA. . . . The rest of Mabika's family remains in Congo. "I call my family every day, and I'm always scared for their lives," Mabika says. "Every day, they hear gunshots and they tell me that there is no food because it is in suppression. Each time they call me, it's usually bad news."[11]

Tamba Hali was a child growing up in civil war torn Liberia when the rebel planes would suddenly come strafing overhead. Hali, now a destructive force of his own as a Penn State defensive end, would scramble for cover. . . . His memories return to Monrovia, the capital of Liberia, where Hali can remember being 5 or 6 and friends carrying AK-47 rifles. He was told of his younger half-brother, Joshua, who was thrown down a well to his death at the age of 6.[12]

The casual reporting of a child being thrown down a well or of an athlete's concern for friends and family members, or the comparison of athletic performance to that individual's experience of war typifies the devaluation of black life and stereotypes of African backwardness in Western media. Western supremacy is maintained not only through the reinscription of Africa as a dangerous place but also through the maintenance of the West as a place where these athletes were "lucky" to have gotten. Western responsibility for postcolonial and neocolonial economic policies is absolved because it "graciously" offers a "safe" space for those able to immigrate. We should also not be swayed by the quotations from the athletes themselves, as they have little control over the final published form of the article and are unlikely to have been asked any sort of detailed question on the topic. The shallow nature of the reporting itself is indicative of a media that is uninterested in finding out about itself.

Of course, the very different experiences of nonsport and nonhighly skilled (or credentialed) immigrants to the West are also ignored in these moments. The construction of the successful athlete as a "good" immigrant serves as a warning to both native and foreign blacks of their unwanted and tenuous positions in Western societies. Ironically, when Drogba left the English Premier League in 2012 to play in China (for Shanghai Shenhua in the Chinese Super League [CSL]) Western media focused not only on the corruption of the CSL but also on the problems black African migrants have in China.

Indeed, China and Africa have ever-deepening links—Chinese officials have signed natural resources and other business deals all over
Africa, while tens of thousands of Africans have migrated to China
for economic opportunities (in lieu of more traditional target destinations[,] places like Western Europe and North America). However, these African migrants (many of whom are of Nigerian descent
and concentrate in the southern city of Guangzhou) have a life that
is light years away from the glamour, adulation and affluence enjoyed
by Drogba. Frequently abused and harassed by police and shunned by
many Chinese who have never seen a black person before, the overwhelming majority of ordinary African traders in China struggle to
survive, much less prosper. In some cases, they face brutal violence,
as the case of the Nigerian who perished in police custody in Guangzhou. Yet, Drogba will never be treated like that—his fame, wealth,
talent make him beloved by China's masses. As with U.S. basketball
superstars Kobe Bryant and Lebron James (who have massive follow-
ings in China) Drogba will never suffer the indignity of police brutal-
ity or routine racism among the Chinese that the humble traders in
Guangzhou encounter daily. This is one of the bizarre end-products of
globalization and migration—some immigrants are better than others. Some people of the same race are adored and championed, while
others are reviled and rejected.[13]

Fear of China and its economic activities on the African continent is palpable and relies on discourse reminiscent of the Cold War
era that frames communism as inherently evil. It is a discourse that
sees China and Asia as competitive and hostile threats that must be
stopped through economic and military action. That African countries ultimately remain under the thumb of Western economic and
military power—that of the U.S. military more specifically—is predictably unacknowledged. China (communism) is recast as the "enemy"
of Africa, capitalism, and "progress." The article in which the excerpt
above appears ends by noting that "poor immigrants from a Third
World country are generally viewed (in China and elsewhere) as an
unwanted burden at best and a danger to life and property at worst."
Hence Chinese society is portrayed as hostile to poor immigrants while

the West's often very same hostilities go unnamed as, presumably, "elsewhere," but not explicitly so. While many news articles dwelt on the corruption of Chinese soccer—again ironic given the 2016 arrests of high-ranking FIFA officials on corruption—this is the only article I was able to find dealing so explicitly with the conditions of African migrants in China. Yet given the short amount of time Drogba was in China (he made only eleven appearances for Shenhua) it carries some extra weight, because in the entirety of my data no article offers similar criticism of Western European or U.S. attitudes toward poor or unskilled migrants of color. The only critique that comes close is one that looks at racism among Eastern and Southern European countries within soccer stadiums and sometimes beyond. However, these critiques tend only to reinforce the European hierarchy of nations— reinscribing Western European nations as racially progressive—while often making black players (Balotelli especially) at least partially to blame for the racism directed toward them.

Some additional examples of mundane Othering are representations of black African athletes as having raw, immature, childlike, untapped, or unrefined ability. These descriptors reinforce the connection between Africa and its presumed lack of development in comparison to the West. As Michelle Wright notes, Western notions of progress—and superiority—depend on a spatiotemporal fixity in order to determine how far "we" have come. "Yet to claim we have progressed is a hard qualitative argument to make: the corruption, violence, and bigotry that infest contemporary societies are no better or worse that the ills of preceding societies, only sometimes different."[14] As they concern this study, discourses of "raw" or undeveloped athletic ability reinforce the hegemonic narrative of progress. These discourses tend to be used in general when discussing athletic prospects who are perceived to lack certain (often normalizing and idealized) skills yet still have the "natural" athletic ability to learn those skills—the technical details—given time. However, in the representations of black African migrant athletes, discourses of raw ability are intra- and intertextually related to those that construct them as Others in the West.[15]

Born and raised in Enugu, Nigeria, Okoye came to the United States late in 1982 to run track for Azuza Pacific, an NAIA school in Azuza, Calif. He speaks excellent English, sometimes pausing to find the precise word. "I think, you know, I think I'm getting better and better. . . . I'm really happy about that." "Christian doesn't have any idea how good he can be," said Chiefs' tackle Irv Eastman. Okoye went out for football in 1984, a rank beginner competing against college athletes who had played the game most of their lives. After a slow beginning, he won NAIA all-America honors with 1,680 yards his senior year.[16]

Imagine how good Christian Okoye of the Kansas City Chiefs would be if he ran properly. If he lowered his shoulder instead of running so upright. If he followed his blockers better. If he tried running past defenders instead of through them. On second thought, don't imagine it. That, truly, would be an opponent's nightmare, a Nigerian Nightmare, as Okoye is so aptly nicknamed.[17]

We observe similar discourses in the representations of Olajuwon, Drogba, Balotelli, Hali, and Mutombo as well. Okoye is thus seen as raw in numerous ways, he is new to the sport and does not have experience, he is naturally talented but unrefined, and he is ignorant of the sport itself, having never played football. This idea of the black African athlete being raw draws upon stereotypical representations of Africa(ns) as underdeveloped. The result is a self-confirming process. The black African immigrant athlete is linked to Africa, and its underdevelopment, through being consistently labeled as African. The black African immigrant athlete is raw because Africa is underdeveloped and lacks technical sophistication, and Africa is underdeveloped because its people are not fully developed, not fully human, and hence raw.[18] Yet Christian Okoye was already an Olympic-caliber track and field athlete for Azusa Pacific before he played football. The athletic histories of black African migrants are thus neatly ignored or trivialized because they did not occur in the West. This finding corroborates what Bale discusses in *The Brawn Drain* concerning the supposed belief that the training of Kenyan distance runners at U.S. universities is what made them able to compete at the international level. Such beliefs rely on the assumption that only Western technology and rationality in creating sophisticated training regimes can produce world-class athletes. That "Africans" might be capable of such things contradicts the invested belief of Western progress. Ultimately, the problems of underdevelopment, poverty, disease, and conflict are no doubt real in many African countries but, as Mills explains, the one-dimensional presentation of these facts does little to dislodge antiblack notions of black cultural deviance or of blacks' inability to self-govern and achieve.[19]

Nicknames

Another aspect of mundane Othering is the use of nicknames. Nicknames are not chosen, they are usually given or earned, so they represent a practice in naming that is entwined in power relations and assertions of status. Nicknames may emerge in a range of different ways, but their adoption and frequent use in the media are most important here. Two athletes in this study have nicknames that typify the focus of this chapter: Hakeem "The Dream" Olajuwon and Christian Okoye, the "Nigerian Nightmare." Both fit within established discourses of U.S. nationalism and African stereotypes. Olajuwon was also infrequently called the "Nigerian Nightstalker" due to his ability to steal the basketball, and because of his nickname and his contemporary status with Okoye, Olajuwon's "dream" status was at times called a "Nigerian Nightmare" for opponents. Two other athletes, Didier Drogba and Tamba Hali, were also nicknamed in questionable ways. Drogba was frequently called "Drog," which shortens his last name and is often alliterated with "dog," and during his brief time spent playing in China he was nicknamed "Devil Beast," which reportedly has racial connotations but was used "without malevolence."[20] For Hali, the nickname "Liberian Nightmare" was briefly floated around on fan websites but has never gained mainstream attention. Finally, it was reported that Mutombo was affectionately called "Deekums" and "African" by teammates, coaches, and classmates during his college career, while media and others most often called him "Deke" during his time in college and the NBA.

If we further our analysis beginning with Christian Okoye's nickname, "Nigerian Nightmare," it is clear that there is a reliance on the dark imagery and exoticism of the African continent in general, Nigeria more specifically. It is the addition of "Nigerian" that makes this nickname an interesting point of analysis. As I have argued, the dominant discourse regarding "Africa," its countries, and its peoples in Western media has often been uncomplicated and focused on the negatives. "Nigerian Nightmare" serves to further illustrate this point with the phonetic pairing of the words *Nigerian* and *Nightmare*, which draw on one-sided imagery of the African continent from Western media sources. This imagery consists of the depiction of Africa primarily in terms of warfare, disease, tribalism, poverty, famine, the "Dark Continent," savages, and so on. The legacy of the nickname is still attached to Okoye and is perhaps most prominent in an otherwise corny poster where Okoye is wearing a Freddy Krueger glove and hat in a bedroom full of cowering NFL players from different teams. The poster is, at the time of this writing, still available for purchase on Okoye's personal website, and it remains possible to buy t-shirts with "Nigerian Nightmare" on them. Okoye may very well be a big Nigerian who was a nightmare to tackle, but we always already know that Nigeria is a nightmare, and that is what makes the nickname compelling and impactful.

Olajuwon's nickname, however much the polar opposite of Okoye's that it first appears, performs a similar function. "The Dream" first emerged as a way to describe Olajuwon's style of play in that it was something you could only dream for, but it quickly and easily collapses into the more familiar notion of the "American Dream." The link between Olajuwon as The Dream and the American Dream became even more evident after Olajuwon because a U.S. citizen through naturalization and was popularly pictured with the American flag draped around his shoulders ahead of the 1996 Atlanta Olympics. Though Okoye's nickname explicitly links race, Africa, and negative emotions, while Olajuwon's links his black foreign Otherness to hegemonic American values in a more positive manner, both remarginalize Africa, Nigeria specifically, and the respective backgrounds of the athletes.

This remarginalization process requires greater explanation for

Olajuwon's nickname. In part, the process of remarginalization occurs through Olajuwon's own words. Throughout his career Olajuwon and his words have been positioned as pro-American and fit into a discourse of U.S. exceptionalism in the media. Early in his career Olajuwon stated, "Everyone in Nigeria dreams of going to school in America. . . . Schools here are much more advanced. That is what I wanted to do."[21] Later he was quoted as saying, "You cannot compare this country with any other. . . . I've traveled a lot—all over Europe and to many other countries. But the freedoms, the opportunities, the people, the system—there are no others like them."[22] Combined with Olajuwon's words, his nickname remarginalizes Nigeria and other African countries against the superiority of the United States, at least for Western audiences. Because of his black foreignness, the dream Olajuwon fulfills is one of escaping Africa and its social ills. Despite Olajuwon's middle-class upbringing, sparsely mentioned in my data, Africa is represented as a place to escape from. Further, the invocation of the American Dream in black immigrant representations of success is more provocative than it would be for native black success, because African immigrants presumably had more obstacles to overcome even before reaching the States. As Olajuwon put it above, the opportunities, the system, and the very people are unlike anything anywhere else. In the end, there is little attempt by Western media to find out more about Africa or Nigeria. Olajuwon is allowed to speak as an authority on the matter because he is positioned by the media to represent all Nigerians. We actually get no sort of understanding as to what is going on in Nigeria to drive Olajuwon's assessment.

Along these lines we can also examine nicknames of white athletes that may seem derogatory at first glance. In a casual intersection with the representation of Okoye, the nickname of Al Hrabosky, the "Mad Hungarian," is mentioned. Hrabosky was a Major League Baseball pitcher who, in an attempt to save his career, developed a warm-up routine that earned him his nickname. Hrabosky's nickname harkens back to when white ethnicity had an impact on the daily lives of some ethnic groups. However, while Hungarian immigrants to the United States likely faced many of the same forms of

discrimination as other members of white ethnic groups, the gradual convergence of Hungarian Americans into the white mainstream
has left few residuals of the kinds of negative ethnic stereotypes that
continue to beset Africa and Africans. Even when Hrabosky was
playing (1970–82), many of those stereotypes had lost any meaningful impact. Today Hrabosky's nickname makes little sense outside of him as an individual. Western media has no preoccupation
with Hungary or its apparently mad population but continues to rely
on commonsense understandings of Africa and its peoples. Thus
for the Nigerian Nightmare there are different inherent meanings
because the moniker is rooted, partly, in persistent negative stereotypes about Africa. Other nicknames of white athletes worth mentioning include Toni Kukoc (the Croatian Sensation); Honus Wagner
(the Flying Dutchman); Nikolai Khabibulin (the Bulin Wall); Steve
Nash (Captain Canada); Ryan Braun, Al Rosen, and Hank Green-
berg (the Hebrew Hammer); Steven Gerrard (the British Bulldog);
Danny Woodhead and Jason Williams (White Chocolate); Marcin
Gortat (the Polish Hammer); Joel Przybilla (Vanilla Gorilla, the White
Kong); and last but not least, Jim Jeffries (the Great White Hope).
Many of these are positive or lack any meaning in Western societies today. The latter three nicknames, of course, betray stereotypical
understandings of blackness and black athletic ability and concerns
about white physical inferiority.

A further example is the nickname of Catherine Ndereba, "Catherine the Great." Clearly the nickname plays on Ndereba's first name
and that of an Enlightenment era Russian empress. Perhaps more
importantly, the name draws on the noble savage stereotype. In this
way Western and European media gives itself away as Western and
European through its own practices. We see similar notions of regal-
ity in the representations of Mutombo and Olajuwon and in the way
Africans, women especially, are discussed. Attention is drawn to their
posture and appearance as being somehow king- or queen-like, with
expressions of dignity and mystical auras. In some ways, the use of
these nicknames in African newspapers reflects just how penetrat-
ing European norms are in former colonial countries.

In a slightly different vein, Tirunesh Dibaba's nickname, the "Baby-

Faced Assassin," appears disruptive but only feminizes a stereotyp-
ically masculine "occupation" that is itself problematic in the realm
of sport and distance running. Female assassins on television and in
movies tend to be beautiful, young, and athletic, or hyperfeminine,
which are qualities Dibaba's nickname draws on and attempts to fix
upon her. Only one athlete, who intersects with Ndereba, was nicknamed in another language, and that is Robert Kipkoech Cheruiyot,
who goes by "Mwafrika," which translates into "being of or pertain-
ing to Africa."

All of these nicknames are biased toward those doing the naming.
It is clear that until the institutional norms of representing African
and black peoples change, the ways in which black African immigrant
athletes are labeled and (nick)named will be problematic.

African Women, Patriarchy, and Motherhood

The well-known concept of intersectionality tells us that women, as
well as men, will be acted upon in society in ways that are simultaneously influenced, but not in a predetermined way, by race, sexuality, gender, and class. Intersectionality urges academics to recognize
that the "black" experience is much more than a heterosexual male
experience and that failing to do so tends to erase those who do not
fit within those confines.[23] As Patricia Hill Collins explains, the problems and solutions that black American communities face require
attention to the politics of gender and sexuality if we wish them to
be solved. She states, "Black women can never become fully empowered in a context that harms Black men, and Black men can never
become fully empowered in a society in which Black women cannot
fully flourish as human beings."[24] In this view race, class, gender, sexuality, nation, and other social categories are not competing frameworks; rather they are "mutually constructing systems of power."[25]
Their dense interconnectedness in any given situation makes untan-
gling their individual effects difficult, to say the least. Historical representations of blackness, African American women, and black African
women reveal fears of masculine women in sport, hypersexuality and
lesbians, pregnancy and reproducing the nation-state, and white feminine beauty standards. The various interconnections among these

representations and the ways in which women are represented differently than men in my research compel my use of intersectionality in this section.

Turning specifically to representations of black African female athletes, we find a tendency in the media to focus on different aspects of their lives and to engage in different types of Othering than they do with men. Aside from the persistent referencing through national origin and the construction of the African continent as primal and (technologically) backward, issues of gender and patriarchy are consistent in women's representations. Aspects of African women's representations are consistent with how women in sport are often stereotyped, as the participation of women in sport remains a contested terrain. (White) women tend to be stereotyped as physically frail and emotional and through their status as mothers, yet black women are often racially stereotyped as being naturally strong because of racist notions of either slave legacies (in the United States) and/ or primal African ancestors. Historically black women have also been stereotyped as hypersexual (savage, animalistic, and/or freakish in body and practice), angry and loud, "welfare queens," and "bad black mothers." In certain times these narratives have been reversed, such as when Wilma Rudolph was described in relation to ideals of white beauty, but these moments have often come at the expense of other (black) women and sexually objectifying the individual in question. Thus there are a number of discursive strategies through which black women in sport can be remarginalized and their achievements devalued.[26]

I have elsewhere begun detailing the practices of representing black African female athletic ability in contradicting ways.[27] There I discuss two emergent themes surrounding the athletic ability of Tegla Loroupe—the "Amazing Athlete" and the "Untethered Mote." The Amazing Athlete theme emerges from media references to Loroupe's gender and sex as they pertain to her performance in races. The term comes from general expressions of awe, surprise, and praise for what Loroupe was able to accomplish during her career. Amazing Athlete encapsulates the profuse praise she receives, much of which is presented as genderless, while the Untethered Mote subtheme speaks to the more stereotypical framings of her body, sex, and capabilities as a woman.

The Amazing Athlete theme, which presents Loroupe as an elite athlete, is more prevalent during the middle to late parts of Loroupe's career, once she was established as an elite runner. Because this theme exists within a sea of more stereotypical representations, sometimes even within the same news article, the genuine nature of such descriptors must be questioned: "Tegla Loroupe of Kenya, the hardest working woman or man in road racing, is back to normal. . . . She's racing at a rate that astounds other runners"; "In the end, she did not win a medal, but she did further the legend of her unbreakable will"; "The Kenyan, who won the Flora London Marathon last Sunday, is one of the world's most amazing athletes"; "She also won the world half marathon title seven days after having won a marathon. Mortals normally ease off for weeks."[28] These examples elevate Loroupe above common gender assumptions, and even beyond what is believed possible for mortal humans. The focus on her overwhelming abilities and determination constructs Loroupe as a strong and dominant athlete and would seem to indicate a positive progression regarding media portrayals of female athletes. Generally, discourse on athletic ability frames men as the only athletes capable of such amazing feats of physical prowess. Rarely are women even in the conversation when the title of "greatest" or "most amazing" is being considered, as such a framing would challenge the boundaries of male-dominated sport. Women cannot be considered "the greatest" because they compete only against women, a situation tennis icon Serena Williams still faces today. The presence of such feelings surrounding Loroupe can be seen as disruptive to the discourses surrounding the hegemonic male sporting body. However, as I will discuss in a later chapter, Loroupe, along with the other women in my study, does not escape racial assumptions concerning the natural, cultural, and environmental "advantages" of black (African) athleticism. Further, as it concerns gender, the Amazing Athlete theme does not exist by itself; it is complicated by and exists alongside the Untethered Mote theme.

The Untethered Mote theme emerges through stereotypical media representations of Loroupe's ability as a female athlete and a woman. Throughout Loroupe's career, many references have been made to her physical stature. Attention is drawn to her small frame and skinny build, as she stands around five feet tall and weighs about eighty-five pounds. Examples include "The tiny Kenyan"; "having the frame of a sprite has its disadvantages, and Loroupe has learned to run through all manner of impairments"; "the fast pace may have taken its toll on her 4-foot-11-inch, 85-pound frame"; "with feet so tiny that even children's running shoes are too big"; and "she needs her running shoes less for foot support than to anchor her to the earth. Without them, she might simply go sailing through the air, a mote untethered by gravity."[29]

While the above discourses seek to pin Loroupe onto stereotypical notions of female athletic ability, frailty, and toughness, other discourses simultaneously raise questions about her sex and sexuality. During the late 1990s Loroupe publicly dismissed allegations that she was not a woman, claiming after one race, "I am pleased to show I am all woman. Some people have been suggesting otherwise, things like I am half man and half woman because I have been running with men." Where these allegations came from exactly is unclear in the data gathered for this project; however, Lewis reported, "The Kenyan was speaking out after cruel gossips questioned her gender after her impressive times in races against men."[30] Later in her career she would be framed along heteronormative lines, with articles drawing attention to shopping sprees, "three-inch glittery pumps," and the problem of "a man . . . I can't seem to find one."[31]

Later I will come back to these persistent problems of gender policing and heteronormativity that seek to limit what women can achieve in sport. Needless to say, it is troubling that a seemingly disproportionate number of black and brown women from developing countries have been accused of being men in recent years. I argue that, among other things, the gender policing and salient fear of black and brown female athletic bodies, as well as their assumed (hyper/homo) sexuality, is an effort by white supremacy to keep sport as safe place for "good" white women. That Loroupe felt the need to respond to the allegations is indicative of the treatment female athletes have historically received, seen more recently in controversy surrounding South African runner Caster Semenya, who is accused of being intersexed. The continued prevalence of stereotypical discourse makes it difficult to truly accept Loroupe or other black African women as gender-transcendent athletes, assuming they would even want to be. Given the examples regarding questions about Loroupe's sex and sexuality, we can see there is often a quick reach to stereotypes and assumptions about the potential and capabilities of women.

Another prevalent aspect of black African female athletic representation is the presence of Western postfeminism in descriptions of African patriarchy. In this aspect of representation it is "African" culture that women have had to overcome in order to achieve their goals. By its nature, the postfeminist approach of media ignores ongoing gender inequality in the West—or sees it progressing toward an inevitable end point—while blaming the condition of women in developing countries on deviant cultural norms in need of repair. Here again, the role of the West in maintaining neoliberal policies that perpetuate poverty, dependency, and conflict goes unexamined. We might argue that "African masculinity" was at once destroyed by colonialism, reconstructed to colonial norms, and then continually embarrassed and infantilized by colonial and neocolonial practices. Without access to the avenues of power or secure material wealth, masculinities that are defensive, aggressive, homophobic, and misogynistic tend to develop regardless of racial or geographic location. Yet still, that is never the full complexity of masculinity regardless of context.

In these narratives, African women are thus stripped of their agency and made into passive actors, while men are uniformly seen as the perpetrators of sexist norms even when most of the women I researched had some sort of significant male figure in their support structure. An account of Loroupe's performance in the New York City marathon recounts, "She surged over the final 10 miles to become the first black African woman to win a major marathon. Her victory became an affirming symbol of achievement for Kenyan women, whose lives are often lived in subservience, and a silencing rebuke for the Kenyan men who had told her she was wasting her time."[32]

Elsewhere Kenya has been portrayed in media reports, quoting Loroupe, as a country where "the traditional system is, you listen to your father until your husband buys you [in exchange] for cattle, then you listen to him."[33] Accounts of Loroupe's early training with African men in the United States often describe the experiences as exploitative, with the male runners asking her to wash clothes, cook, and do their chores and Loroupe often feeling compelled to oblige them because of her upbringing.[34] Indeed, the issue of men assuming that the women they train with will clean for them is something that Lornah Kiplagat experienced as well and has addressed by establishing her own High Altitude Training Centre (HATC) in Iten, Kenya. Kiplagat, a contemporary of Loroupe and Ndereba, explains in an interview for PBS's *Frontline* that she tries to instill a sense of confidence and a different way of thinking about relationships between men and women among the women who attend her camp. Kiplagat, who labels herself a social pioneer for Kenyan women in the interview, is well aware of the economic and familial roles women play in rural Kenya and has designed her camp to make sure the burdens of cleaning and cooking do not fall by default to the women, who should be focused on training. She goes even further by explaining that her camp makes no concessions on this point, and any man who asks a woman to do domestic work for him while at the camp runs the risk of being asked to leave.[35]

I do not argue that these recollections and experiences of Loroupe, Kiplagat, and others are somehow inaccurate or false. Yet to Western media and its target audience, Loroupe and others represent all of Kenya, or "Africa." While I cannot speak as to whether Loroupe felt that she was personally representing all of Kenya, we must wonder, when she speaks of traditional systems, whether she is talking about a traditional Kenyan system in general or about the Kalenjin, or even more specifically the Pokot. There is a level of detail and complexity missing that could help us understand which system Loroupe is actually talking about, but Western media does not ask the appropriate questions and Loroupe does not offer the information. Hence it is worth noting that Loroupe, Ndereba, Dibaba, Kiplagat, and other women who have succeeded in sport very often have strong examples of family support, including that of their fathers. The dominant discourses of Kenya and

often, by association, Africa as being culturally backward and static—
while the West remains a beacon of progress—are left unchallenged,
with any deviance from the "single story" treated as an exception.

When we begin looking further at the role of men in the lives of
female African athletes we find some interesting things. For example, Ndereba's relationship with her husband is a point of interest for
the media because she is considered the "breadwinner" of the family.
The way that her marriage and the raising of their child, as well as her
winnings, are discussed betrays Western media's bias regarding "African" culture and its expectations of how relationships work in Kenya.

> She is unique among African female runners in having a husband
> who is happy to stay at home and raise the couple's daughter while
> she travels the world earning a living. This unprecedented combina-
> tion has turned Ndereba and her husband, Anthony Maina, into role
> models in Kenya, where their relationship is seen as a whole new way
> for men and women to regard each other . . . Maina's willingness to
> care for their four-year-old daughter Jane when Ndereba is abroad
> enables her to ignore criticism in Kenya that she should stay home
> and be a "proper" wife. She never asked her husband for his permis-
> sion to carry on with her running career. . . . He never considered try-
> ing to stop her. "I said it in my heart, I should not discourage her," he
> said. "I should let her go until she feels it is enough." When Ndereba
> became pregnant in 1997 he agreed to stay home with the baby while
> she travelled. Since giving birth, her career has blossomed.[36]

Ndereba and her husband are held up as examples of a "new" and
"progressive" relationship in Kenya. Representing female subservience as the "accepted" norm makes African cultures and societies historically static and ignores the various ways African women
have resisted and continue to resist male dominance. The histories
of African women supporting and helping each other and their children are discursively marginalized in the West by accounts of the
relatively recent success of "the black African female athlete." At the
same time, there are faint concerns over how Ndereba still manages
to be a mother and how her husband deals with her absence and
her salary. We must remember that there have long been questions

about whether women who work can be good mothers, and for black women even more so. Ultimately those concerns are calmed by defining Ndereba through motherhood and framing her as loving mother who desperately misses her child.

> It was time. In 1996 Catherine Ndereba was at the top of the running world, universally recognized as the top female road runner in the world. But it was time. Time to start a family. She had married. She was home in Kenya. Her maternal instincts called. "I just wanted to be a mother," she said, matter-of-factly. So, in her prime, she stopped running. A full year passed. She gave birth to daughter Jane in May of 1997. Seven months later she was training again. . . . While she admits it was difficult, missing the competition, she has no regrets she took the time off. "I considered it part of my life," she said. "I was there to start a family."[37]

Ndereba is variously cast as a "working mom" who knits for her daughter, works away from home, gets homesick, and yet keeps it all together—the embodiment of Western postfeminism. Other great distance runners who are mothers and wives, such as Paula Radcliffe and Derartu Tulu, who intersect with Ndereba, are similarly represented. A similar focus on fatherhood, along with the travel and time away from family, among the male athletes in this study is almost nonexistent. While wives and children may get mentioned, there is not the same casual and consistent labeling of athletes as "father" or "husband." Further, the gendered political dynamics of Ndereba's husband ranking above her in the Kenyan prisons system (national athletes in Kenya often work for government bodies) go unexplored. That Ndereba's husband remains hierarchically above her in certain social aspects remains normal and natural even in this "untraditional" relationship. The true nature of their relationship is actually unknown to us, given the partial nature of the information available, but my argument is that the complexity of any given relationship gets reduced to a simple comparison between an "African patriarchy" that is never well explained and Western postfeminism. A similar discursive strategy occurs in Ndereba's intersection with Derartu Tulu. Tulu's husband and their relationship are given to us as examples of progress out of traditional gender and relationship norms in Ethiopia. The notion that "African tradition" precludes women from being primary wage earners freezes African cultures in time, ignores the ongoing changes in those societies concerning relationships, and erases the continued misogyny and patriarchy of Western societies.

Conclusion

Representation of Africa and the peoples of Africa have long and well-documented histories. My focus in this chapter was to explain some of the more mundane and everyday ways in which black African athletes are Othered by Western media. These processes are consistent in keeping the foreign black Other in the position of an outsider, even if—as in the cases of Drogba and Balotelli—they were born or have spent most of their lives in the West. This discourse keeps the racial imagination of the Western nation-state white while simultaneously exteriorizing all those considered "Other." That these simple processes of labeling quickly and assuredly link to deeper understandings and stereotypes of "Africa" and "the black athlete" is indicative of the dense intertextuality of sports media with the larger context outside of sport. That athletes themselves are positioned to "corroborate" media assertions gives these discourses an aura of truth. The stereotypes I discuss here are not recent developments, as we see with Olajuwon and Mutombo, but what has indeed changed is the level of exposure, through sport, of Western societies to peoples (athletes) from African countries. The opening up of the global South to exploitation by sport leagues in the global North has led to the formation of various types of migration and talent pipelines. This new and changing level of exposure creates complex forms of representation, a complexity I have begun to tease out in this chapter. It is not hard to look toward other migrant groups and discern similar phenomena. Whether it be Latinos in American baseball, South Americans in European soccer, Arabs and Asian Indians in English cricket, Asians and Asian Americans in basketball, or Indigenous populations in Australian rugby, the discourse is often similar if not the same. Those at the margins are actively excluded from the nation or used in such a way as to whitewash imperial or colonial pasts.

3

Model Minorities

Origin Stories, Hard Workers, and Humanitarians

In the previous chapter I discussed the mundane processes of boundary making and maintenance and how they link to more explicit, often stereotypical, forms of Othering. In this chapter I will go further in examining specific discourses that elevate either the personality of the individual or the personal history of struggle black African migrant athletes have experienced. Many of these discourses seem to include or accept the black African migrant into (white) Western society, or the nation, and establish these athletes as exceptional individuals—or model minorities. They also serve to fix the black African migrant to an immediately knowable "Africa" while also teaching "us" about that very same "Africa."[1] I use the term *origin story* here purposefully, as in popular culture it is often used to explain the mythic beginnings of heroes and villains. For my work, an athlete's origin story begins with the athlete's emergence in the media, establishes a foundation for how we know the athlete, and is further developed through the athlete's continued success—or failure—in sport. These media-created origin stories and the later human interest and humanitarian pieces that accompany them accomplish a great deal through their explicit discourses and silences.

The concept of the model minority originated in the 1960s era of civil rights and changes in U.S. immigration law. As East and South Asian communities were increasingly reported as having found "success" in the United States and "overcome" race, that very same reporting often served as a rebuke against African American communities that were irrationally "rioting" and too "sensitive" about race. Claire

Kim explains that the model minority "is diligent, disciplined, possessed of strong family values, respectful of authority, thrifty, moral, self-sufficient, and committed to education."[2] Because of the "discipline" and "respect for authority" attached to the concept, the model minority is also an apolitical subject who goes along with the status quo. Asian Americans (primarily Chinese and Japanese immigrants) have succeeded because of these cultural values and have "assimilated" into (white) society, while African Americans have not due to their deficient culture and constant talk of race. Of course, whiteness and white supremacy go unnamed, as does the fact that Asian Americans remain an inferior racial group in the United States and are not "assimilating" so much as serving as a buffer space for white supremacy against other racial groups. Despite the relatively high rates of education and income among Asian Americans, as "model minorities" they are constructed as passive, uncreative, and lacking in leadership abilities. Asian women, as with black women, face racially specific stereotypes that put them in an unwinnable double bind, portraying them as either passive sex objects or overbearing "dragon" women. As such, both men and women continue to be underrepresented at the highest levels of their occupations and make less than similarly accomplished or educated whites. More importantly, if the "model minority" complains about the white, patriarchal, heteronormative, and capitalistic system, she or he very quickly discovers the nature of his or her tenuous position in the racial order. In the end, we find that the model minority stereotype keeps certain immigrant groups in a liminal status of forever-deferred economic and social gratification—the model minority myth is an inhuman mechanism of social and political control.[3]

I designed this chapter to address three interrelated themes that construct the black African migrant as an exception to other forms of blackness, or a model minority. Under the first theme, "Origin Stories," I discuss the positioning of black migrant athletes against their African "origins" or backgrounds. Second, under "Hard Workers and Friendly Faces" I draw attention to the self-presentation and representation of black migrant athletes as hard working and extremely friendly individuals. Finally, under the "Humanitarian" theme I discuss the humanitarian narratives surrounding the athletes in my study. I find that such discourses often draw upon the same commonsense understandings and rhetoric found in the origin stories, that of African underdevelopment and hardship. What I argue in this chapter is that consistent processes are making model minorities out of black African migrant athletes and simultaneously remarginalizing native black communities, reinscribing African underdevelopment, valorizing hegemonic neoliberal notions of development and aid, and, at times, using African athletes as a background for white humanitarian action.

Origin Stories

The origin stories discussed here represent efforts by the media to make intelligible the backgrounds of black African immigrant athletes. Because they are created by and for Western audiences, such stories tend to be simplistic and rely on commonsense understandings of African societies and politics. In reading through the careers of these athletes, I also find that their origin stories tend to be contradictory, inconsistent, and subject to revision over time. Often these stories are first pieced together through what the recently migrated athlete tells a reporter and the opinions of people around the athlete, such as coaches and teammates. This initial impression is often what "sticks" and gets repeated in different media outlets. It is usually quite some time before Western media seeks to clarify the origin story or even go to the athlete's home to ask questions. When the latter occurs, problems emerge of the sort that are predictable when the West covers Africa. One of the first things an origin story describes is the upbringing or the childhood of the athlete: "One of seven children, Loroupe began running the way many Kenyans begin running, to and from school, barefoot, with a book bag strapped to her back. She grew up on a farm outside of Kapenguria on the Ugandan border. It was six miles each way to school, she said, and 'if you were late you were punished.' Her parents raised cattle and grew corn and potatoes, she said, and sometimes she chased the herd as far as 12 miles. 'I didn't know I was training,' Loroupe said."[4]

The discourses surrounding the childhoods of Loroupe and Ndereba, and to varying degrees the other athletes in this study, draw on notions of backwardness and naïveté. For Loroupe and Ndereba specifically, this discourse temporally retards African societies. That "we" in the West do not walk to school or that "they" do not have cars positions readers as observers looking at societies that are locked in the past. In other words, African societies are kept static in part through the representations of its athletes who migrate to the West. This retardation also provides a convenient explanation for the athletic success of these athletes as a kind of cultural and environmental essentialism. Kenya and Ethiopia (in Dibaba's case) become places that simplistically, easily, produce elite athletes because of a convergence of culture and environment. Simultaneously, this discourse also explains the downfall of the Western distance runner—predominantly the white male, but it applies to females as well—in that with greater technologies and busier lives (mind) comes a greater separation from nature and the capability for physical pursuits (body). Black African athletes, separated from technology and sophistication, are thus reified as natural and achieving without effort, high-level competition, or disciplined training.

Common in the representation of Mutombo is his rise from an inexperienced and "ungainly" prospect speaking "African dialects," while Olajuwon carries a similar origin story with a focus on education and raw athletic potential. Yet despite the favorable appearance of each origin story there is an underlying devaluation of "Africa" in different ways.

What's most remarkable is that Mutombo, 25 [years old], has been playing basketball for just seven years. He grew up in Kinshasa, Zaire, and his first day of hoops turned into whoops. Mutombo fell during a routine drill and . . . suffered a gash in his chin. . . . When he enrolled at Georgetown, Mutombo was a language wizard, fluent in French, Spanish, Portuguese and five African dialects. But initially there was a communication breakdown—he couldn't speak English. . . . As a player, Mutombo was ungainly, a possessor of crude skills who rapidly refined them. He averaged just 9.9 points and 8.6 rebounds in his three-year Hoya career, but there were dominating moments that told of the possibilities.[5]

As noted previously, the devaluation of African languages is prominent across the stories of the athletes in my analysis. Only twice in Mutombo's career were the names of the languages he speaks mentioned in my data, but even then the list is sometimes incomplete. Mutombo reportedly speaks Swahili, Lingala, Luba-Kasai, and Kikongo. Each of these languages is spoken by millions of people. In particular, Swahili, spoken by 140 million people, is the official language of four countries (Uganda, Kenya, Tanzania, and the Democratic Republic of Congo) as well as the African Union and is taught in more than fifty universities in the United States. That these languages are often hierarchically devalued as "dialects" and "tribal tongues" betrays the ethnocentrism of Western English-speaking societies as well as the failure of Western media to ask a simple question in order to gather a little more information about Mutombo and his background. Also unquestioned is why he knows any European languages at all, a relic of colonialism and the establishment of European educational systems in African countries. As Said notes, part of the discursive power of an institutionalized knowledge form like Orientalism is the ability to make authoritative and evaluative distinctions between different forms of language.[6] In the quote above we can also discern tropes of noble savagery, innocence, and naïveté and some of the casual Othering that separates foreign from native blacks, as I will discuss in the next section.

Balotelli, as a second-generation immigrant, has an origin story that differs in that it revolves around his adoption by a white family, his citizenship status, and race relations in Italy. Discourses surrounding Balotelli's adoption not only keep him foreign in some ways, as an African/Ghanaian, but also tend to depict Italian (Southern and Eastern European) society as deviant from the West on issues of race and racism.

> Balotelli was born—and immediately abandoned by his Ghanaian parents—in the Sicilian capital, Palermo. He is an Italian passport holder and was brought up by adopted parents in Brescia from the age of two. He speaks with the accent of his region, but has received far more racist abuse than other black stars in Italian football because his Italian identity is seen by some as a provocation. "The difference

[from other black players] is Balotelli is totally black and totally Italian, and that has provoked a short circuit among fans," said Sandro Modeo, a correspondent for Corriere della Sera. As Italy's immigrant total reaches 7%, the treatment of many of the "Balotelli generation"— the half-million children of immigrants born in Italy who qualify by law for Italian citizenship on their 18th birthday—is becoming an increasingly controversial issue in a country which still, overwhelmingly, considers itself white.[7]

Balotelli's case is certainly interesting, mostly because early in his career he shunned his Ghanaian parents, has declined requests to play for the Ghanaian national team, and seemingly spurns any notion of being "African" altogether. His disruption of expectations through his rejection of national identity based on race and heritage has made visible (at least partially) an entire Italian generation—now named the "Balotelli Generation." Still, the "problem" is placed and kept in Italy, and any larger self-reflection by the West stops there. Second-generation immigrants throughout Western societies confront the everyday racism and discrimination of native black populations, which, at least in part, gives rise to our current notions of diaspora. In the marginalized spaces of Western cities there is a growing awareness of the global nature of white supremacy and its links with neoliberal capitalism.[8] Though we cannot escape the particular of the local, the consistent placing of the problems of race and racism elsewhere in Europe by Western media makes it difficult to fight the hegemonic color-blind narrative that marginalizes the ongoing impact of racism in "developed" countries.

In a different manner, the origin stories of both Tamba Hali and Christian Okoye are centered on violence and the civil wars of Liberia and Nigeria. They demonstrate the fetishized nature of war and warfare in Western media. In the representation of Okoye, those few articles that do seek to illuminate Okoye's life in Nigeria portray it as "vaulted straight out of post–civil war Nigeria."[9]

[Okoye] was 6 and living in a small village named Nri when insurgents from his native Ibo tribe seceded from Nigeria and formed the republic of Biafra. It started a 1967–1970 civil war that killed 500,000 to 2 million people, most of whom died of starvation. . . . "People carried machine guns in the streets," Okoye said. "We hid in people's basements. I can remember the sound of guns and the explosions. We had to stay on the move all the time, to stay ahead of the fighting. When the shooting got too close, we'd move on to the next village."[10]

If anyone ever deserved to live in a place called Happy Valley, it's Penn State defensive end Tamba Hali. Born in Suacoco, Liberia, he was six years old at the outbreak of the 14-year civil war that ripped his country apart. He was eight the first time he fled gunfire, nine when his family abandoned its home in the village of Gbarnga to live in the wilderness, subsisting on cassava root and cabbage while hiding from brutal bands of soldiers who roamed the countryside.[11]

The backgrounds of Okoye and Hali differ from those of the other athletes in this study because theirs are linked directly to experiences of war. The repetitive narrative of Africa as a troubled and war-plagued continent in Okoye's and Hali's origin stories reinforces well-established and historical stereotypes that often lack context or understanding, despite their graphic detail. The intense media focus on Hali's experiences in war positions him as a mimetic object, a representative for the whole of Liberia. Hence Hali becomes *the* source to learn about war in Liberia, particularly as it concerns his childhood and immigration to the United States. Because of Hali's mimetic status, we receive only answers from his perspective, and because he is a mimetic object, the questions are posed to him rather than by him. Thus there is a failure to probe the causes of Liberia's problems and how or what Hali feels about such causes. Any insights Hali may have regarding the causes of or historical forces shaping the conflict in his country are left unrevealed. As startling as Hali's experiences are, they represent only a piece of a much larger picture in the context of Liberian history (including the role of the United States, slavery, religion, and colonialism) that is passively hidden from us. African wars are thus presented as current but also the result of longstanding ethnic conflicts from time immemorial and not the effect of historical or contemporary (neo)colonial practices.

The often casual insertion of a war narrative into a sports article is also unfortunate because of the way war intersects with sport in the context of American football. Football in America is often described in militaristic terms, with many parts of the game, including the players, being referred to as missiles, bombs, battlefields, tanks, soldiers, and so on. This terminology all occurs within the rigid bureaucratic structure of football that subjects players to brutal disciplinary training regimes at nearly every level, but especially in college and professional football. Yet the lines between this war "play" and actual war are often blurred, primarily in American football with its jingoistic national displays of military might, the national anthem, and the parading around of active and veteran military service members. Such settings celebrate the West's war-making power while at the same time obscuring two elements: few athletes have military experience, reflecting changing military enrollment dynamics since the twentieth century, and some athletes have experienced war in their home countries and could possibly have been its innocent victims—akin to the hundreds of thousands innocent lives lost in the recent and ongoing Iraq and Afghanistan wars and wherever there is armed conflict. Instead of learning from those who have experienced war, which would require critical self-reflection, Western media and professional sport instead push further militaristic nationalism and jingoism— indeed, in the United States they are paid to do so by the Department of Defense.[12]

Despite the overwhelming presence of the aforementioned discourses, counterexamples do exist, even though they were exceedingly rare in my sample. However, even as the counterexamples seemingly tried to dispel myths surrounding a particular athlete, they often managed to reinforce stereotypes of "Africa" more broadly. Hence the statements are often imperfect and contradictory.

Akeem Olajuwon—"The Dream," they call him—is a middle-class young man with skills so pure, so spontaneous he is frightening. Olajuwon did not walk barefooted around the continent and wear a leopard skin. He is from Lagos, principal city in Nigeria. His only material problems were his size. At 6-feet-11, he was so tall by Nigerian standards that it was difficult to find the proper clothes or shoes. . . . He learned that because he is a black foreigner, he was assumed to be ignorant. "People don't think I can count. They say, this is a quarter, 25 cents. It is four in a dollar. They don't think I can look on the coin and see for myself it is 25 cents."[13]

Thus there is a counter discourse that seeks to dispel some of the stereotypes surrounding Olajuwon as a Nigerian and recent immigrant. In particular, this example is a rare acknowledgement that Olajuwon faced assumptions of ignorance specifically because he was a black foreigner. Yet if Olajuwon does not own a spear, walk barefoot, or wear leopard skin, apparently someone (most people?) in Africa, Nigeria, or Lagos does or is believed to. Our previously held beliefs are deconstructed only so far. Olajuwon here is constructed more as an exception (and certainly in some ways he is) than the norm, as the focus is on him and his family and how they are different from the "Africa" we "know." If articles were to more fully explore Nigerian culture and society, even just focusing on urban life and the mere existence of a middle class, they might carry more progressive potential than they do by singling out Olajuwon. These origin stories generally tend to lean on stereotypes of Africa to construct the African migrant as exceptional—a "good" (im)migrant—when coming from an otherwise negatively racialized space.

Hard Workers and Friendly Faces

Immigrants, particularly black immigrants, generally come to their host countries with economic goals and the desire to fit into society. While historically black immigrants have done better economically than native blacks, over time black African immigrants to the United States have seen their wages fall below those of African Americans. One of the explanations for this phenomenon is that black immigrants, without knowledge of the Western labor system, are employed for lower wages and willing to work longer hours than African Americans. Black immigrants are lauded by whites (Western societies) for their hard work ethic while they are actually being exploited due to their lack of labor experience in the West. With Western economies ever more reliant on exploitable workers—often with liminal legal status—African immigrants are increasingly joining Latino and Southeast Asian migrants in low-wage service industries.[14]

My focus in this section is on representations of the work ethic of black African immigrant athletes and their "front" or "front stage," to use Goffman's terminology, when being questioned by the media. For my purposes, *front* refers to the attitude and manner of the athletes while they are in public. As Goffman finds, individuals will attempt to portray (perform) a positive or favorable image of their selves, a tendency that is no doubt stronger when individuals face uncertain or novel social settings, such as adapting to a new country and culture. Hence we should not be surprised to find among migrant African athletes very friendly dispositions, at least initially, which is then picked up on by the media. These friendly face representations do not really tell us anything about the athletes in question besides the fact that they are trying to manage their impression. Additionally, Goffman notes, performances of the self are not solo acts. Western media is thus implicated in this process by encouraging certain behaviors and denouncing others in an attempt to frame the individual as a certain kind of person, athlete, or celebrity. The media attempts to construct athletes in such a way as to make them easily accessible and knowable to a white male middle-class target audience. This process necessitates the reduction of individual complexity into stereotypes. We must also remain cognizant of the fact that these athletes in the United States perform in a context dominated by native black athletes and are thus inherently compared to that population and the native black population in general.[15]

The most provocative examples of the "hard workers and friendly faces" theme can be found in the representations of Tamba Hali, Hakeem Olajuwon, and Dikembe Mutombo. These three have been consistently lauded for their work ethic, both on and off the field, and/or their friendly temperament and disposition. In the example in the Origin Stories section, Hali is described as "deserving" to live in Happy Valley (Penn State), a notion that in part comes out of a discourse on his work ethic. Of course, what is also problematic is that by constructing Hali as deserving—a discourse related to his foreign Otherness—the valid presence of others is put into question. Further, this theme of hard work constructs these athletes as exceptional individuals and "good" migrants while also invoking noble savage imagery. The athletes are seen as having some kind of purity or naïveté about them that whites in the West have lost through technological "progress." In the trope of "the foreign black athlete" as noble savage, native black athletes in the West are seen as "spoiled," "soft," or "arrogant."

> [Mutombo is] as endearing as he is awe-inspiring, more likely to react with a pained look to a low-post elbow planted in his chest than with any sort of retaliation. . . . The accent and the voice—which rumbles at an octave that seems as low as any human possibly can produce— are just part of the wealth of idiosyncrasies that lead Thompson to call Mutombo his "filling station." . . . "He has come out of a different way of living, a different system of life," Thompson said. "It's easier to communicate and to deal with him without him being fragile. He has a refreshing freshness about him . . . because he has not been Americanized since he was in elementary school, with somebody recruiting him or somebody trying to convince him that he's the best thing that's happened to the game since the tennis shoe was invented."[16]

That Mutombo would go on to be well-known for giving elbows throughout his career makes the quote above somewhat ironic. The description of Mutombo as awe-inspiring and passive in the face of aggressive play clearly infantilizes him. Yet his masculinity is rescued later in the passage when Georgetown coach John Thompson clears him of any fragility due to excessive "Americanization." Given Thompson's history of activity in the African American community and his status as one of the few black coaches in major college basketball programs at the time, it is perhaps unlikely that his intent was to blame young black athletes for excessive ego. Thompson rightly points to the larger system of recruiting and, indirectly, how corporate shoe money (historically, Nike and Adidas) influences young basketball players, but the article is directed at differentiating Mutombo from the "crowd" (African Americans), not the institutions that push young black Americans into sport or the problematic concern with young black male masculinity, and so the critique is unacknowledged and rendered moot.

> There is a precious innocence surrounding Akeem Abdul Olajuwon. . . . On the floor, he is a picture of raw talent in bloom. . . . He epitomizes a simple, sincere love for the game that other players only speak of having. That love, combined with the hard work at mastering a game he has played for only four years, has made the 20-year-old Olajuwon, who came to the United States from Africa, the spotlight of the Final Four this weekend in Albuquerque, N.M. . . . Speaking in a soft, low tone, he seemed almost shy as he stood towering above a group of reporters, trying to answer politely each question put to him. At times, he appeared to strain for the right answer, as if something had been lost in a translation. He speaks English well, having learned it many years ago in his hometown, Lagos, Nigeria, in a school that charged students a dime each time they spoke their native language in class. But sometimes, Olajuwon said, "People go too fast for me."[17]

As with Mutombo, the attributes given to Olajuwon frame him as a shy man-child worthy of adoration. Olajuwon's masculinity is never put into question, however, due to his existence and performance in sport but also because his model minority status puts him "above the fray" so to speak. Thus because Olajuwon does not do "childish" things like trash talking or bragging about himself, he is actually "more manly" than "other" players. In the U.S. context, because Olajuwon does not engage in young black hip-hop culture, which was becoming more and more popular during his career, he is effectively used to shame and denigrate the fellow players around him who do.

In some ways this invokes issues related to but different from the model minority stereotype. The "good black"/"bad black" dichotomy has long played a role in American and European sport, often falling along class lines within the black community. Whether it is middle-class blacks in the early twentieth century shying away from Jack Johnson or athletes such as Joe Louis, Jesse Owens, Frank Bruno, and Michael Jordan steering clear of race issues during the height of their careers, the "good black" has nominally stood for racial "progress" while the "bad black" has been indicative of base nature. Indeed, we might re-read "The Dream" as a construction of American (and similar to other Western societies') desire for only certain kinds of (black) masculinity—ones that submit to white authority—and thus as saliently speaking to the deviant masculinities of black youths specifically. This despair and fear of black youth in the West is reflected within the general global "crisis" of masculinity among the poor and working classes more broadly. The ongoing impacts of neoliberalism and austerity programs have left many underemployed (if that) and unable to find meaningful work to fulfill the masculine obligations society holds them to. The turn toward forms of masculinity that are damaging to the self, family, and community—in various forms, including different types of radicalization—may be expressed differently in different contexts but is linked to larger systems of opportunity and self-realization. In the next chapter I return to this topic again in order to address the underlying fear that the model minority is actually just another one of "them."[18]

The quote above states that Olajuwon's hard work and dedication have allowed him in four years to succeed at a sport that others have been playing their entire lives, and yet Olajuwon's athletic history of playing netball and soccer throughout his youth gets glossed over. The notion that basketball or football are so complicated that "we" are surprised when individuals with athletic backgrounds succeed at them again betrays how Western-centric these sports are and the underlying belief in technical superiority. It is not that professional athletes do not work hard or have not trained for years; rather, it speaks to an underlying belief in sport that young athletes must specialize early on if they are to succeed, when that is not the case. In this instance the intersection of a certain belief about youth sport and foreign Otherness produces racist discourse.

> Olajuwon's humility is charming. After he conquers his foe, Olajuwon is ready with a smile and a handshake. He deflects praise, redirecting it to teammates. Hakeem speaks English, French and four Nigerian dialects. But you won't hear him talking trash. That would violate his dignity. . . . He became a U.S. citizen two years ago and has applied to compete for his adopted country in the 1996 Olympics. Hey, Team

USA needs Hakeem. This noble Nigerian can remind the world that there's more to the NBA than self-absorbed Ugly Americans. This isn't a shining stretch for the NBA. There are too many young, unproven players cashing in for doing little, and that's created a selfish environment. Olajuwon's performance in the postseason has elevated the entire league. He's restored respect. He's back in the NBA finals. Scoot over, Michael Jordan. Hakeem is the man.[19]

The interrelated nature of these themes makes talking about any one of them in isolation a difficult task. Olajuwon is positioned as the cure for an NBA dominated by African American athletes who are described, basically, as taking advantage of team owners and dictating the work environment. Further, by playing on Team USA Olajuwon can remind that world that Americans—though Olajuwon himself remains a "noble Nigerian"—are not so bad. Clearly this kind of discourse takes for granted the global impact African Americans (especially Michael Jordan) have had among the African diaspora—and beyond. The "problems" of the NBA were only truly a problem for the predominantly white male executives and managers who wanted to make sure the sport was not becoming "too black" for their white middle-class fans. Similarly, it is not black America, or black Europe, that the rest of the world has a problem with. There is a certain irony in the black and brown populations of the West often being (used) put in a position to recuperate the nation's image when internally they are also seen as the ones damaging it. U.S. goodwill tours to foreign countries by athletes such as Althea Gibson, Arthur Ashe, Bill Russell, and Kareem Abdul-Jabbar demonstrate that such usage is not a one-time mistake but rather has been a particular maneuver of white supremacy to hide its existence and power throughout history.

Many of these descriptors occur early in the career of these athletes and then dissipate or change over time. That for Olajuwon and Mutombo they have been maintained consistently speaks to the length of their career, their quality as players, and their celebrity status. Tegla Loroupe was similarly received in the United States after winning the New York City Marathon in 1994 and 1995. Conversely, Didier

Drogba and Balotelli were both represented early in their careers as friendly and likeable in British media before later being represented in more negative ways. This initial framing reflects the more amenable reception black immigrants have tended to receive in the West because they do not reflect the racial history of Western countries back at themselves.[20] Admittedly, this framing process has become more complicated in the twenty-first century, particularly in Europe, with increased migration from black African refugees and asylum seekers. Yet with the prestige that comes with being an athlete, it is understandable how black African athletes, particularly those who succeed early in their careers, are seemingly welcomed with open arms. As some of my examples show, it is precisely the *foreign* Otherness, the lack of "Westernization," that privileges the African athlete above other black athletes. This "welcoming," however, is really a tendency to portray the foreign black Other in a childlike, simple-minded, or innocent manner. These tendencies invoke a long history in the West of representing black men and women as children, with the adult alternative being to frame them as physical or sexual threats to whiteness.[21] Those who fail to continually validate this idealized media construction, such as Drogba and Balotelli, are quickly subsumed into the more negative stereotypes of blackness that we often see applied to native blacks. Hence blackness remains marginalized and subhuman, and no black athlete transcends race. In the next chapter I will discuss in greater detail the contingent nature of foreign black acceptance and explore discourses that link the black foreign other to criminality, ugliness, and the irrational.

Humanitarians

Black African migrants' humanitarian and charitable efforts in their home countries, as individuals who have left and found "success" in the West, serve as another means of elevating the individual and reinscribing the problems of African countries. Similar charitable efforts undertaken in the West by native or foreign black athletes, usually in cities where they play and live, are often ignored. The growing problems of inequality and racism in the West go unnoticed in favor of a focus on the more remote problems of "Africa," the individuals trying to solve the problems, and at times, what "we" can do to help. As Jonathon Glennie explains, long-term development aid from Western governments may hurt the development of democracy in African countries by making African political institutions more dependent on the West and less accountable to their constituents.[22] This, of course, is the old story of aid conditionalities—economic restructuring or structural adjustment programs—that developed with the formation of the World Bank's and International Monetary Fund following World War II. When elected officials in developing countries have to have their economic program approved by the International Monetary Fund before it becomes law, there are valid questions of who exactly lawmakers and institutions are responsible to and who is really running the country. While populations suffer, the West has benefited from a massive and ongoing transfer of wealth from the global South—hence neocolonialism. Meanwhile "we" in the West are often guided toward short-term emergency aid when famine, disease, or natural disasters strike but away from thinking about the root causes of these problems. Giving will be enough.

Most of the athletes I analyzed were involved in some kind of humanitarian or charitable activities. For example, Loroupe organized and still runs the Tegla Loroupe Peace Academy to help stem pastoral violence and help women and orphans in Kenya. Catherine Ndereba was involved in charitable races to help raise awareness of HIV/AIDS and corruption. Mario Balotelli gave his time and money to charitable causes for kids in Brazil (among other causes), and Olajuwon was heavily involved in the Muslim communities in and around the Houston area. However, it is in the representations of Didier Drogba and Dikembe Mutombo that we find significant attention placed on their humanitarian efforts in Ivory Coast and the Democratic Republic of Congo, respectively. Drogba is popularly credited with "stopping" the civil war in Ivory Coast (a war that was already winding down at the time) and has created a foundation to build hospitals and schools. Comparably, Mutombo has spent his time and millions of his own dollars to make a hospital in the Congo, dedicated to his mother, a reality.

Didier Drogba

Drogba is routinely represented in Western media as a deity figure for the people of Ivory Coast. It is, of course, Drogba's status in the West (his success and wealth) that gives him a platform and drives this representation of him as a kind of savior for his country of birth. Drogba and the West are linked in a way that celebrates the accomplishments of the black migrant in helping his homeland and celebrates the West for making that possible by simply "being" the opposite of Africa. The status of the West as advanced, modern, civilized, and democratic is thus reinscribed via the representation of Drogba and similar athletes for those—in the West as well as in African and other developing countries—who increasingly access sport through Western media. As Daniel Künzler and Raffaele Poli argue further, Drogba's corporate sponsors, along with those of other Ivory Coast players such as Kolo Touré and Aruna Dindane, often promote neoliberal discourses of hard work and achievement within their Ivory Coast advertisements. These advertisements have been criticized by organizations that help unsuccessful migrant soccer players for relying solely and simplistically on the careers of those few who find success. The situation is further compounded by local Ivorian media that focuses overwhelmingly on players like Drogba to the detriment of local leagues. The aura of ease, of soccer as a "way out," that is created around these players and the sport itself is completely contradicted by the circumstances of Drogba, who was primarily raised in France, never played in a local Ivorian league, and apparently does not speak the Ivorian languages (Bété, specifically) very well.[23] Again, this is not to discount Drogba's popularity or argue that he is somehow not "Ivorian," merely to state that there are other, additional and problematic, forces involved that, in both Western and local African media, preserve the hegemony of Western neoliberal democracy.

> Blessed are the peacemakers—which is why Didier Drogba enjoys the status of a saint in the Ivory Coast. . . . After he inspired the Ivory Coast to qualify for the 2006 World Cup finals in Germany, television crews entered the dressing-room and Drogba seized the microphone. He said: "Ivorians—in qualifying for the World Cup we've shown you

the whole of the Ivory Coast can share the same goals. We promise
the celebrations will bring everybody back together." And then, after
kneeling with his team-mates in supplication, Drogba announced:
"We beg you on our knees to lay down your arms and organise free
elections." And they did. The warlords agreed that the fighting had
to stop. The years of killings and revenge attacks that had left thousands dead, wounded and mutilated came to an end. . . . He is hailed
as "The King of Africa."[24]

Drogba's immense popularity in Ivory Coast does not appear to
be a mirage or a solitary product of media filtering. He has a beer, a
dance, and a town named after him, and, we are told, he can call the
president of Ivory Coast whenever he wishes.[25] Certainly it is increasingly rare for any athlete to attain that kind of celebrity.[26] My primary
concern is with the background upon which Drogba's celebrity is
played out, or represented. That background consists of repeatedly
reading that the average citizens of Ivory Coast has a life expectancy
of forty-seven years and that Drogba is in regular contact with the
president, all while glossing over the fact that Drogba uses money
from companies such as Nike, Samsung, and Pepsi to further his
humanitarian efforts.[27] These transnational corporations are interested in selling products through Drogba, not changing the neoliberal order from which they benefit wildly. Because we already know
that the African state is often portrayed as undeveloped, diseased,
and corrupt, the representations here of Drogba as close to godlike
only simplify Ivorian (and African) politics and sport culture. It is
made to seem reasonable that an athlete is in such a position when a
similar phenomenon would be unthinkable in the West.

Relatedly, we can examine Drogba's participation with musician
and activist Bono's RED campaign to fight HIV/AIDS. The campaign,
which markets items colored red and then makes donations, for example, to the Global Fund to Fight AIDS, Tuberculosis, and Malaria,
has received a lot of attention and criticism over the years. The link
between commerce and charity, development through consumerism,
is uncritically embraced by media outlets in Drogba's representation.
Nothing is said about the continued pressure put upon developing

nations to adhere to neoliberal Western norms or the history of structural adjustment programs, and it is worth considering whether athletes caught in this system are unknowing pawns or are using their fame and wealth in the best possible way under constrained circumstances. Drogba's intersection with Bono and the RED campaign—as well as with other white celebrities—receives a great deal of media attention, at times even more so than the efforts of Drogba by himself. This predominant focus on the activities of whites is another part of the industry of charitable donations and aid, which the novelist and social critic Teju Cole has called the "White-Savior Industrial Complex."

The White-Savior Industrial Complex relies on simplistic portrayals of Africa's problems in order to make white donors and activists feel that they can make a difference by making a financial contribution or by directly intervening on the ground. Taking the popular Kone 2012 video and Uganda as an example, Cole explains that this approach ignores the political realities of African countries and the agency of African peoples to contribute and solve their own problems. As Cole has put forth, the White-Savior Industrial Complex is not about social justice that would result in the change of Western policies toward developing countries but rather it is about donors and activists having strong emotional and sentimental experiences of giving that serve to justify their privilege. In this instance, the privileged white athlete and white activist represent the West and its "efforts" to aid people in African countries.[28] By focusing on the white activist to a greater degree than the black African athlete or the actual politics of African countries, the West is absolved of further political responsibility.

Dikembe Mutombo

The discourse surrounding Mutombo's humanitarian efforts differs from that surrounding Drogba's in that Mutombo spends a significant amount of his own money toward building a hospital in his mother's memory. Though Mutombo was active in local charitable efforts in each city he played in throughout his NBA career, the majority of media focus is on his efforts to build a hospital in the Democratic Republic of Congo. I argue that the representation of black African human-itarian efforts has its own place within the White-Savior Industrial Complex. Black African migrant athletes are seen as benefiting from migrating to and living in Western communities. Because their expe-riences with racism are marginalized or go unnoticed, black African athletes can be positioned as having benefited from Western society and thus being able to help the communities from which they came. Here again, the West is elevated and congratulates itself for having "given" the black African immigrant the opportunity to help others (themselves). Yet the humanitarian activities of the black African ath-lete should not pass our critique either because they often are linked to corporate concerns (as noted with Drogba) and frequently inter-vene without consulting local communities or politics. In the end, the best thing potential donors and activists could do to help peo-ples in African countries would be to convince their Western govern-ments to stop the oppressive neoliberal economic controls that have been forced upon African nations—often taking money that could go toward education, health, jobs, and infrastructure and spending it on debt services to Western banks.[29]

> "Africa is dying," Mutombo said in an interview this week. "Whole villages are being destroyed. Whole cultures are being diminished. Some peoples' histories are gone." In the face of the epidemics, fam-ines and wars that are ravaging his native Africa, Mutombo poses the question: "What is the world doing about it?" Mutombo . . . has been doing something about the dire conditions for years. In 1997, he estab-lished the Dikembe Mutombo Foundation, which works to prevent childhood diseases in African poverty zones. His foundation also is building the first new hospital in more than 40 years in his homeland, the Democratic Republic of Congo (formerly Zaire). He has contrib-uted more than one third of the projected $29 million cost of the hos-pital, which is scheduled to open next year.[30]

Mutombo has very clearly decided to do something to help the peo-ple of the Congo and his efforts should be acknowledged, as his hos-pital provides services, particularly to women, that otherwise would be unavailable. However, we learn little more about the root causes of suffering in African countries than what is provided above. Instead, Mutombo is positioned as the person who will be doing something for the people of Africa even if the rest of the world is not. Western media is essentially a bystander providing us no other solutions. What is different and important is a concurrent and parallel discourse concerning Mutombo's disappointment with the level of charity from his fellow NBA players. This discourse developed after Mutombo first decided to build a hospital and demonstrates how Mutombo is represented differently from African Americans.

> "I thought about a clinic, maybe 30 to 100 beds. My cousin said that would mean nothing in terms of really helping. He said 300 beds. He said, 'Don't worry, you can do it. You have power. People will respond.'" . . . That is a difficult subject for Mutombo. At last season's All-Star Game in Washington, Alonzo Mourning, his old Georgetown teammate, was soliciting funds for kidney disease research. Mourning recently had been diagnosed with a kidney disease that was threatening his career, if not his life. Mutombo, on the spot, wrote out a check for $50,000. But when Mutombo asked players in the league to help him with his project, he says he got little meaningful response.[31]

Much of the discourse on Mutombo's troubles finding donations from NBA players draws upon a familiar background—the lazy and selfish (black) athlete—to distinguish Mutombo's efforts. The assumption that NBA players are wealthy and have money to spare hides the reality that many face financial challenges and bankruptcy after their playing years are over.[32] What we have here is a process by which the recognition of the attitudes and efforts of black African migrant athletes can serve as a vehicle for whites to praise certain black (migrant) athletes while simultaneously denouncing and remarginalizing others, primarily native blacks, in a moment of color blindness. Often Mutombo's efforts are taken as a simplistic indication that he has "not forgotten" his homeland, suggesting a problematic temporality in which Mutombo—a "good" immigrant—will return home while other migrants unwantedly stay. As in society at large, as long as black African migrants conform to how white society wants or expects them to behave they gain contingent acceptance, which, of course, means suppressing any questionable form of cultural or ethnic expression. Their difference must only ever be superficial. As long as black African immigrants present themselves in a way that does not remind whites about the racial histories of the United States, or France, Germany, or Britain (among other former colonial powers), that "acceptance" remains in place. That black immigrants are often willing to suppress, yet at certain times stress, their cultural distinction is indicative of the kind of differences they have with native blacks in political and economic outlook and goal attainment, which sometimes causes friction between the groups.[33]

Conclusion

A great deal of work is being done within these origin stories, discourses of hard work and humanitarian narratives. The representation of "the black African athlete" as humble, hardworking, humanitarian, or from an extremely tough background is recurrent and thematic within a globalized Western sport media. The obstacles they are said to face are "Africa" itself or their particular "African" cultures, never the result of a continuing colonial legacy. That the "history" of African countries seemingly begins after formal independence is another salient tendency in the representation of black African athletes. The backwardness of the African continent and peoples is thus reinscribed through their representation in media discourse. This tendency also makes alternative readings difficult. For example, learning that Mutombo knows multiple languages could offer a point where we think about the necessity to communicate in order to understand other peoples. Instead, Mutombo's knowledge base is at times derisively defined in terms of the one language he had not learned yet, English. The fact that athletes from different countries have had to learn English is often lost on those in the West and reflects a bias toward learning the languages of others, especially in the context of the United States.[34]

As celebrities, black African athletes are discursively made to stand for and reaffirm a political system, neoliberal democracy, built on notions of individual achievement.[35] Though their life stories sit alongside the often similar life stories of native blacks, the life stories of black immigrants are somehow *more* primal and *more* terrific. "Africa," always already the Dark Continent, produces athletes with unimaginable backgrounds, yet they emerge humble and honorable. That these athletes have overcome their brutal situations is a lesson for all, men and women, but even more so for native black populations in the West. In sports such as American football and basketball or European soccer, we frequently see discourses that charge black athletes with laziness or accuse them of having "diva" complexes or of being spoiled, undeserving brats.

What I want to stress are the different modes of alterity that are placed on the black African migrants in this study and how that alterity is used to reinforce Western understandings of race and Africa. Through the descriptions of their backgrounds and the empty valorization of their work ethic, the athletes in this study are privileged in the media against a backdrop that often consists of stigmatized native black athletes. Similarly, the simplistic elevation of the importance of the black African athlete in his or her country via humanitarian work contributes to the self-aggrandizement of the West. A focus on the activities of Africans who find wealth in the West and give back to Africa allows Western societies to continue ignoring their native black communities and similar efforts of native black athletes. Unsurprisingly, this way of covering what happens in black communities keeps us consistently running into variants of the time-worn neoconservative question "What about black-on-black crime?" As if black people are not concerned about their neighborhoods, as if the racial geography of crime does not reflect ongoing racial segregation, as if policing practices are unimportant to how neighborhoods respond to crime. It also positions black Africans as "good blacks" who might succeed if only their own governments would get out of the way—a somewhat paradoxical neoliberal assertion that what African peoples need is "less government." Of course, we also know that most black African immigrants to the West do not receive the welcome of the superstar athlete and that they are increasingly treated with hostility and disdain, something that also remains hidden in these representations.

Further, it should be made clear that the role of discourse in society is important and has implications for the actions individuals take, but at the same time it is not everything. My research explores the dominant narratives, or the *re*-presentations, of Western media on the subject of "African" athletes, and therefore it essentially deals with what the dominant powers would like to think about themselves and society. Since we are in a historical moment where blatant racism has given way to color-blind racism (although the former seems to be making a comeback), much of the discourse I examine predictably falls in line with color-blind rhetoric—especially as it concerns suffering on the African continent. Despite the sense of concern dominant discourse often portrays, including that of publications considered "liberal," it is underlain with a distinct and *naturalized* antiblack racism as it regards "African" poverty or development. Under the color-blind rhetoric and despite the academic appeal of color blindness, race is still a naturalized and tacitly accepted phenomenon.

This thinking has its roots in what Moon-Kie Jung, building on the work of Pierre Bourdieu, calls "symbolic coercion" and "symbolic perversity." *Symbolic coercion* refers to the counterdiscourses of marginalized groups that are willingly ignored by dominant society. Dominant society is not willing to listen to the legitimate concerns of the oppressed and continues to use naturalized racist schemas—patterns of thinking—in the ongoing oppression of the oppressed.[36] There is perhaps no better contemporary example of symbolic coercion than the state violence consistently directed at black protesters—in America and elsewhere—advocating for their very lives. That recently in Ferguson, Missouri, the Oathkeepers, a white antigovernment armed militia, arrived to "maintain order" and were not arrested, while unarmed black protesters were, further illustrates this point. The state acts from a point of naturalized racist beliefs on black criminality and violence in such a way as to often provoke and bring about that very violence—thereby reinforcing racist beliefs and validating further state oppression.

Symbolic perversion points to the overwhelming abundance of data on disparate racial outcomes produced by dominant state institutions, and yet nothing is done, no outrage evoked, to promote social change. Jung examines *New York Times* coverage of unemployment during the 2008 financial crisis and finds a disparity in how black unemployment—almost always twice as high as white unemployment—was covered. In brief, there were more articles—and more articles expressing urgency—when white unemployment reached 9.4 percent in fall 2009 than when black unemployment reached that same number a year and a half earlier. Such reporting points to the ongoing indifference to black suffering not only in America but around the world, and we can extend this thinking to other colonized indigenous peoples, Latinos, and Asians as well. This indifference to the sufferings of black and brown peoples around the world and in the West means that the antiracist beliefs of whites and liberals are just beliefs in principle—beliefs without action behind them. Beneath the surface of antiracist and color-blind beliefs lies an accepted and naturalized concept of race that we have yet to disrupt. That the empire-states of the West are foundationally built on the naturalized inequality of different races and not the horizontal citizenship of the nation-state that they assume they uphold makes working within the system (state) for change difficult, to say the least.[37]

My work investigates how we can read for various racisms and naturalizations within ostensibly color-blind discourses, because I doubt any of the publications I examine would admit to being "racist." Their casual Othering and contingent acceptance of African athletes, as well as their explorations into "African" problems and humanitarian advocacy, compose an antiblack racism that keeps blacks—all blacks—in a marginal and tenuous position. As we will see, the discourses of Western media not only work to maintain race as a naturalized concept but also portray an indifference to the suffering of both foreign and native black communities. The next chapter explores the contingent nature of these processes of making "model minorities" out of black African migrant athletes. It becomes ever more apparent that a majority of these representations are made by the West and reinforce Western hegemony.

4

"Bad" Blacks

Contingent Acceptance and Essentialized Blackness

As Paul Gilroy tells us, "In this world of overdetermined racial signs, an outstandingly good but temperamental natural athlete is exactly what we would expect a savage African to become."[1] The praise and acceptance in Western society that I documented in the previous chapter is viable only as long as black migrant athletes remain silent to their racial position in the West. It is also viable only while the athlete manages to succeed athletically, maintain acceptable behaviors, and remain out of negative news coverage. As mentioned in earlier chapters, the exploitation involved in the recruitment of black Africans to European soccer clubs results far too often in athletes being cast aside with no place to live, no way to get back home, and no kind of quality education. When this happens black African immigrants certainly fall into highly stigmatized modes of representation, as they are both black and foreign. In essence, they become just like any other black person. This exploitation demonstrates the tentative position occupied by black migrant athletes in Western countries and correlates with the exploitation black immigrants face in the job market in general.[2]

As Yoku Shaw-Taylor and Steven Tuch point out, despite being considered a kind of model minority, black African immigrants in the United States experience relatively low levels of household income and often live in poorer neighborhoods. Similarly, in Europe African immigrants can increasingly be found in the *banlieues* of France, shantytowns of Portugal, and poorer areas of London. The economic success of immigrants, their ability to utilize their human capital, is dependent on their reception into their host countries. In brief, Western countries have been making immigration more difficult and putting immigrants under greater surveillance while simultaneously dismantling social welfare programs.[3] Recent economic recessions have only worsened these trends and fostered antimigrant sentiment in the West. Concurrently, black African immigrants are arriving with less education, and the education they have is devalued in the West due to the harm done to African institutions of higher education by various dictators and the strictures of neoliberal development programs. Thus black immigrants, both men and women, often have to take poorly paid jobs and, because they may initially be unaware of the (racialized) labor structure, are often exploited for more work with less pay and little chance for upward mobility.[4]

Antiblack Discourses

In this chapter I continue to interrogate the representations of athletes who have "succeeded" and, as I have shown, are often lauded—turned into model minorities—for doing so. Yet this success does not mean that their representations escape the stigma of blackness or are immune to Western fears of immigration. I have divided the rest of this chapter into three sections, or themes. In the first section, "Anger, Greed, and Selfishness," I begin by talking about a time when Hakeem Olajuwon struggled with physical violence, a contract dispute, and lawsuits and then make links with representation of similar aspects of Dikembe Mutombo's career. The second section focuses on discourses alluding to the "Intelligence, Ignorance, and Sanity" of the black African athlete. This time, beginning with the representation of Mutombo, I look at the contradictory ways in which he is simultaneously represented as intelligent and sophisticated, simple and unintelligent. Then I analyze the ways in which Didier Drogba and Mario Balotelli are represented as mentally unstable, irrational, and even crazy. In the final section, "Black African Women in Sport," I look more closely at the representations of Tegla Loroupe and Catherine Ndereba in particular in order to talk about the stereotypes surrounding black women in sport.

Anger, Greed, and Selfishness

Although Olajuwon was favorably constructed early and late in his career, a set of events in the 1980s and early 1990s began to turn his representation in the opposite manner. Numerous fights on the court, harsh words for teammates and management, and a personal life reportedly going out of control started to turn the discourse around Olajuwon toward questioning his demeanor and temperament. In reading this period of Olajuwon's career, I find that he begins to be portrayed as just another selfish and arrogant player at time when some felt the NBA was becoming "too black."[5]

One of the first of many publicized "outbursts" by Olajuwon was in the wake of an NCAA finals loss in his senior year of college. After the University of Houston's loss to Georgetown, Olajuwon criticized his teammates and the officiating. "'What will they think when they read this? I don't care what they think,' said *Akeem the Steam*. 'This game was very important and we blew it. They just didn't get me the ball.'"[6] He added, "When some of our players drove to the basket, Georgetown went for the block and I was wide open. But we blew it. We didn't play as a team. We were selfish." For the media and those around the game, Olajuwon's criticism of his teammates went against the accepted "team first" way to discuss defeat. Of the officials he said, "'Before the game the referee says, 'I'll let you play.' . . . But he didn't. Sometimes he did. Then he came down on me. Nobody would have called me for those third and fourth fouls.'" Olajuwon's comments drew criticism from his own coach, Guy Lewis. "'Bing, bing, bing, fouls every time,' Lewis said. 'He had one silly foul, where the guy takes one pump fake and goes up. He knows everybody's gonna do that.'"[7]

Following this game Olajuwon declared for the NBA draft, and early on in his career he had a number of physically violent encounters on the court. In one instance he was fined $1,500 for punching the Utah Jazz's Billy Paultz, who had been frustrating him during a game. "'He was pushing me,' Olajuwon said. 'And every time I would push him back, they would call a foul on me. I was just trying to get the ref's attention. I was trying for the referee to make it equal. I am satisfied I did it.'"[8] Scotty Sterling, then the NBA's vice president of operations, remarked, "He [Paultz] was in no way prepared for the punch and totally defenseless. . . . While the flagrant act was undetected by the officials working the game, it nonetheless violates all of the NBA's principles of fair play and sportsmanship."[9] The fight was Olajuwon's second time receiving a league fine; the first was for an earlier fight with the Dallas Mavericks' Kurt Nimphius. Some were surprised that there was no suspension for the second incident. Olajuwon was also criticized for showing no remorse for his action, which was interpreted as a display of smugness.

Yet while he was still considered to be a well-tempered individual for the most part, an accumulation of incidents through the rest of the 1980s would eventually begin to sway opinions of him the other way. In the 1986 NBA playoffs Olajuwon was ejected once for shoving one player and grabbing a referee during a series with the Denver Nuggets. Against the Los Angeles Lakers, Olajuwon threw punches at a player who had been frustrating him, much like Billy Paultz, and in the NBA Championships Olajuwon was again fined $1,500 after yet another fight. An Atlanta newspaper reported that Olajuwon's "Achilles heel is a habit of fouling excessively in his still-reckless, undisciplined style and a temper that has raged out of control."[10] Teams suddenly realized they could get Olajuwon in foul trouble or even ejected if they sparked his temper, and the media became more critical of him. Olajuwon's constant criticism also appeared to make referees less sympathetic to his pleas for fouls in-game.

Olajuwon's off-court troubles also raised media interest and contributed to his growing reputation as a malcontent. In the summer of 1986 Olajuwon was ordered to pay $150 after pleading no contest to an assault by contact charge for allegedly striking a convenience store clerk who called him a name. The following January it was reported that Olajuwon and his brother fought outside of The Summit (the Houston Rockets' home arena) after a game. Near the end of that year Olajuwon fought his teammate Robert Reid over Reid's comments regarding rumors of cocaine use by Olajuwon. Such rumors surrounded Olajuwon that winter and prompted him to make a public denial. "Olajuwon had said he would submit to a drug test any time someone wants to put up $1,000. If he passes the test, he would donate that money to a drug treatment center. If he were to fail the test, he had promised to give $50,000 to the challenger."[11] The accusations were deemed to be nothing more than rumor, but soon after Olajuwon gained critical attention again by voicing his unhappiness with coach Bill Fitch and teammate Sleepy Floyd. "'All I know is that the players say they are afraid to make mistakes,' Olajuwon said. 'If they make mistakes, he [Fitch] takes them out.'" Regarding Floyd, the team's point guard, Olajuwon declared, "We don't have a playmaker on this team. . . . A point guard is a guard who makes something happen, who creates things."[12] Fitch would eventually be fired during the 1988 off-season, something he would publicly blame on Olajuwon in the immediate aftermath. For all intents and purposes, Olajuwon's representation as a malcontent would come to a head in the summer of 1988:

> For as long as we've known him, Akeem has been a Dream. But lately he's beginning to look like Freddy Krueger. It's a real "Nightmare on Elm Street" over at The Summit. It seems like every time the Rockets try to close their eyes and relax, Akeem Olajuwon has been there to give them a rude awakening in this summer of his discontent. If Olajuwon isn't assuming the role of coach and making demands about the Rockets' offense, then he's playing personnel director and suggesting wholesale changes. If he isn't swapping lawsuits with former companion Lita Spencer, then he's got his hand out looking for more money or his fist raised to deck a TV cameraman. Then there are the veiled threats to pack up his slam dunks and go to Italy.[13]

Olajuwon went from being a "Dream" in terms of his personality to a nightmare akin to the horror film icon Freddy Krueger. Aside from what could be taken from the *Nightmare on Elm Street* reference—a popular movie at the time—the quotation describes Olajuwon as a malcontent who is power hungry, looking for more money, personally irresponsible, and threatening to leave America altogether. In short, Olajuwon is recast as the embodiment of instability, hostility, and, with his hand out like an obstinate beggar, blackness. I make this link between Olajuwon's blackness and his increasingly negative representation because of the larger historical context of the NBA and

Reagan-era politics. As mentioned previously, at this time the NBA feared "losing" it white audience because the league was "too black." Physical play leading to fights on the court and in the stands, increasingly baggy shorts, "rampant" drug abuse, tattooed bodies, and the emergence of hip-hop culture were becoming problematic for the image of the league and its white ownership. These fears, of course, resonated with the larger Reagan-era political and penal crackdown on black communities and depictions of social welfare programs that (re)stigmatized blacks as inherently lazy, criminal, and dependent on welfare (black women in particular, with the image of the "welfare queen").[14] Hence we see the representation of Olajuwon begin to gain similarity with those of some of his more "problematic" African American contemporaries.

The events of the late 1980s would earn Olajuwon a label as a kind of troublemaker early in his career and going into the 1990s. In his autobiography he recalls this period as one in which he simply did not have patience.[15] It does not seem that the representation of this "bad behavior" was linked to Olajuwon's immigrant status in the same ways that his immigrant status was used to frame him early and late in his career as a role model. However, during a contract dispute in 1992 Olajuwon was often described as selfish or greedy, and attention was brought to his nature as a shrewd businessperson, a stereotype of Nigerians (yet no evidence emerged in my research to suggest that such a specific link was made in the media). Regarding the fan base, however, sportswriter Jackie MacMullan later recalled the hostility toward Olajuwon and his contract dispute in 1992:

> There was a time when he did complain—loudly. Two years ago, Olajuwon wanted a new contract, and the people of Houston began wondering if he'd ever be happy. They said he was greedy, and some said he should go back to the jungle and see how much money he'd make there. Ugly? Yes, it got very ugly. Olajuwon said he was injured, and the team said he was faking it to punish them for not extending his deal. Olajuwon, a man who wishes nothing more than to be called a gentleman, called the team owner, Charlie Thomas, a coward, and the general manager, Steve Patterson, a fool. It took a long plane flight

to Yokohama, Japan, for the owner and his unhappy star to finally make peace.[16]

MacMullan gives us a fleeting glimpse into how people were making sense of Olajuwon and his attempts to get a new contract. Throughout the accounts included in this study, athletes in general were derided for their social exploits and contract demands in the multimillions of dollars, euros, or pounds. Yet MacMullan's account acknowledges that Olajuwon's status as a black African immigrant is far from forgotten. The notion that he should "go back" (to Africa) demonstrates a white racist sentiment toward migrants, and blackness in general, that makes them disposable and holds that they exist in the West only because the white nation-state allows them to—even if, in the case of African Americans, they were fundamental to its construction. Additionally, immigrants should feel "lucky" that they are in the West and take what is given to them, or else they are free to go back to their "jungle," a space discursively denigrated as representing pure wilderness and savagery. This tenuous acceptance of Olajuwon finds resonance with the case of the Canadian sprinter Ben Johnson, who was (re)labeled as a Jamaican immigrant after he lost his gold medal because of doping. As Steven Jackson points out, the reinscription of Johnson explicitly as a Jamaican immigrant was done not only in a racist fashion but with a white ethnocentric zest that sought to punish both Johnson and the Jamaican community more broadly. That members of the Jamaican community felt the need to distance themselves from Johnson speaks to both the aggression of the backlash and the community's awareness of the position they occupy in Canadian society as black foreigners.[17]

At various points in his career Mutombo, similar to Olajuwon, was described in a variety of ways as angry, selfish, and greedy. If these representations existed in isolation they perhaps would be more innocent. However, in leagues that are or are becoming predominantly populated by people of color, both native and foreign, the discourses of selfishness, greediness, and anger are tied to what is already "known" about black athletes. Native black athletes might not be named, but we see complaints about a generally unwanted "culture" of professional sport. There is often a sense of fear or concern that the migrant athlete will "fall" into this degenerate sports culture.

> The easy excuse is to suggest Mutombo's effrontery is the product of a foreign culture we don't understand. That's a cop-out, not to mention an insult to Mutombo's family and his native Zaire. . . . If he's a product of any strange culture, it's pro sports in the 1990s. Mutombo came to America in '87, but he's a quick study. The Nuggets center knows NBA success is defined by your shoe contract and your TV time. All Deke really wants is to be like Mike, Grandmama [Larry Johnson] or Shaq. Why does the honesty of Mutombo's ambition make folks so nervous? Maybe it's because his obsession with celebrity says as much about us as Mutombo. . . . Mutombo owns a big ego and a bigger heart. You can neither shut him up nor dampen his spirit. The big man talks his mind, ignoring what's politically correct. While many pro athletes define charity as a celebrity golf tournament, Mutombo volunteers for duty in war-torn or starvation-plagued African countries.[18]

Here we have Mutombo's unwanted behavior being blamed on the sport culture of the time, which is represented by predominantly black athletes, specifically Michael Jordan, Larry Johnson, and Shaquille O'Neal. There is an unstated fear that Mutombo already is or is becoming like one of "them," which of course would be a reason to be "nervous." Through the description of his personality as "Mutombo being Mutombo" we are told that we should not expect Mutombo to be predictable or pleasing all the time. Simultaneously, he remains different, better than, other professional athletes because, while he still may want a shoe contract and television time, he at least helps out in war-torn and starvation-plagued African countries. While this example is rather provocative, it speaks to the ease with which the alterity, the blackness, of the foreign Other is made similar, intelligible, to that of native blacks.

Intelligence, Ignorance, and Sanity

Throughout his career the representation of Mutombo has also contained subtle, underlying assertions that he was mentally slow, stupid, and childlike. Despite attention often being drawn to how many languages Mutombo speaks, that he wanted to be a doctor before switching majors to diplomacy, the effort that he puts toward his foundation, or that he is intelligent in very general terms, there is evidence to suggest that some of the plaudits Mutombo receives mask another reality, that below the model minority stereotype presented on the surface of media articles lies an antiblack cynicism. At times Mutombo has attempted to push back against such characterizations, but most articles are not designed to validate Mutombo's views.

> "I felt the critics, about knowing the offense, had kind of crossed the line," Mutombo said. "I've been playing [NBA] basketball for 12 years and I've played for so many coaches and I did so well on all the teams. Why would I struggle here? It's not complicated. It took maybe a week but it's not complicated. . . . Because we lost two, three games on the west coast, everybody was saying the offense was not working because Mutombo does not understand. . . . I have a great career. If I didn't know offense what the hell was going through the mind of all the coaches I played for? Even Larry Brown, to play me all the way through to the NBA Finals? That means I was doing something right."[19]

Mutombo rightly gets upset when his intelligence is questioned. The situation with the Nets in 2002 changed Mutombo's representation by making it acceptable to discuss his intelligence on and off the basketball court. Mutombo's deep voice, accent, and linguistic gaffes are treated as evidence that he is lacking in some ways. Often his voice is compared to that of the Cookie Monster from the popular U.S. children's show *Sesame Street*. Cookie Monster talks in a gruff manner, has a lazy eye, is comically obsessed with cookies, and regularly drops prepositions and articles out of his speech. The reduction of Mutombo to a comical children's character devalues his discourse and him as a human being. Again, the lack of appreciation for Mutombo's ability to speak English, as one of a number of languages in which he is conversant, betrays a certain arrogance and ethnocentrism. As we will also see with the representation of Mario Balotelli, if we approach Mutombo with the expectation of amusement and entertainment, then we are approaching him as a fetishized object, not a full human being. Anything he may have to say is irrelevant because we are only interested in being entertained. Thus there are links with the long histories of black populations being infantilized and seen derisively as objects of (white) entertainment, while there are also ties with the difficulties many black immigrants face with being treated poorly because of their accents.[20]

Mutombo's age also became a popular topic of debate when, late in his career, questions arose as to whether he is as old as he says. This is another discourse that arises suddenly and is evoked repeatedly. It is a discourse that emerges in stereotypical ways common to athletes migrating from the global South based on the assumption of poor or nonexistent record keeping.

> In one corner, you have O'Neal, who was born in Newark. In the other corner, you have Mutombo, who was born in the Congo. O'Neal, we know, is 29. Mutombo, we are told, is 34. Some feel he has underwear older than that. O'Neal spent one summer working on a rap record. Mutombo spent one summer in Africa, getting malaria. O'Neal is barely audible. Mutombo talks like he's calling audibles. O'Neal's middle name is Rashaun. Mutombo's middle name is one or all of the following: Mpolondo Mukamba Jean Jacque WaMutombo. (Personally, I don't understand why Dikembe, who obviously chose to go with just two of his names, didn't pick "Jean Jacque." He could play basketball and design hair products.)[21]

Clearly a lot is going on in this example—and by now much of it should be unsurprising. The 2001 NBA Finals matchup between Mutombo and Shaquille O'Neal was treated in the media almost as a kind of minstrel show. Both Mutombo and O'Neal were treated as man-child objects of entertainment and Otherness. Yet the focus on Mutombo's age accomplishes more than an easy joke on his physical appearance. The accusation of giving a false age is an accusation of cheating—age cheating—and it assumes an intent to deceive. That those in developing countries are most often accused of age cheating fits into the construction of blackness as lacking morality, honesty, trustworthiness, rationality, objectivity, and so on. There is a feeling among whites that blacks are using the system unfairly—again akin to fears about welfare fraud. What is being

taken for granted (valued) is the privilege of Western record keeping and the institutions that rely on and reinforce a strict separation of ages. That many (postcolonial) developing countries have
been unable to invest the resources to adhere to these demands of
Western rationality speaks to their historical and ongoing underdevelopment in the global economy. The inability to engage in the
rationality of age also has implications for the movement of individuals in these countries, thus impacting their ability to travel
and improve or enjoy their lives. In the sport context we recently
saw such an example when a Little League team from Uganda was
denied entry to the United States based on "irregularities" with
their birth records. Hence what seems like a very simple and routine part of life in the West—having a birth certificate—is caught
in a web of ongoing power relations and (neo)colonial histories.
And while Mutombo often jokes about things such as his age and
talking like the Cookie Monster, he appears to tell us how he actually feels at other, infrequent, times.

> Despite his prodigious talent, Mutombo has found respect elusive. The
> Denver sportswriters used to say that Mutombo spoke nine languages,
> but English wasn't one of them. His voice is incredibly hoarse: Radio
> personality Howard Stern calls him the Cookie monster because he
> sounds like the Sesame Street character. . . . He remembers each affront.
> The questions about his age provoke particular scorn. "Some people
> say I'm not 35 years old, I'm something like 40. I don't know why they
> say that. It hurts my feelings. It's like they're insulting my parents for
> not being smart enough to know when I was born."[22]

As with most cracks in the hegemonic discourse, Mutombo's counterdiscourse is rare and receives no follow-up attention. There is no
doubt that Mutombo is a gregarious, outgoing, and likeable individual. Throughout his career, there are plenty of examples of him jok-
ing with reporters and teammates. It also seems as though he was
perfectly willing to make a joke of himself, which is evident in his
television commercials for the insurance company GEICO and his
singing a song about himself on Jimmy Kimmel's late night television

show—a song that is reminiscent of "Hakuna Matata" from Disney's *The Lion King*. However, the example above gives us an insight into Mutombo's awareness of the media discourse around him.

Within this theme of temperament and mental ability we can draw some parallels between the representation of Mutombo and representations of Didier Drogba and Mario Balotelli. Drogba's initial acceptance in England as a "grounded" individual was specifically attributed to his upbringing in and migration from Ivory Coast as a tough but "character building" experience.[23] Over time, however, that discourse eventually turned into one about his "mercurial" or "enigmatic" nature.[24]

> The Drog . . . has become so irredeemably pathetic, he's bringing the Premier League into disrepute. . . . He was a preening, prancing, diving, moaning, whingeing waste of time. . . . The highlight of his histrionics was his hyperactive child impression when he pursued Michael Ballack across the pitch because he was upset Ballack had tried to take a free-kick off him. . . . Ballack may not have excelled himself since he joined Chelsea but the way he ignored Drogba's raving as if he was a lunatic let out for the weekend was beautiful. . . . What a shame that Drogba should be the opposite of a courageous centre-forward like Alan Shearer or a brave dribbler who rolls with the punches, like Cristiano Ronaldo. . . . What a pity Drogba lets down teammates who are men of character like John Terry, Michael Essien, Frank Lampard, Joe Cole and Claude Makelele.[25]

Here we see Drogba's sanity and character questioned and infantilized at all points. His masculinity is also inherently questioned, much in line with historical tropes, as not being the "right" or "appropriate" kind of masculinity for English soccer. Though Michael Essien, Joe Cole, and Claude Makelele are mentioned as men of character, their inclusion in this type of article is less likely than the relatively constant presence of the white English players Frank Lampard and John Terry. Indeed, along with Steven Gerrard, Terry and Lampard (and others) often serve as "examples" of how soccer should be played in reference not only to Drogba but to foreign players in general. When foreign black athletes go against established norms, their Otherness is often used to marginalize them and self-serving attempts are made to understand how or why they make the decisions they do.

The media's effort to understand or make knowable—often in order to dismiss—the mental state of the black athlete is a hallmark of Mario Balotelli's representation. This is primarily due to the fascination of British tabloids with Balotelli's personal life. Who he was dating or thought to be having sex with, where he went out to at night, what he was wearing, his hairstyles, what cars he bought, where he was living, or what he did with his free time were all issues of popular concern, with their importance greatly exaggerated. In many ways Balotelli became a symbol for any "crazy" or unbelievable act, as many reports of things he did turned out to be false.

Two aspects of Balotelli's representation are important to explore. The first, and most explicit, is the constant representation of Balotelli as "crazy" or unthinking, and the second is the focus on Balotelli's personal life. Both representations are routinely presented to us in a dramatic, often criminalized, fashion and relate to stereotypical notions of blackness.

> When I look at Mario Balotelli, I feel nothing but sadness and regret. Not just for the Italian, but for a large portion of modern footballers in general. Roberto Mancini, David Platt and dozens of other people at Manchester City did everything they could to help the striker settle in; to help him fulfill his potential. But they were facing a losing battle from the start. "Why always me?" he once asked. Well, Mario, it was probably because of all the stupid, misguided and crazy decisions you made along the way. . . . I love people like Gary Neville, Frank Lampard, Paul Scholes, Ryan Giggs and even John Terry. Because they all have a real passion for the game.[26]

> So how DO you solve a problem like Mario? . . . When he sets foot on to the pitch he has no idea what he's doing. I genuinely believe that Balotelli hasn't got a vicious bone in his body. What he's got is stupid bones and he's got a lot of them. His nickname is Super Mario. It should be changed to Barmy Balo. Because as a footballer he's as daft as a brush. He doesn't think. He just does it and then regrets it. The

only thing wrong with Balotelli is his age. He's a child wearing a man's body. And like animals, children do the daftest things.[27]

Reading Balotelli, what we see is his construction as an unpredictable, crazy, and temperamental individual—if a "naturally" gifted athlete. His off-field activities are often labeled as "crimes" by the media, thus playing on assumptions of black male criminality both in Europe and the United States. That he is considered a "problem" in need of solving has particular resonance with the "negro problem" of the twentieth century as analyzed by W. E. B. Du Bois.[28] Balotelli, like Drogba, is compared to white, primarily English, soccer players and constructed not only as crazy and stupid but using the familiar trope of the black man-child. The historical construction of black men as children is rooted in colonial ideology as a way to emasculate and dehumanize blackness.[29] Appropriate to the representation of Balotelli, the colonial opposite of the black man-child is a hypersexual criminal threat. Balotelli is made to encompass both.

It should come as no surprise that the media is aware of its treatment of Balotelli. This persistence in the face of knowing carries with it an undercurrent of antiblack racism via casual disregard for black suffering. I argue that Balotelli becomes an acceptable conduit through which white supremacy can voice its feelings and concerns about blackness—inside and outside of sport. Even in articles that seem to be sympathetic toward Balotelli he is solely blamed for bringing his problems on himself. This lack of restraint concerning Balotelli—and empathy as it concerns the rote nature of describing African suffering—points to "an underlying racial logic that implicitly assumes radical difference between categories of people and renders the suffering of some incommensurable with and less worthy than the suffering of others."[30] Hence the media can and does know exactly how it treats Balotelli, as something to be used and discarded without any sort of true remorse.

Balotelli has become Baloo-telli, the dancing bear—prodded and tormented until he roars, then whipped and sent to his cage for roaring. There's a vicious circle here, in which we're all culpable. And by the way, I'm sure I should include myself in that. Anyway. So long now,

Mario Balotelli. It was fun winding you up, then pretending to be offended by you. May you thrive in Italy, score a silly hatful of goals every season and stick it to English clubs in the Champions League until the day of your retirement. Let's give this story a happy ending.[31]

Mario Balotelli's night began less than 30 seconds in with an innocuous volley from 40 yards out. Italy kick off, some tidy if unadventurous passing and then Mario just whacks it to nowhere, a bit like Peter Kay in that old lager advert. Was he trying to catch Joe Hart off guard? Was it just a way of steadying the nerves? Had the switch in his brain been flicked to "mental"? Nobody knows, but we can all speculate. That's the nice thing about Balotelli. He's a big, blank canvas on which anyone can project anything they like.[32]

Within all of the "craziness" that embodies the representation of Balotelli and the psychological analysis that comes with trying to "solve" Balotelli, he, more than any other athlete in this study, becomes a media-created abstraction divorced from the actual human being. The construction of Balotelli ensures that we never know him in even the most remote sense. He thus becomes another object in our meme culture—and indeed his stern pose after scoring a goal in the 2012 European Championships was a highly popular Internet meme—where anyone can put words to "him," his representation, and it "makes sense," however ridiculous. This kind of representation occurs whenever blacks fail to follow the expectations of white supremacy—deference, docility, humbleness—in whatever social institution. The need to put the out-of-place ("crazy") black individual back into place in an emphatic, unusually cruel, manner has long been the hallmark of whiteness offended. It has its roots in colonial ideology concerning the supposed unwillingness or inability of the colonial subject to work and the white imperative to make him or her do so. Interestingly, in his autobiography Drogba notes that the "laziness" he is criticized for on the field is actually a strategy to lull defenses to sleep during the course of a game, yet he was never asked about such a strategy in my data— black laziness is assumed. That much of this discourse appears raceless, or color-blind, only hides the ongoing reality of naturalized beliefs of black inferiority.

Black African Women in Sport

This contingent acceptance into Western societies is, of course, not a fine line for black men alone to walk. Black women in the West have historically been constructed outside established notions of white femininity. While today African American women have been subjected to this exclusion most noticeably, representations of the black female body as grotesque, hypersexual, and deviant have their roots in early precolonial ideology and exploitation. The most provocative example remains that of Saartjie Baartman, who was so named after she was orphaned by European military action in South Africa and who is also known variously as the "Hottentot Venus" and the "African Queen." Baartman was taken to London from South Africa in the early nineteenth century and put on display in human "freak" shows because of the size of her buttocks and genitalia. Her relatively short time in Europe ended with her death and dissection by a French surgeon who put her "famed" body parts on display. It was not until 2002 that her remains were returned to South Africa. Her dehumanizing story resonates with the ongoing fetishization of black women and their supposed hypersexual qualities. The body of the black female athlete is caught in this history and inherently put under the normalizing gaze of whiteness, which finds it deviant both physically and sexually. Especially in sports traditionally popular within higher socioeconomic classes, such as tennis, figure skating, and gymnastics, we often see black women depicted as masculine and subjected to critiques of both their personal style (hair and clothes) and their body type or figure, Serena and Venus Williams being prime examples.[33] The black African migrant women in my study were often represented in the same ways as native black women, but also women in general.

Beginning with the issue of masculinity and heteronormativity, I earlier told of how distance runner Tegla Loroupe was moved to publicly defend herself from speculation that she was not a woman and that she was somehow a man or had male sex organs. It is worth digressing a little here, as such representations carry extra weight given the more recent controversy surrounding the South African runner Caster Semenya—among other women from developing countries—who was coerced to undergo a process of gender verification and was temporarily banned from competition. After winning the 800M at the Track and Field World Championships in 2009, Semenya, then eighteen years old, was publicly accused of being a man, and it was increasingly suggested that she should be barred from competing with women and undergo gender testing. Ultimately it took almost a year for Semenya to be cleared for competition. Reportedly, Semenya, along with a number of other black South African women, underwent a form of "therapy" to help whatever apparently "unnatural condition" she has.[34] It is generally believed that Semenya was required to take medication that would lower her natural levels of testosterone—a "treatment" that often comes with side effects that impact metabolism and hydration. Perhaps it is no coincidence, then, that her performances following the treatment suffered greatly compared to earlier results.

Accusations of elite female athletes being men are nothing new, as there is a long and unfortunate history of such accusations. Often they have ended careers or publicly embarrassed the accused, as in the recent examples of Santhi Soundarajan and Dutee Chand.[35] There are two important intersections at work here. The first is the desperation by the track and field governing body, the International Association of Athletics Federations (IAAF), and the International Olympic Committee (IOC) to make a clear demarcation between the sexes. While previous gender testing relied on "nude parades" (physical exams) and then chromosomes, since 2011 the IAAF and IOC have used "normal" female testosterone levels as a threshold that women must remain under in order to compete. If that threshold is passed then a woman must undergo hormone therapy or surgery (usually to remove internal testes, a characteristic of intersexuality) to lower her level of testosterone. This method is, of course, flawed in its own right, as there remains a great deal of ambiguity concerning what is natural and normal for men and women. It is also not clearly established that higher natural testosterone levels consistently produce

better athletic results.[36] In 2015 the IAAF policy regarding testosterone levels was suspended by the Court of Arbitration for Sport for
want of solid evidence. With the IOC following suit, Semenya was
able to race at her natural levels in the Rio 2016 Olympics, as was
Dutee Chand. Semenya easily won her 800M event, while Chand
failed to advance to the final heat. For some, Semenya's victory was
evidence of testosterone having a clear impact on her return to top
performance, although they conveniently ignored Chand's defeat.
Others, such as Katrina Karkazis, argue that the side effects of the
medication Semenya was forced to take were a more likely factor in
her depressed performances in the previous years and that we are
still trying to understand how hormones like testosterone are taken
up and utilized in the body.[37]

The second issue, directly related to the first, is a more nuanced
public conversation about the socially created definition of the category of "woman." What is different here is that our increasing knowledge of biological markers has made simple divisions between what
is male or female more difficult.[38] Thus, in media discourse, Semenya
is often referred to as "intersexed," or having a combination of "male"
and "female" sex organs and hormones, of which there can be a multitude of possibilities and combinations. Whereas a chromosomal test
sufficed to distinguish men from women in the recent past, "greater
understanding" of sex and bodily processes necessitates a more varied and nuanced knowledge base in order to maintain some semblance of two genders. Yet while there is greater recognition and
nuance in the debate, the inability to move beyond sex-dichotomized
sport also points to the fact that society is not quite ready to dissolve
the sex/gender binary and often makes gender judgments based on
appearance—the adherence to white feminine norms. That Semenya's performances at the World Championships in 2009 and 2016
(1:55.45 and 1:55.33, respectively) and her Olympic gold medal time
of 1:55:28 did not even break the top ten all-time seems to confirm
the visual aspect of suspicion.[39]

This intense focus on women only reinforces male supremacy
by allowing us to ignore how athletic ability rests on a continuum

between the sexes and is not a binary. As a result, women remain excluded from the category of "athlete" because "too much" athleticism calls into question their status as women. Men are never tested to see if they have enough, or too much, testosterone to compete in men's sport. Thus, despite recent movement and continued contestation of the sex/gender threshold, the dominant ideology concerning women and intersexuality in sport persists. It remains important to "know" or determine the "truth" about athletes, whether it be about doping or a socially constructed category such as gender. As Jaime Shultz explains, though recent efforts by the IOC or IAAF may seem progressive, elite female athletes remain stigmatized and intersexuality remains pathologized. There are also significant ethical and health questions regarding testing and medically unnecessary "treatments" involving drugs or surgeries that can have lifelong consequences. Women should not have to drastically alter their bodies to play a sport. By highlighting the complexity and interdisciplinary nature of these issues, Shultz implores us to stop trying to define "woman" and instead ask different questions, specifically, what conditions, natural or unnatural, create unfair advantages in sport.[40]

A final concern to raise here is the salience of race in many of the most recent popular accusations concerning the sex of female athletes. Through gross mishandling of the cases of Semenya and Soundarajan and in popular discourse about Serena Williams and WNBA player Brittney Griner, women of color have become the primary objects of suspicion in this public debate. After Semenya's gold medal victory, when black African women from Burundi (Francine Niyonsaba) and Kenya (Margaret Wambui) took silver and bronze, respectively, the fifth-place finisher, Joanna Jozwik (white European/ Polish), stated that she felt like the "silver medalist," adding that she was the "first European" and "second white." Further, the sixth-place finisher, Lynsey Sharp (white European/British), questioned the fairness of the race and the inclusion of women with higher levels of testosterone. Neither Niyonsaba nor Wambui have been identified as having higher levels of testosterone, so the discourse of Sharp and Jozwik assumes that all black women have natural, but unfair, advantages in sport. Again, any notion of work or training, or the relative disadvantage in terms of funding of athletes coming from developing nations, goes unexplored. These are just recent events in a long history of the sexist and racist masculinization of black femininity within sport, and, as alluded to previously, such characterizations rely heavily on appearance (muscularity) and sound (voice), correlating with a deviance from white social norms in which women are expected to be minimally athletic (muscular) and petite and to have high voices.[41] In this era of color-blind racism the public questioning and talk about the sex of black female athletes, often via social media, occurs with no explicit reference to race or its ongoing historical relevance in sport.[42] For example, a 2012 article by Stephanie Findlay comments on Semenya's intricate circumstances (the actual results of her "gender verification" were never released to the public, but that did not stop media speculation and leaks) and then proceeds to explain how issues of intersexuality, in various forms, are prevalent in South Africa, making the country "ground zero" in the debate over inter-sexed women in sport.[43] Findlay goes on to cite an interview with a "scientist" who claims that some African women's soccer teams are essentially made up of men, Nigeria's specifically.[44] Though the article reads sympathetically, the specter of race goes unaddressed in a debate increasingly focused upon the black female body. With little exploration or explanation of how or why such a propensity for intersexuality might exist among the black South African population (or throughout Africa in general), we are left with the salient (colonial) formulation that black sex and sexuality equates to the abnormal and pathological—and is in need of correction. The partial acceptance of black African female athletes means that high-level performance and physical appearance can quickly bring their femininity into question. The role of gender in athletics is already a contested terrain, regardless of race, yet we can see that there is often a quick reach to stereotypes and assumptions about the physical capabilities of black women both native and foreign to the West. That more recently such accusations appear to be almost solely located on black and brown female bodies from developing countries is particularly concerning but unsurprising.

Great White Hopes

In a different manner, black African athletes, both men and women, can sometimes find their successes turned against them. For example, Loroupe's accomplishments were at first very highly heralded yet became less newsworthy as her career progressed. While part of this is due to the media focusing more on Loroupe's competition, fellow Kenyans Joyce Chepchumba and Catherine Ndereba, there is a more noteworthy and intense focus on white Western runners. More specifically, the media positioned white female runners as "Great White Hopes" in relation to Loroupe and Ndereba. At times Ndereba fell out of the conversation about top women runners completely as the media tried to construct "dream" races between, for example, the United Kingdom's Paula Radcliffe and the United States' Deena Kastor. Western media outlets also tended to support their own runners. Hence British media tended to focus on Paula Radcliffe while Irish media focused on Sonia O'Sullivan. However, the media focus on nationality may not be as important as that on race in this context. Theresa Walton and Ted Butryn found that in considering who counted as a "true" American runner, the conversation tended to exclude both naturalized Africans and African Americans. I argue that this logic translates fairly well to most Western nations. Thus the favoritism Western nations show to "home grown" talent is inherently raced and nationalistic.[45]

The most provocative evidence of media construction of a Great White Hope concerns Loroupe's world marathon record. In 1998 Loroupe set the women's marathon world record at Rotterdam with a time of 2:20:47. The controversy started when the London Marathon race organizers claimed Loroupe had unfairly used male pacemakers. Understandably, Loroupe felt aggrieved and had a strong response for the race organizers. "I felt a little bit upset at what people were saying. I was the one who ran the race, not the men running alongside me, and I ran most of it on my own. No one has bothered mentioning that Kristiansen also ran in London with men."[46] Ingrid Kristiansen, from Norway, was the previous record holder, a record that was never brought into question despite her use of male pacemakers. Eventually London Marathon organizers decreed all women's times set in mixed marathons ineligible for world record consideration. Then, in 2003, London organizers slackened this regulation for British runner Paula Radcliffe. At this point, Radcliffe owned the official women's world marathon record of 2:17:18, set in Chicago, and wanted to improve on that time. Though her Chicago time was faster than Loroupe ever ran, the hypocrisy of London race organizers was evident. "Radcliffe, who wants to break the record of 2hr 17min 18sec she set in Chicago, will be paced by men in what will be called a separate mixed race. Loroupe said: 'When I ran my record, the London people started to complain. They were pointing the finger and now they're doing it themselves.'"[47]

When Loroupe owned the world record, or when Naoko Takahashi (Japan) broke the 2:20:00 barrier, race organizers never felt the need to give them pacemakers to try to improve their time. It was only when Radcliffe, a white woman racing in her home country, was in position to further her legacy that London organizers dropped their protests and provided male pacemakers. Previously London race organizers had claimed, "We believe that to maintain the integrity of women's marathon running it is essential to recognise times set in women's only races. We are putting our money where our mouth is."[48]

Stereotypical discourses surrounding the athletic ability of women are inherent within this issue. The previous quote speaks of integrity in women's races, but how exactly do male pacemakers hurt the integrity of women's races? Historically men have used pacemakers, first to win races and split the money and, later, to set records. Most famously, Roger Bannister's first successful attempt at a sub-four-minute mile was disallowed because the pacing was *too* blatant. As sport has professionalized, it appears that most of the debate around men using pacemakers has subsided. In the era of endorsement deals and speaking engagements, where winning triggers payments or the ability to charge more money, pacemakers are often paid (and paid well, as they themselves have to be elite runners) to help secure favorable outcomes. Campbell tells us that Radcliffe was paced in Chicago by Weldon Johnson and others, who were paid by the Chicago race organizers to protect her from wind and other runners. Though

Johnson's fee was not divulged, Campbell also mentions an incident with Ben Kimondiu, who was hired by Chicago marathon organizers for the legendary Paul Tergat in 2001. Set to be paid $7,500 for his efforts, Kimondiu would end up holding off Tergat at the end and winning the race, instead receiving the winner's purse of $90,000.[49] Hence, with pacemaking being a common practice, the idea that men and women are different in such a way that any form of interaction in sport destroys the "purity" of a woman's accomplishments is problematic. What is actually happening is the continued stunting of the athletic development of women. While few women might be able to set a fast enough pace to keep up with Loroupe (or Radcliffe or Ndereba), perhaps it is more likely that no women in her class would be willing to potentially give up a marathon victory to help her set a world record.

It is clear that, as with black men, the assumed physical advantages of black women remarginalize blackness as a whole. Though often an object of interest, perhaps adoration, early in her career, the black female athlete is always in danger of becoming just another dehumanized and undifferentiated part of the black masses. Particularly in distance running, as more women from Kenya and Ethiopia began to compete at an elite level they become, to an extent, a nameless and faceless "mob." Little attention or effort is put into seeing them as individual personalities. In other words, we are given the feeling that there will always be another Kenyan, or Ethiopian, to replace the one who just won or just retired. The construction and elevation of the Great White Hope is a distinct response to a feeling of racial inadequacy among whites in Western countries. It is also a set of discourses that inherently devalues the accomplishments of Loroupe, Chepchumba, Ndereba, Kiplagat, and many others.

Conclusion

My argument in this chapter is that favorable representations, at least initially, of the athletes in this study are contingent on their perceived "good" behavior. When their behaviors or level of play fail to match expectations, there is a turn toward derisively stereotypical representations of their mental states, physical capability, intelligence, materialism, work ethic, and propensity toward violence. Because my study is focused on highly successful athletes, it is also worth considering the applicability of my findings to the "failed" athlete or the migrant nonathlete (unskilled labor migrant) in the West. I have found that the high expectations of success initially placed on the athletes in my study drive their popularity and initially shield them from negative stereotypes. Among athletes who face high expectations and then fail we see a rapid and startling application of negative stereotypes. Most notably, we see this process in the case of Yinka Dare, who was supposed to be the "next" Hakeem Olajuwon but lasted only four seasons in the NBA, as remarks about him—particularly concerning his passing ability; he registered only four assists in his career—pulled not only on his blackness but his foreign alterity as well. We are left with the impression that Dare was a black African who failed to take advantage of the opportunities given to him.

Similarly, when we consider a photo of Mario Balotelli that an Italian politician digitally altered to depict him working in a field like an African migrant worker, we gain insight not only into the workings of race and racism but also into how Balotelli's foreign Otherness, and the stereotypes around it, are never quite forgotten. Nonathletes or unskilled labor migrants immediately confront these negative stereotypes upon arrival because they lack the status to shield themselves. Based on the broader literature, we should expect nonsporting migrants to initially form an identity around national origin or religion in an effort to protect themselves from the psychological and sometimes physical damages of racism in the West. Though my study does not directly focus on the failed athlete or the unskilled migrant laborer, they are inherently included and their social treatment is implicated precisely because of my focus on the marginalization of the foreign black Other and foreign black communities. In other words, in focusing on highly visible actors we can observe certain phenomena impacting the broader community. Of course, as the previous chapter explored, even seemingly "positive" representations are often stereotypical and essentializing. This is a part of the contradictory nature of representing the foreign Other in the West, as different modes of alterity can be placed on the Other at different times and achieve similar racializing or discriminatory effects.

Often evading scrutiny is the salient heteronormativity and misogyny in the representations of the men included in this study and their masculinity. Hegemonic masculinity and its normative influence often evade critical engagement in Western media due to the media's own paternalistic tendencies; however, a few examples are worth mentioning. First, Mutombo, along with Patrick Ewing and Dennis Rodman, was called to testify before a grand jury in 2001 for allegedly receiving sexual favors at a strip club in Atlanta as part of a larger criminal investigation. Second, a story is told about Mutombo during his time at Georgetown, more of an urban legend, in which he walks into a party, shouts "Who wants to sex Mutombo," and then leaves with two women. Not only is the story still being repeated, despite Mutombo's denial of it, but it is often told humorously in interviews with Mutombo. Third, the intense focus on Balotelli's love life consistently details his involvement with numerous women. Not only are we led to think he has sex with all of these women, but the tabloids eventually find a former lover who testifies to the size of Balotelli's penis. Again, these are usually told as humorous stories in the UK press.

None of these activities or the reporting about them disturbs the current form of hegemonic masculinity, namely its aspects of heteronormativity and misogyny. If anything, the reporting of them reinforces the notion that athletes in general have a lot of sex with women. With Balotelli, those understandings, linked as they are with black male virility, shame the women he is "with" because they should have known better. That many of Balotelli's reported love interests have been white only exaggerates the racial undertones of this discourse, as does the inevitable curiosity with how big his genitalia are. Though these examples are brief, and the number of articles covering them few, the discourse of hegemonic masculinity is one that makes no difference with respect to foreignness. Men are men and blackness remains hypersexualized.

More anecdotally, it is necessary to at least reference the former English soccer player Justin Fashanu, as he serves as an example of the hostility of the sports world to homosexuality. Born in England, the son of Nigerian and Guyanese parents, he was left at an orphan-age after his parents broke up, raised in foster care by a white family, and eventually became the first black soccer player worth £1 million. While rumors had circulated that he was gay, after he came out he was subjected to the homophobic environment that sport often fos-ters and faced problems with fans, management, and other players. He also faced rejection from his brother, John (who also played pro-fessional soccer), who went as far as saying that he would not play with Justin, that Justin was not really gay, and that he came out only to get attention. While the institution of English soccer certainly did its part in trying to force Justin out, John stands at the intersection of preserving hegemonic sporting masculinity, black masculinity, and African masculinity. The issue with African masculinity referring to the salient feminization of blackness (the historic denial of black masculinity—especially at a time when black players were few and stereotyped as weak) and the feminized African nation-state (pater-nally controlled by the West—which continues to have problems with homophobia, in part because such states have been and continue to be so thoroughly "penetrated" by the West).[50] Due to what Justin Fash-anu faced—ultimately committing suicide in 1998 after an allegation of sexual assault—it is unsurprising that to this day few (black) gay athletes have tried to come out during their playing careers.

To conclude, the athletes in my study are privileged in Western societies due to the success and wealth they have attained through sport. Though some athletes are able to speak out against their treat-ment in the media and society, however minimally, that is certainly not the case with most black African athletes, black immigrants, or black communities. The hegemonic discourses of Western societies also contain a normalizing element that seeks to circumscribe black political actions and identities by stigmatizing activities that could be resistive or contrary to white neoliberal norms. Such pressures act to the detriment of native and foreign black populations, within and between each other, both politically and culturally. In the West, though foreign black immigrants are conceptually black before they immigrate, a reification of their blackness is necessary because of the immediacy of the black immigrant. In my study this process happens through their inconspicuous comparison to native blacks. This comparison makes the black immigrant knowable, but this knowledge is derived from blackness always already being at the bottom of the social order. Black immigrants are no longer "outside," in some other country, but "inside," and their place in the dominant social order, where they are overdetermined as black, requires confirmation.[51]

The representations in this chapter draw to mind the works of Frantz Fanon and Lewis Gordon. Both of these intellectuals, the latter an expert on the former, critique colonial and antiblack racist discourse for essentializing and exoticizing blackness—equating blackness with an absence of morality, rationality, and humanity. The discourses of black African athletes I have explored in these pages resonate with the supposed missing human qualities of blackness. The contingent nature of black migrant acceptance in the West rests on the migrant's ability to avoid behaviors that are not conciliatory to white society. Though unknown to the athletes in my study, at least at first, the pressure to adhere to forms of blackness that whiteness can accept is dehumanizing in that it sets a standard that is impossible to attain. It requires athletes to denounce their own humanity and maintain an unnatural, robot-like existence in exchange for having a social presence that is often unacknowledged and under constant threat of expulsion. In essence, blacks are required to perform a higher level of humanity than whites.[52]

5

Immigrant Reception

Nationalism, Identity, Politics, and Resistance

In order to better understand the full complexity of the immigrant experience it becomes necessary to examine the politics and social dynamics surrounding the construction of immigrant identities. Identity construction among black immigrant populations is an attempt to negotiate their position in the antiblack Western racial order. Though black immigrants often arrive in their host countries eager to meld with the host society and work toward success, they find the racial barriers to full integration difficult to ignore. Hence, despite initially shying away from issues of race that often concern native black communities, black immigrants and their children become increasingly aware of their racial marginalization. How black immigrants are received into their host countries and how their experiences with race and racism shape their identities is my concern in this chapter.[1]

The athletes in this study represent highly skilled labor and are often privileged, meaning that their reception in the United States and European countries is different but no less important than that of unskilled migrants. Materials such as interviews, autobiographies, and news articles allowed me to piece together the context in which athletes arrived. This chapter uses Dikembe Mutombo, Hakeem Olajuwon, Didier Drogba, and Mario Balotelli as entry points into different aspects of the immigrant reception process. By exploring the contexts and backgrounds of these athletes while drawing links with some of their contemporaries, this chapter begins to differentiate between the person and the representation. If we also keep in mind that representations are an interpretation based on an event, something that actually happened, then we can offer a rereading, or a reinterpretation, of that event. Thus this chapter is primarily concerned with offering a reinterpretation of the representations of immigration, nationalism, and identity that the athletes in this study present. "The Utility of Citizenship" takes into account the circumstances surrounding black African migrant athletes' reception and experiences in the West, allowing us to read against the hegemonic nationalist Western narrative regarding the decision to naturalize. Next, in "Generation and National Belonging," I take Drogba and Balotelli, generation 1.75 and second-generation immigrants, respectively, and their intersections with athletes of the same generation in order to further discuss issues of racial identity, racism, and national belonging. "Religious Identity" looks more closely at Olajuwon and his refusal of a racial identity in favor of a religious one in the form of Islam. Olajuwon's efforts to embrace Islam and distance himself from issues of race provide us an example of an alternative way immigrants may construct identity within the West.

The Utility of Citizenship

In order to demonstrate the intersection between immigrants, their host societies, and the state, it is informative to look at the acquisition of citizenship. While the taking of citizenship in Western countries is often presented to us in nationalist terms and understandings, the transnational nature of athletic migration blurs the boundaries (sovereignty) between nation-states. To be clear, there is more going on than the simple "growing irrelevance" of the (Western) nation-state that has been thrown about in the past. Transnational, or diasporic, athletes (and others involved in globalized sport) must navigate contexts controlled and determined by nation-states and neoliberal capitalist markets. Aihwa Ong, in describing her term *flexible citizenship*, brings attention to the fact that "globalization has made economic calculation a major element in diasporan subjects' choice of citizenship, as well as in the ways nation-states redefine immigration laws."[2] She goes on to explain how highly skilled migrants often attempt to evade and manipulate nation-states for their own benefit while, simultaneously, nation-states are engaged in adjusting to global capitalism in such a way as to benefit the country at minimal cost—often in the form of changing immigration laws to attract "capital bearing subjects" while limiting unskilled laborers. In sport, these processes are best highlighted when an athlete "changes" nationality in order to compete internationally and in the interactions between international governing sports bodies and nation-states in order to limit athletes' ability to do so. To have flexible citizenship puts one in a privileged position that infers the ability to manage the multilayered interrelationships between states and global capital. Flexible citizenship is a form of neoliberal capital that allows movement and (tenuous) inclusion to those who have it and exclusion (expulsion) for those who do not. As highly skilled laborers, transnational athletes can be conceptualized as Ong's "capital bearing subjects"—as long as they are productive.[3]

The (hyper)nationalist, post-9/11 athletic discourses those of us in the West are routinely exposed to ignore the contemporary realities of globalized sport for athletes. Despite an increasingly foreign workforce, transnational athletes are still being "asked" to fit themselves unproblematically within local particularities and sport lore.[4] Upon further examination, we find that the media's nationalist discourse can be interrupted by what the athletes in this study say and do. I begin here with Dikembe Mutombo before moving on to athletes with similar activities and motivations regarding citizenship. What the case of Mutombo demonstrates, while keeping in mind individual histories and motivations, is that immigrant reception is vitally important in the formation of identity and experiences in the West for black African immigrants. This fact, of course, has been borne out in the literature but is worth taking a look at here because it is possible to examine how athletes with similar celebrity status end up forming very different identities and holding different attitudes and concerns regarding where they grew up or immigrated to. Mutombo grew up in a household where education was stressed, a number of his siblings attended college, and his father was educated in France and involved in the local school system. He attended Georgetown University on scholarship and chose the school so he could be close to a family member, a cousin working as a doctor, in Washington DC.[5]

His sophomore year he joined the Hoya basketball team with head coach John Thompson and future Hall of Fame basketball player Alonzo Mourning.

John Thompson is well known for being one of the first prominent and successful African American head coaches at the Division I level. Aside from his own status as a black coach at a wealthy and historically white university, Thompson was very involved with recruiting black players, helping them graduate, and preparing them for life after basketball. Thompson was also heavily involved with the black community at the university and in the surrounding neighborhoods in Washington DC. He often was on the receiving end of media spite for policies that limited access to his athletes but nonetheless served as an example of black achievement. Suffice to say, Thompson was well aware of the racial attitudes of the time and the challenges that young black men faced. As an example, Patrick Ewing, another future Hall of Fame player from Georgetown, endured racist chants and statements on placards from fans at various schools during the 1982–83 season, including "Ewing Is a Ape" [sic] at Villanova, "Think! Ewing! Think!" at Seton Hall, "Ewing Kan't Read Dis" [sic] at various Big East schools, and several game disruptions when bananas were thrown on the court. That season, upon checking with Ewing to make sure he was holding up okay during a return flight, Thompson recalled being profoundly saddened when Ewing replied that he had become used to the abuse.[6] Incidentally, Ewing left Georgetown for the NBA right before Mutombo arrived but was nevertheless an important figure in welcoming Mutombo to the United States. Ewing, another child of the black diaspora, emigrated to the United States with his parents from Jamaica early in life and was only a few years ahead of Mutombo at school. While his immigrant experiences were likely very different from Mutombo's, who immigrated much later in life, it would seem rather likely that they—Mutombo and Ewing, as well as Thompson—discussed matters such as dealing with racism and being black in the United States. This notion is reinforced by reports that they often spent time together off the court and discussed political issues of the day, especially as they concerned what was then Zaire.

"We were sitting at dinner before we played Villanova," said George-town coach John Thompson. "It was myself and Alonzo, one of the managers and Dikembe. We were talking about some recent devel-opments in Africa. Now, there's no way we would have been talking about that if Dikembe hadn't been sitting there."[7]

For most of his days at Georgetown, Mutombo was constantly reminded of Ewing's success, and even though their games are nothing alike, their journey to the NBA is similar. "He was a great footstep to follow because he almost came from the same path that I came from," says Mutombo, who played at Georgetown from 1988–1991. "He came from a poor country in Jamaica. He came here to look for a livelihood with his parents. He didn't play basketball that much."[8]

This reporting is a part of the trend of representing Mutombo as an intellectual individual. Throughout their NBA careers Mutombo and Ewing would spend time together and develop into a kind of Georgetown brotherhood, which included Alonzo Mourning as well. Mourning and Ewing would later be among the first players to con-tribute significant amounts of money to Mutombo's humanitarian causes when he was having trouble finding other NBA players to do so. It is also worth mentioning that Mutombo and Ewing were very involved in the NBA collective bargaining sessions between play-ers and owners in the 1990s. Meaning that, at a time when interna-tional players were still rare, black immigrants who were Georgetown alumni were overrepresented on the players' side of the negotiating table. From early on in his collegiate career Mutombo appeared to be aware of the global power relations that shape the significance of race. He often professed a strong pan-African identity along with his Congolese identity, but—as with many immigrants—his views on naturalization changed over time, and for interesting reasons. As a young player in the NBA Mutombo objected to the notion that he would ever become a citizen of the United States.

Olajuwon is delighted to be playing basketball for his adopted home country in the Olympics. Mutombo, meanwhile, doesn't get it. Mutombo, who says he will never apply for American citizenship, paid a visit to the Rockets' locker room following a late-season game and chided Olajuwon by pulling his Zairean passport out of his pocket. He waved it, telling Olajuwon that instead of playing for America, the two of them should be banding together to lead an African squad.[9]

[Mutombo's] not a U.S. citizen and has no intention of becoming one. "No, I will not. Not for this country," he said. "I will live here and work here, and when I retire I will go home. I think I represent my culture, where I come from. It means a lot to me to be from another country." Dual citizenship doesn't make any sense, he says. "For which purpose?" he said. "If Uncle Sam would say I could pay 25 percent in taxes, I would. It (not being a citizen) really doesn't affect me. . . . It has something to do with the soul. Africa has been abandoned by the West, not just the United States."[10]

In the above examples Mutombo is certainly direct. His attachment to a pan-African identity strongly values African and Congolese culture and unity. Mutombo criticizes Olajuwon—not for the first time—for naturalizing to U.S. citizenship in time to play for Team USA in the 1996 Summer Olympics. (Ironically, on August 1, 2015, years after their careers ended, Mutombo and Olajuwon would "come out of retirement" and play in the NBA Africa Game—the first NBA exhibition game held on the African continent, in South Africa, featuring Team Africa vs. Team World.) He even dismisses the idea of dual citizenship and reduces the concept to purely economic terms. Mutombo's insistence on being African and creating an African team, which I critique later, is reminiscent of the difficulties that have faced black (African) philosophy and intellectuals. Kwame Anthony Appiah explains that throughout history European intellectuals have posed their problems of authenticity (search for the authentic self) against other Europeans ("my people") in an otherwise private and individual affair. Meanwhile, black (African) intellectuals have not only tried to find a place for themselves in society but also been engaged in (re)creating a culture. They ask what it means to be, for example, Embu or Kenyan or African or "Black." The question is not "who am I?" but rather "who are we?"

because "we" share the same or similar problems across the continent and beyond. Appiah goes on to advocate for an African identity (and pan-Africanism), insofar as it can avoid racial ideology and is engaged in coalition building, because so far an "African" identity has been defined as inferior by Europeans.[11] It is these questions of identity and belonging that Mutombo appears to be trying to get Olajuwon on board with.

What is odd about Mutombo's stance toward American citizenship is that it is never questioned or critiqued in the media. I believe we can read this silence as part of the dichotomous nature of media discourse on naturalization. On the one hand, immigrants—those the West wants—are congratulated for becoming citizens because it feeds the narrative of Western supremacy. On the other hand, a peculiar discourse in the West encourages those from elsewhere to maintain their cultural heritage (pride in where they come from), but only insofar as there is the promise of return to their home countries. Immigrants who hold fast to their cultural or national identities but stay are viewed suspiciously and are thought to be benefiting unfairly from Western "hospitality"—in other words, not assimilating as they should. Hence Mutombo's desire not to become a U.S. citizen but also not to permanently stay can be seen as unproblematic. Stuart Hall explains a similar phenomenon in his recollections of emigrating from Jamaica to England in the 1950s: "In the first generations, the majority of people had the same illusion that I did: that I was about to go back home. That may have been because everybody always asked me: when was I going back home? We did think that we were just going to get back on the boat; we were here for a temporary sojourn. By the seventies, it was perfectly clear that we were not there for a temporary sojourn. Some people were going to stay and then the politics of racism really emerged."[12]

And yet in 2006 Mutombo would reverse course and become a U.S. citizen. Different reports on why Mutombo became a citizen emerged and most were fairly consistent in their questioning of Mutombo and his responses. There was not much fanfare in the media around his decision and there were no questions as to why he changed his mind after being so adamant. Further, Mutombo seems to have reconciled taking U.S. citizenship with remaining Congolese. As with many first-generation immigrants, Mutombo appears to have realized that, despite having the material resources to return (in which he differs from most other immigrants), his life and that of his family are now intricately tied to the United States.

> Houston Rockets center Dikembe Mutombo will soon be sworn in as an American citizen. He was told by the U.S. Department of Homeland Security on Wednesday that his paperwork had been approved. "It's more joy and more happiness," Mutombo, who was born in Congo, told Houston television station KRIV. "My blood is still going to be Congolese. This is where we are going to call home, so it's good to be an American."[13]

> Houston Rockets center Dikembe Mutombo is expected to be sworn in as an American citizen on Thursday. . . . The NBA star said he hopes becoming an American will help his cause of building a hospital in his hometown of Kinshasa. "*I think it will open up the door more to the government assistance in this country*," he said.[14]

The latter example gives a glimpse of Mutombo using U.S. citizenship as a vehicle through which to secure further funding for his projects in the Congo. Around the time of his naturalization Mutombo was becoming increasingly involved in and known for his humanitarian activities. It is certainly within the realm of possibility that being an American citizen—with its greater access, privilege, and power— would help Mutombo in these endeavors. As with many cracks in the dominant narrative, the above quote appears only once in my sample of news articles about Mutombo. I argue that this use of citizenship to accomplish certain goals is a conscious effort on Mutombo's part and resonates strongly with statements he made at a presentation he gave later at the University of Georgia's Terry College of Business. At that presentation an audience member asked about his foundation and what the hardest part was in building his hospital. Mutombo chose to focus primarily on the fund raising process and he explained to the audience what you need to do in order to be an effective fund-raiser.

You have to be articulate, how you talk to people, 'cause sometimes you can turn somebody off right away as soon as you start your speech. You've got to know how you are approaching somebody to make sure he opens his wallet by the time you finish speaking. You know, I don't walk in a room and say, "Hey give me money, my name is Dikembe Mutombo, hey can I have two hundred dollars from you." No, I'm not going to give it to you even though I have it. First you've gotta tell me some story, you gotta give me some numbers, some statistics, you know. When you're telling somebody that I'm from the place where the life expectancy is 45 and 47 for women, and the way my people have perished because of this pandemic of HIV/AIDS, which has destroyed the fabric of our society, and has killed more than 30 million people so far and left more than 20 some plus million people living with the virus in Africa. You tell people, I mean the children in Africa today, more than half a billion [*sic*] of children in Africa under the age of 15 are orphans, they don't have no parents and they don't know where their future holds for them. And you tell people, how's the continent itself, you know, there are more than almost 800,000 children under the age of 15 years old, which is the youngest population in the world today as we live in. And you talk about all of those diseases that killing them. If you're not doing [that], my sister [audience member], you're not going to get no money from nobody. Those are some of my lessons, they may not teach you that at graduate school but, uh, those are the lessons you learn in life.[15]

Mutombo seems very well aware of his position and the necessity to play upon the single story of Africa in order to secure funding. The statistics Mutombo recalls in his example are real and are terrible, but Mutombo seems to deploy them in stereotypical and uncomplicated ways. For the purposes of my analysis, what Mutombo does or does not know or intend is irrelevant, if not impossible to determine given my methodology. My point is that there is an industry of charitable giving that forces Mutombo into certain modes of discourse and action. Those modes prohibit Mutombo from engaging in criticism of the United States and its policies toward Africa. Earlier in his career, when he was not as involved in charity efforts,

Mutombo still struggled with being silent about the political actions of the United States and the nature of its international military interventions in the 1990s.

> "It's tough the way the American government has responded to Kosovo that quick. We have had the same ethnic cleansing going on in our country for the past year. Our next-door neighbors in Rwanda and Uganda have been fighting. You see that the rest of the world didn't respond to that. It's tough, especially for someone like me who lost his mom. People are getting killed every day." Mutombo feels the reason Kosovo has become such a cause and Africa has not is a racial thing, although he'll never verbalize it. "Y'know, I'm a student of diplomacy," he said. "That's what I studied at Georgetown University, so I can see the answer, but I'm not going to give it to you."[16]

Mutombo demonstrates his awareness, indeed anger, that race and racism (if only indirectly and saving for possible deniability) impact the military interventions of the West and that, as an athlete, he is not in the position to be overly critical. Thus the need for Mutombo, as a black African, to reflect back to primarily wealthy white audiences their preconceived notions of African poverty, disease, and helplessness is an exercise in self-confirmation. The aspect of helplessness specifically relies more on the current state of governments in African countries than on the lingering and contemporary legacies of colonialism. Because African governance has "failed," the inability of blacks to self-govern is discursively confirmed in the West and African peoples are suffering through no fault of their own. This construction of "African" peoples is in distinct contradiction to the situations of black populations in Western countries, who, presumably, could benefit, if they wanted, from the opportunities available to "everyone" in Western societies through meritocratic effort and state support.

Yet still, Mutombo, as a black foreign Other telling well-known narratives about Africa, gives legitimacy to those stereotypes and the industry of charitable giving. As a mimetic figure, Mutombo represents the entire society and culture of the Democratic Republic of Congo, at best, or all of Africa, at worst. That Mutombo seems to accept and even welcome this role while maintaining a singular discourse on "Africa" is problematic because he does little to explode the myths of Africa. However, in the quoted explanations from Mutombo, we can see that he is negotiating an industry—the White-Savior Industrial Complex[17]—from which he has learned that in order to accomplish his goals there are certain simplistic discourses he needs to engage in. As I have mentioned, the White-Savior Industrial Complex is not about social justice that would result in the change of Western policies toward developing countries; rather it is about donors having strong emotional and sentimental experiences of giving that serve to justify their privilege. Mutombo's discourse seems purposefully constructed to accomplish such a goal.

I have focused on Mutombo because he represents the most provocative example in my study. However, if we look at Tamba Hali and Hakeem Olajuwon we can discern comparable reasons for pursuing citizenship in the West. In each instance we see a consistent narrative of Western exceptionalism. The West, here the United States specifically, is reified as a place where freedom, dreams, and equal rights are a reality. However, it is only through Western citizenship that these things can be achieved. This reality is problematic in that it means valuing some lives over most others. It also means that individuals must strive toward certain forms of national belonging in order to achieve certain basic rights and freedoms. For Hali, U.S. citizenship became a tool for family unification, as he had been separated from his mother for most of his adolescent and adult life because of civil war in Liberia. "Getting anyone from one country to another is never easy, and I'm sure a lot of other people are having the same problems," he said. "They say to do it this way, but that doesn't work. We try it a different way, and that doesn't work, either. We think that when we become citizens (Hali is completing work on his naturalization) it will become easier. Our other way is through humanitarian reasons, showing that her life is in danger."[18] While the media is sympathetic to Hali's cause, questions are never raised concerning U.S. policies on family unification and asylum or concerning why such things are "never easy." Because Hali's parents were not married—before immigrating Hali grew up with his mother, stepfather, siblings, and stepsiblings—his father could only petition for his children to come to the States. Why U.S. immigration law is so inflexible regarding complex family situations, which we may expect in situations such as Liberia's, goes unquestioned. Hali's use of citizenship and the necessity of gaining citizenship in order to live a certain way or to have your family with you put into question the boundaries and morality of the nation-state. The current system of human rights and benefits being tied to national belonging only produces human suffering and reinforces racist nationalisms.

We can further complicate this discussion on morality and citizenship by examining the words of Hakeem Olajuwon. Olajuwon often rationalizes U.S. citizenship into his worldview and lifestyle. His naturalization came just in time for the 1996 Atlanta Summer Olympics—where he won a gold medal as a member of Dream Team III—and also corresponds with a reinvestment in his religious faith in the early 1990s, which I will discuss in more detail later. It also came at a time when Olajuwon, often noted as a shrewd businessperson, was actively seeking mass-market advertising opportunities, something his presence on Dream Team III helped him finally achieve. Regardless of the possibility that Olajuwon aimed to use citizenship to further enrich himself—something he has never admitted but was probably never asked—he often advocates for a worldview that inherently privileges the United States. As we will see, this worldview is also linked with his religious beliefs. These beliefs encourage Olajuwon to see and elevate the transnational character of Islam while simultaneously downplaying the impact of various power relations on the lives of Muslims around the world. Hence Olajuwon places Islam above all else yet simultaneously practices a version of Islam that is amenable to being (safely) put under the power of the Western nation-state. At least this is how Olajuwon and his views are represented in the media and his autobiography.

> [Olajuwon] considers himself "more global" and avoids political involvement. . . . "I just don't want to get caught in the politics. I believe in equal rights, justice, fairness and being a good example." Consequently, Olajuwon's focus is wider than small corners of Africa

or Texas. . . . "Everybody is supposed to live in peace and take care of each other—without color issue. You have to look beyond and look into the soul of people and for the good and fight against evil, greed, power struggles. When that comes into play, then there is selfishness. Everybody is living for today and there are moral (problems) and we lose focus of the quality of life."[19]

Throughout his career Olajuwon has stayed far from critically engaging the power structures around him, often taking the conservative approach instead. I earlier discussed how we should not expect migrants to openly critique their host societies, as they are aware of their tenuous position. It is quite clear that the media enjoys Olajuwon's "can't we all just get along" rhetoric, as it points to qualities and principles Western societies supposedly value yet do little to achieve. Ultimately, Olajuwon's discourse of being a good citizen by ignoring politics and race is more of the consumer-citizen variety, which in his case further extends to the freedom to promote consumption by advertising name-brand products, the most controversial of which was Uncle Ben's Rice. Similarly, Didier Drogba signed on to do questionable ads for the cocoa industry (often accused of child labor abuses) ahead of the 2010 World Cup in South Africa.[20] These athletes may be transnational and challenge national borders, but as highly skilled and valuable labor their actions are more indicative of the declining importance of the nation-state and the increasing importance of capital. Put another way, though they may appear to transcend the state in some respects, they still belong to and reaffirm the dominance of neoliberalism, which is currently centered in the West. Western countries are (re)valorized because individuals must attain Western citizenship in order to conduct their affairs "freely."

The situations I have discussed here are thus very different from the more straightforward concerns in the media that migrant athletes naturalize in order to "unfairly" compete for the host country. Such a discourse often reinforces authentic notions of national community and refuses to see immigrants as true citizens. Some evidence of this issue arose in my research concerning distance runners who intersected with Loroupe and Ndereba, such as Lornah Kiplagat, who married a Dutch citizen and began running professionally for that country. Yet what is most important is that the concept of immigration and naturalization for the sake of competing nationally for another country reinforces national boundaries and creates hierarchies of citizenship within the state. Conversely, the actions of the aforementioned athletes use citizenship in the nation-state to further their more transnational goals, even if those goals are "simply" family unification. Media representations of the naturalization of black African immigrant athletes, often using their own words through interviews, put a nationalist gloss on what could otherwise be considered a transnational act hampered by the Western state.

Generation and National Belonging

Second-generation immigrants and those who immigrate as children or teenagers (generation 1.5 or 1.75) face a different set of experiences in their host societies than adults who immigrate later. Because of their experiences in youth culture and the educational system, we can think of the second generation as being more "integrated" into the host society than their parents.[21] The second generation in Europe and the United States frequently display signs of political integration and citizenship that refute fears of national decline because of immigration. As Gilroy notes, the second generation feels entitled to the full citizenship denied their parents and thus refuses to be relegated to the marginal category of "second generation" in nationalist discourse.[22] Of course, they still face a number of barriers to full participation (citizenship), chief among them being continued discrimination in education and the job market.[23]

We can begin by looking at Didier Drogba's experiences with racism growing up in France and his later attachment to Ivory Coast. Despite being born in Ivory Coast Drogba spent most of his childhood in France. Throughout his playing career, Drogba has intersected with a plethora of African- and European-born black soccer players. Perhaps unsurprisingly, then, many of the players he seems to spend time with socially tend to be some combination of African, Afro-French, and Ivorian. In his autobiography Drogba makes clear that such a division does indeed take place, particularly in England. He explains that his teammates at Chelsea made clear to him that the (white) English socialize with the (white) English, Brazilians with Brazilians, and Africans with Africans. Such divisions appear to make Drogba uncomfortable as they regard being a member of a soccer team, but he also makes links between such self-segregation and his childhood experiences as a black African immigrant in France.[24]

Drogba recollects being the only black child in his school classes, people closing their window shutters when he walked through neighborhoods, being called racist names while playing youth soccer, and later living in cramped quarters with his parents and siblings in a Parisian *banlieu*. He tells us that he saw family members struggle to find jobs despite being overqualified and how he saw soccer as a way to succeed. These experiences in France stand in stark contrast to the freedom and joy he experienced, and *remembers*, when he would make trips back to Ivory Coast. It is the stinging experiences of racism contrasted with the euphoric, if at times idealized, feelings of belonging that pushed Drogba toward identifying and playing for Ivory Coast, despite having spent most of his youth in France.[25] This history, from Drogba's autobiography, gives us some insight into his later efforts to bring awareness to the marginalization and racism faced by players from Africa.

[Drogba explains,] "To be an African player is not an advantage. A French international or an Ivory Coast international have totally different status. An African of equal value will earn less than a European. We don't start on a level footing. When you talk to a sponsor about a contract or with a club, they say to you: 'That is the way it is.' If you were in the France team, the negotiation would be pushed further and in the end you would earn a lot more money. Let's stop the lie." Drogba also rapped "a lack of respect" for the Africa Cup of Nations in the Premier League. He said: "When I see a player like Fredi Kanoute was stopped by Tottenham from going to the 2004 CAN for Mali, it lacked respect-not only for the player but for the whole of Africa."[26]

Didier Drogba has claimed that black African footballers are subject to racism and unequal treatment during their commercial nego-
tiations with clubs and sponsors. The controversial Chelsea striker
revealed he has fought against such disadvantages all his career and
has only overcome them now as he is successful and famous. . . . Chelsea, who have not only Drogba but John Obi Mikel, Salomon Kalou
and Michael Essien on their books, will be disappointed not to be
excluded by name from the striker's accusations, especially as they
now pay him £100,000 a week.[27]

Athletes like Drogba are at times given a platform by major news
outlets in the West enabling them to make their views heard. It is
unfortunate, however, that the causes of the continued devaluation
and mistreatment of black and African players are treated abstractly
by the media. Drogba's accusations are loosely aimed at soccer clubs
and the advertising industry, but there is nothing to make us think
that something will change anytime soon. Additionally, Drogba's
discourse on racism and discrimination is given token treatment by
the media. As a highly paid athlete Drogba is deemed to be making
too much money to complain about his treatment by fans, media,
and society at large. That his words are often truncated and articles
quickly move to other, generally trivial, news is evidence of his devaluation. Hence race and racism are often embodied in the stereotypical soccer "hooligan" or passively defined as a problem that blacks just
have to deal with—no action is required from readers or the media.

Drogba, of course, is still privileged as an athlete. He is able to identify with Ivory Coast without complication because he became popular in the country, fantastically so, as his playing career in France
began to develop. However, if we look at players who intersect with
Drogba, we can see that great celebrity within an African country is
not necessary to develop an affinity for playing for that country. For
example, the lesser known Benoit Assou-Ekotto chose to play for
Cameroon instead of France because of what he describes as a certain feeling he gets while in Cameroon:

I have more feeling with, uh, Cameroon or Africa. . . . [When asked
why, he says,] I don't know you know . . . for example . . . when I go

to Spain and there is not a . . . there is not a lot of black people in Spain . . . and when we see each other they give you a sign, you know, means you're cool. . . . I'm cool . . . but when I go to France I don't see . . . I don't see a . . . a white person who do that to me. So it's just only about the feeling and the spirit.[28]

Assou-Ekotto would go on to explain in the interview how he had been visiting Cameroon since he was five years old and had made numerous trips when his father was still alive. Such experiences in the lives of individuals like Drogba and Assou-Ekotto play an important role in their decisions to represent African countries in international competition. Their experiences and travels on the African continent give them a lens through which to look back at their lives in Europe and see the contradictions in their treatment by Western society.

In the media a conservative discourse questions why, or is confused as to how, players with African backgrounds who were born in Europe and have never been to Africa or have limited experience in Africa can choose to play for an African country. Doubtless, some players may take advantage of their African backgrounds just to be able to play internationally or because their path to playing time is blocked in their European country. However, the questioning and confusion over how a person who has never been to Africa could choose to play for an African team shows a lack of understanding of the black diaspora and how black immigrant communities and families construct identity.

Here we enter into a complex maze of possibilities and outcomes, none of which are easily predetermined, which speaks to the postmodern politics of identity creation, however forced and constrained they may be. Some athletes of African background born in Africa immigrate to Europe and eventually compete internationally for their host countries, while others do not, and some athletes of African backgrounds born in Europe play for their African country, while others do not. The decision often rests on where the athlete feels most at home, or where she or he *imagines* his or her home to be, if such issues of identity are indeed ever so simple.[29] For athletes who choose to represent African countries, even without ever having been there, Africa, in some respects, acts a place from which the athlete can draw meaning and belonging while living in societies that are hostile to black life. For athletes like Drogba and Assou-Ekotto, their choices appear to be driven by feelings of belonging combined with positive personal experiences. There are times, however, when we can see the pressure put upon black African immigrant athletes by the media and sport institutions to choose their national team loyalties. The cases of Mario Balotelli and Wilfried Zaha are particularly instructive. Balotelli has often defended his choice of the Italian national team over the Ghanaian by claiming he is, contrary to the opinion of some, Italian. "Due to his Ghanaian heritage, Ghana have tried to convince him to join their national team set-up but Balotelli is determined to play for Italy instead. He is only 17 years old but has already scored four goals in three cup appearances this season and has twice come off the bench in the league. 'I refused the call-up from Ghana because I don't feel Ghanaian,' he said. 'I was born here, I'm Italian, I don't know anything about Africa, I've never been there.'"[30]

Balotelli had spent his whole life in Italy and had never been to Ghana or any other African country. His case is further complicated by his rift with his birth parents and his subsequent, almost hostile, denial of being Ghanaian in his youth. This denial was only fueled by his early experiences with racism during youth football and his desire to take the name of his adoptive family, which he legally could not do until he was eighteen. However, once Balotelli cemented his choice by finally playing with the senior Italian team the debate subsided.

Wilfried Zaha's choice, on the other hand, received much more attention, in part because it played out in the British press, which was overrepresented in my data. Zaha, whose representation intersected with Drogba's in my analysis, was eligible to play for either Ivory Coast or England before accepting a call-up to the senior England team in 2012. Despite being born in Abidjan, Zaha immigrated to England with his family when he was around four years old and never returned to Ivory Coast. Zaha eventually choose to join England, but because most of his life was spent in England, the notion that he had any kind of choice to make was sometimes met with confusion.

[English manager] Hodgson finds the whole debate slightly odd. Given the chance to play for England, he does not feel there should be any choice to be made. "It is very simple," he said. "England, for me, is very important. To be asked to play for England is a major honour and a major feather in people's caps. I am not interested in people who are deciding whether England is where they want to be. When people are called up I expect them to come running, get on a bicycle and cycle to the training session if they have to, then shake hands with everyone and tell them how happy they are to be there. All this nonsense about players receiving phone calls [from Didier Drogba] and being enticed away, if they are going to be enticed away, they are not the right player for us."[31]

Despite Zaha's choice being a "simple" one from the perspective of the English national team's manager, Zaha is never asked how English or British he feels or if he feels he belongs in that society. In the Assou-Ekotto interview mentioned previously, the interviewer, before asking Assou-Ekotto why he chose to play for Cameroon, states that many players who play internationally for African countries have never been to the continent, and he also makes an offhand joke about Assou-Ekotto insisting he is not a "traitor" to France. The statement assumes—and primes us to think—that these players are just taking advantage of the ability to play internationally, almost defrauding African national teams. Additionally, because they have never been to the continent they could not possibly know anything about Africa or "be" African. Such thinking takes for granted black African migrant communities in the West, their transnational activities, and the transmission of culture and values to their children.[32] The influence and expectations of Zaha's family go unexplored. At times Zaha briefly mentions what playing for Ivory Coast would mean to his family (a lot), but the conversation ends there. Instead, the influence of Drogba and his efforts to get Zaha to join the Ivory Coast team are what pulls Zaha into my analysis. The "interference" of Drogba and other Ivory Coast officials is treated almost as an intrusion upon English property. We are not privy to the conversations between Drogba and Zaha, but it would seem unlikely, given Drogba's own choices and experiences with race and racism in France (as well as his pan-African outlook), that they were simple conversations about playing time.

Athletes like Wilfried Zaha, Benoit Assou-Ekotto, and Drogba, among many others, who have choices to make about which country they represent internationally, challenge hegemonic notions of race and nationalism and national coherence. Laurent Dubois's work on the French national team throughout the 1990s and early 2000s demonstrates the discomfort the presence of such players brings to those who cling to a "pure" vision of their country.[33] Dubois, significantly focusing on the French-Algerian relationship, illustrates the hostility of the French nation-state to the idea that it is possible to simultaneously love, identify with, and be from two different nations. Western European national soccer teams have been slow to realize that immigrants and their children are not automatically going to choose to play for either their host country or their country of birth. For some time now African countries and their national soccer teams have been active in courting youth players in the diaspora to play for their teams, though often relying on a similar, essentialized, form of belonging. The lack of such courting of black immigrant youth players by European national teams can be interpreted as a continuation of the salient exclusion of immigrants from mainstream Western society and is thus indicative of how racialized the processes of claiming nationality are. Concurrently, the expectation that an athlete could get "lured" away or play for another country without having been there speaks to the fears of immigrants not wanting to be a part of the Western nation-state. The discourses above are reminiscent of and certainly linked to the familiar notion of the "Tebbit test" that supposedly checked an immigrant's allegiance to the United Kingdom by asking which national cricket team he or she cheered for—the "test" was particularly aimed at Asians and West Indians.

Though the test was initially uttered by the British politician Norman Tebbit in the 1990s, the racism underlying it has intensified in our post-9/11 era as Western countries—especially the United States and United Kingdom—have waged continuous war against pan-global "Islamic" terrorism. In addition, Western countries have witnessed a dramatic rise in far-right political activity that often blames immigrants for, well, everything, while promising to return "their" respective countries to an imagined past. Because sport exists as one of few sites where people engage in public displays of (hyper)nationalist behavior it gains tremendous symbolic value for the nation's very character. Yet at the same time the contemporary composition of these national teams is at odds with the symbolic reification of the (white male) Western nation-state and "being" English, French, American, and so on. When it comes to athletes and their behavior, as Gilroy might put it, there is a certain melancholia and longing for the colonial subject who would do as told or expected.[34] It is a discourse that, again, reifies the link between race and nation so that speaking about the people of Western nations means speaking about white people, white men more specifically. Choosing to play for a national team is a very public declaration or form of nationality that actually means very little. It is an act given exaggerated importance because it happens in sport, but the Western discourse around it is compelling because it already expects (fears) these athletes to choose "Africa." Such a high-visibility discourse obscures the important ways in which the second generation tries to engage and integrate into Western societies.[35]

Religious Identity

As with many sport autobiographies, Olajuwon's is a journey through his career, yet it ends (capitalizes) somewhat prematurely on his second straight NBA championship with the Houston Rockets in 1995. At this point in his life Olajuwon is ten years into his NBA career, has rededicated himself to (Sunni) Islam, and has attained U.S. citizenship. Throughout the book Olajuwon weaves personal information and thoughts with events both on and off the basketball court, which gives us some context regarding his life. Of course, Olajuwon's narrative has significant drawbacks and biases. Without digressing too much, the account Olajuwon provides is often unapologetic, absolves him of any shortcomings or blame, and is often absolute and moralizing. Throughout the book—and in his representation during the time of its release—Olajuwon decries "trash talking" in the NBA and the lifestyles of basketball players as they involve women, money, "the night-life," and drugs. Though never stated directly, these intentional acts, combined with his downplaying of racism in the United States, demonstrate Olajuwon's awareness of race and racism in the United States and the social position of African Americans, from whom he actively tries to differentiate himself. In reviewing media accounts about him, it becomes clear that this shifting of blame is something Olajuwon has done throughout his career.

The autobiography touches too briefly on Olajuwon's relationships, upbringing in Nigeria, and thoughts on Islam, although to ask for more would perhaps be too demanding, given that academics are not the intended audience. Given these shortcomings and biases, what we are left with is, again, a *glimpse* into how Olajuwon perceives and acts upon his life in America. This glimpse begins with Olajuwon's upbringing and eventual immigration to the United States. Throughout the book, Olajuwon's experiences resonate with the literature regarding black immigrants to the United States and Western Europe, which explains how black immigrants enter their host countries with different experiences and expectations than native black populations.[36]

Early in his autobiography Olajuwon explicitly recalls activities that distanced him from his African American teammates. For example, he writes about how he purposefully wore traditional Nigerian clothes and bowed when greeting (white) Houston alumni boosters in order to create his own identity. Being different, being distinctly "Nigerian" or "African," seemed to be important for Olajuwon during his time at the University of Houston. He also recalls wanting to engage with African Americans but being rebuffed at times because of his clothing and behavior around white alumni. He also had difficulty understanding African American slang and disliked their stereotypes of "Africa," as he tells us that he was sometimes called "the big African" and heard comments (jokes) about "living in huts."[37]

Because of these issues, Olajuwon states that he spent a lot of social time in college with the Bahamian basketball player Lynden Rose and his friends because they understood him the most, had a culture similar to his, and clued him in to issues of racial prejudice. Olajuwon would also spend time with a fellow Nigerian national team member who immigrated to the United States soon after him. Clearly Olajuwon attempted to navigate U.S. society in his own way during his college and early professional years due to his experiences with race and racism and his foreigner status. Even in his media representation it is notable that both college and professional teammates at times commented on how they did not know him very well. Overall, however, Olajuwon's autobiography only briefly touches on such topics, so we are left in the dark on many of his motivations as well as on where he stood in relation to the relatively large Nigerian population in the Houston area.

Olajuwon's relationship and experience with Islam in the United States features prominently throughout his autobiography. He recalls his early experiences and conversations with African Americans about Islam and, significantly, the Nation of Islam (NOI) early on in his immigrant experience. He explains that once he learned what the Nation of Islam was and stood for he stopped having conversations with its members, who had initially approached him. Without acknowledging the role of the Nation of Islam in its historical context of the mid-1980s or its place in the black community, Olajuwon denounces it as not practicing proper Islam. He never tells us what this "proper" Islam is, although he does discuss his parents' faith and practice while he was growing up in Nigeria. We might assume Olajuwon practices Islam the way he observed growing up, but we must also remember that his return to Islam was fostered in the United States. Despite this, for someone practicing Sunni Islam the beliefs of the NOI would be odd indeed, even if by the mid-eighties its cohesiveness had completely shattered and many members had converted to Sunni Islam. The emphasis on nationalist self-segregation by race, seeing whites as "blue-eyed devils" created in a lab by a black scientist, an apocalyptic "Mothership"/"Motherplane" that would come to bomb Earth, and other departures from traditional Sunni Islam teachings likely are not aspects of the faith that Olajuwon was used to.[38]

Olajuwon admits that early in his college and professional years he drifted from religion and was not as dedicated as he later felt he should have been. The culmination of events in the late eighties, from domestic problems to on- and off-court fights and allegations of drug use, appears to have driven Olajuwon's return to religion. He describes how, when seeking to rededicate himself to Islam, he began reading the Koran, attending mosque, and having other religious meetings with, primarily, other immigrants to the United States from African and Arab nations. After having invested himself for nearly three years, Olajuwon took a well-publicized pilgrimage (hajj) to Mecca in 1991. From that time on Olajuwon's status as a Muslim would be popularized and become a significant part of his representation, especially as he became a more popular and successful player in the midnineties.

For the rest of his career, then, Olajuwon was the "authority" in the NBA on Islam, the person to whom media would go to for everything "Islamic." Hence "Islam" was added to Olajuwon's representation of foreign Otherness. At different points he would be discussed as Nigerian, or Muslim, or both. Theoretically, this situation gave Olajuwon opportunities to try to clear up some of the harmful stereotypes of Islam and Muslims. However, Olajuwon's insistence on his version of Islam being the only acceptable or "proper" version is difficult to accept in that it works well as a nonthreatening, "ideal" version of Islam that Western media is willing to accept. In some ways Olajuwon ends up acting as an apologist for Islam and policing the actions of other Muslims.

For example, Olajuwon was given uncontested space to talk about and pass judgment on the actions of Mahmoud Abdul Rauf. Abdul-Rauf refused to stand for the U.S. national anthem and flag before NBA games as a politico-religious stand against a "symbol of tyranny and oppression." When the media went to Olajuwon, he told them that "Mahmoud either misunderstood the Koran when he read it or he was given bad information or bad interpretations from other people." Regarding Louis Farrakhan, leader of the Nation of Islam, Olajuwon explains, "He is not teaching Islam. The call of Islam is not based on race or color but is universal. It is available to humanity, not to specific people." Finally, Olajuwon describes in his autobiography how he once visited the boxer Mike Tyson, who was in jail for rape, because he had heard that Tyson had converted to Islam and wanted to make sure he had learned it properly.[39]

Olajuwon's approach to the practice and political utilization of

Islam in a right or wrong manner ends up marginalizing the political history that gave rise specifically to NOI and more broadly conflates black American Muslims and the Nation of Islam. The latter process is evidenced by the salient media assumption that Abdul-Rauf was a member of the NOI. On the other hand, because of the general confusion around Islam, it was at times assumed that Abdul-Rauf was Arab or African and thus foreign, capable of being excluded or deported from the United States.[40] By shifting the conversation to Islam and its correct practice, or "use," the radical political critique (whether we like it or not) otherwise contained in the words and actions of Abdul-Rauf, or Farrakhan, or even Malcolm X, is neatly ignored. Instead, Olajuwon fuses a Western discourse about freedom and rights with a religious discourse in which Islam is "a complete code of life" and "the solution to all problems, and a way for you to fight for justice and fairness and peace."[41]

> [Olajuwon] said, "I wanted to become an American citizen because I wanted to be able to travel and to have the honor that any individual deserves—if they live in a way that is honorable. Being an American citizen, if you are a good American citizen, gives you respect. . . . My goal is to lead a life of righteousness, to conduct myself with honor, to let those other Americans know that I am as good a citizen as I can be," said Olajuwon, who is a Muslim. "That is the basis of Islam. There are no nationalities. We are all different colors, all different races, but all brothers."[42]

As with most media interviews, we would ideally like to see more of what Olajuwon thinks, but the questions are not asked nor is the information voluntarily given. During his playing career, Olajuwon was never questioned by the media on his assertion that Islam is the answer to all problems—something that would not seem possible today. Islam is reinscribed as absolute and unchanging, leaving no space for those who inevitably practice it otherwise (or not at all). It is clear that Islam is an important part of his identity that prohibits any sort of affiliation based on racial, ethnic, or national ties. Yet it also appears that becoming an American eased Olajuwon's travel, especially considering that he began making more frequent trips to the Middle East. That act in itself is somewhat transgressive in that it constructs citizenship as a tool more for crossing boundaries than for love of country, however the hierarchy of American versus Nigerian citizenship, and thus humanity, remains untouched. For his part, Olajuwon tells us that he genuinely felt that Americans had made him one of their own and that by becoming a citizen he was repaying the love he had received over the years.[43] However, Olajuwon is never pushed to account for the contradiction of his taking U.S. citizenship. Despite his desire to keep the two separate, Olajuwon ends up conflating being a good (U.S.) citizen with being a good Muslim (person).

The media may not have questioned Olajuwon on these points, but Dikembe Mutombo did, as he once criticized Olajuwon as "too busy being an American" to be interested in African causes. Olajuwon's response is telling, as he takes noticeable offense, questions Mutombo's motives, and ultimately explains that another Muslim is more of a brother, and knows him better, than someone who is Nigerian but not Muslim.

"Now, there are only two of us [Africans in the NBA], Hakeem and me, representing 100 million, maybe one billion Africans," Mutombo said. "That's why it is so important that we retain our identity, not as men from separate countries, but as Africans. It is very important that we represent our continent, that we present a true and accurate picture of life in Africa, that we help Africa." Twice, Mutombo has returned to Africa with missions to strengthen bonds of understanding and to bring financial and medical assistance. . . . But Olajuwon never goes home to help his people. Mutombo finds this disturbing. "He is so busy being an American he has lost his heritage," Mutombo said, "and this I cannot understand. . . . He is like my brother. He tells me he is proud of the work I do, but he will not accompany me. I feel disappointment for that."[44]

While his roots remain in Africa, Olajuwon explained that his belief in Islam has flowered to encompass humanity. . . . "I cannot think tribal, ethnic or national," Olajuwon said. "No. My cause is universal, for all people. How can he [Mutombo] say he represents Africa when in one country—just one country—you have so many ethnic tribes that are killing each other? Why do you want to represent that? These are wars for power. Simply for power. It is ignorant. Islam is trying to erase that. You are told that you must wish for your brother what you wish for yourself. That is all over the world, not just in Africa. I will give you an example. If a person in China is practicing Islam, and my blood brother is not, then that brother in China is closer to me naturally than my own blood brother who is not practicing. That is Islam. It is natural because that is my instinct. You must look at the spiritual, not the physical. We are above that. . . . I cannot understand such nationalism.[45]

Mutombo and Olajuwon are clearly approaching the subject in different ways. Islam is certainly a part of Olajuwon's, and Africa's (West Africa's and Nigeria's in particular) heritage, to which Olajuwon returns, but Mutombo is more interested in issues of race and racism. Olajuwon further explains that he does return to Nigeria and prefers, in line with his practice of Islam, to do his charitable acts anonymously so as not to draw attention. Unfortunately, the subject was dropped and never publicly appeared again after the two had a private conversation. Olajuwon's focus on brotherhood between Muslims gets contradicted in light of his criticisms of Abdul-Rauf, who, coincidentally, was a teammate of Mutombo's during this time. Reportedly, Mutombo and Abdul-Rauf were friends who often talked about political issues. When Abdul-Rauf was suspended from the NBA for not standing during the anthem, Mutombo lent his support and vouched for the character of Abdul-Rauf while making comparisons to the behavior of athletes like Dennis Rodman. At the time, Rodman was a controversial figure because of his changing hairstyles and colors, piercings, and off-court behavior (once wearing a white wedding dress to celebrate his autobiography). Mutombo engages Abdul-Rauf's actions as a reasoned political stance, while Olajuwon approaches it through a religious lens.

While this is a provocative history, I want to refocus on the fact that Olajuwon has chosen to build and express an identity around an aspect of his life that is marginalized in the West. Despite the inconsistencies that arise when reading Olajuwon, it is clear that Islam and his identity as a Muslim provide a way for him to navigate his social reality. Notably, Catherine Ndereba also projects a strong religious identity, often being called "devout," a term we more often see used for Muslims, but she does not receive the same treatment for or focus on her beliefs. Olajuwon's lack of political message and active condemnation of "different" ways of being a Muslim make his version of Islam "safe" or "good," insofar as that is possible, for the U.S. mainstream. However, both Olajuwon's personal discourse and his representation construct for us an "Islam" that is in line with the romanticized version of the Orientalists, in that it is static and thus essentialized. Hence we already "know" what "Islam" Olajuwon is involved with because of its Orientalized existence in Western societies, even within a contemporary context where Islam is increasingly demonized and defined by terrorism.[46]

In his autobiography there is no mention of Olajuwon facing discrimination or harassment for being a Muslim, and he goes as far as saying that he became an American citizen in part because America is where he "found" Islam.[47] I argue that Olajuwon knew very well the stereotypes of Islam and Muslims and actively stayed away from controversial statements. As Zareena Grewal explains regarding the Abdul-Rauf suspension, many Muslim Americans, including African American Muslims and immigrant Muslims, distanced themselves in order to avoid political scrutiny.[48] However, as Michael Hedges reports, Olajuwon raised eyebrows in 1995 for stating at a meeting of the Muslim Arab Youth Association that "America needs Islam, Islam is the only solution and the only way of life. . . . The morality of America is almost bankrupt. There is no morals [sic]." Hedges also reports that Olajuwon spoke to the same crowd about his attempts to convert NBA players to Islam in order to help them be happier with their lives.[49]

Olajuwon's statements were similar to what one might hear in churches throughout the Bible Belt of the United States and in right-wing media. Yet the Muslim Arab Youth Association and other organizations to which Olajuwon donated money were later linked to Western-defined terrorist groups, including Al-Qaida and Hamas, and it is the links to these organizations that Hedges was reporting on at the time. Olajuwon and his activities were quickly brought into the public spotlight and he was forced to defend his work in spreading Islam. Though Olajuwon was absolved of any intentional wrongdoing, it is a reminder of the duality of colonial Othering and how it can quickly change sides. That Olajuwon never expressed an opinion such as the one above in any media interview is an indication that he is aware of when to publicly engage in some discourses and disengage from others. In identifying with such a highly stigmatized and marginalized religion in the United States, he surely felt pressure to be selective in his media presence if he himself wanted to avoid being stigmatized. That in my data Olajuwon never publicly raises the issue of violence toward Muslims in America remains perplexing, given the opportunities. Despite such silences, Olajuwon served as a role model for Muslims in Houston and elsewhere, something he took pride in. I will discuss Olajuwon's meaning to Muslims in the United States in the next chapter.

The interplay between the representation of "Islam" through Olajuwon and Olajuwon's own identity as a Muslim is certainly complex. As is evidenced in some of the above quotes, Olajuwon was seemingly searching for a place to belong, which he found not only in the Islamic community around Houston but around the United States and Canada, as he often attended Friday prayers in different cities when playing on the road. For our purposes here we can say that Olajuwon, through interactions with the media and media reporting of him, develops a public "Islamic" identity that displaces his blackness both for himself (it seems) and for the media. Yet we would not normally expect an "Islamic" identity to be represented any better than a black African model minority's identity. I would argue that the role of the Nation of Islam in American history during this time—with its calls for black self-segregation in schools, jobs, policing, and so on—made the black American Muslim particularly suspicious. We must remember that the rise of Louis Farrakhan occurred during the 1980s and the Million Man March was held in 1995, when Olajuwon won his second NBA championship. During this time, the Nation of Islam represented black American Muslims in the white imagination and a forceful native black critique of white America, and yet Islam was inherently foreign—hence Abdul-Rauf could be accused of being a member of the NOI *and* a foreigner. Olajuwon, as a foreign Muslim with an apolitical (safe) version of Islam, reconciles the complexity of "being Muslim" and American history. Through his denunciation of Farrakhan and the NOI Olajuwon could be seen as bringing a "true" version of Islam that is uncritical of white America and in line with American neoliberal values. As he becomes an "approachable" Muslim his blackness is displaced (always temporarily) and he stands out even more as a model minority compared to black American Muslims.

Conclusion

Hegemony is never a completed process, so in hegemonic representations we should expect to find cracks and inconsistencies. These cracks allow us to glimpse a different reality than the one given to us and to "reread" what is presented to us in a more nuanced manner. Through these inconsistencies and the inclusion of other source data, we are able to investigate aspects of the representation of these athletes that we otherwise could not and to begin constructing a counternarrative. This chapter focuses on exposing the inconsistencies in the hegemonic (hyper)nationalist discourse and reading for how (im)migrants navigate their host societies as black foreign others.

When we look closely at representations of immigration and naturalization we can see that these events are filtered through a Western-centric lens. That lens, used by Western media, is generally incapable of seeing the complex lines of power and transnationality at work within the black (im)migrant experience. An important critique of Western nationalist notions of space and belonging is posed not only by the black African migrant athlete but by the black foreign Other and blackness itself more generally. Post-9/11 Western nationalist discourse actively works to maintain some semblance of past national history or tradition that is still linked with previous racisms and xenophobias. Whether in maintaining the Other as foreign, re-creating essentialist notions of the nation through sport, or continued paternalistic attitudes toward African cultures, Western nationalist discourse has yet to fully confront contemporary issues of (im)migration that are largely driven by their economics and by war making. Instead, it attempts to freeze and defer issues of migration while continuing to idealize its past traditions as simple and pure, morally and firmly rooted in a homogeneous cultural identity.[50]

Of course, the discourses of the foreign Other are not unproblematic either. For example, Mutombo at times leans upon an essentialized African subject—a creation that tends to make static the concept of race and its fusion with culture and nation. Essentialized notions of (black) African identity and culture also have the potential to fix Africa and African cultures in the past. They also tend to naturalize and dehistoricize race, creating and maintaining essentialized identities and experiences that often work to hide other forms of marginality—such as gender, sexuality, and class.[51] Stuart Hall explains that while "little" or "strategic" essentialisms are tempting, what we require in a transgressive politics is a dialectic—Gramscian wars of position—that can reach people through their multiple and contingent identities.[52] In short, there are no certainties in a politics based on (contingent/unguaranteed) identity and we cannot "conduct black politics through the strategy of a simple set of reversals, putting in the place of the bad old essential white subject, the new essentially good black subject."[53] Though the development of a transgressive politics is slow and frustrating, a continued reliance on racial thinking and racial organization only stops us from dealing with problems as they stand today.

6

The Diasporic Athlete

Blackness and Meaning in the African Diaspora

So far I have been primarily concerned with representations of black African migrant athletes who maintain a kind of transnational consistency between media in Western societies. I have argued that black African migrant athletes are meant, first and foremost, to mean something for white audiences, not black. In the previous chapter I read beyond the media representations of black African athletes in order to provide an alternative reading, a counternarrative, of historical life events and identity formation. My counternarrative, however, is only a part of how blackness is lived and constructed transnationally. In this chapter I refocus on the concept of diaspora, the black African diaspora more specifically, and how we might begin fitting recent (sports labor) migrations into our thinking about it. In other words, in this chapter I explore the representational inconsistencies of these athletes that allow us to see that these athletes do indeed mean something to black populations in the diaspora. Hence I begin this chapter by revisiting Gilroy's notion of the black Atlantic and its extension into sport, what Carrington has called the "sporting Black Diaspora."[1] These works prepare us for thinking about the (new) African diaspora as a space where black African (sport) celebrities are symbolically appropriated by black peoples and used to construct meaning and identity in black communities.

The work of Appiah, Mills, Gordon, Gilroy, Wright, Said, and Hall, among others, has been useful in framing parts of my analysis in terms of antiblack racism, global white supremacy, diaspora, and blackness.[2] In particular, Gilroy's influential work over the years on the concept of the black Atlantic has been useful outlining a politics of the black diaspora without relying on essentialist or authentic notions of blackness. Gilroy and other intellectuals tell us that, though their analyses are grounded in populations linked with the African diaspora, it is impossible and undesirable to create a politics of antiracism or radical humanism based solely on race or racial unity. Any attempt to build an antiracist politics must fundamentally recognize the humanity of each individual regardless of race—a "planetary humanism," in Gilroy's terms.[3]

Hence what is necessary is a politics that recognizes the cultural and experiential hybridity of the black Atlantic but can then expand and make links with other groups of people. These other groups include peoples of color on the spectrum of blackness who face racism (such as Latinos, Asians, American Indians, Asian Indians, and Arabs), racialized religions (such as Judaism and Islam), and forms of oppression (where gender and sexuality remain stigmatized).[4] For Gilroy, the compression of time and space via the progression of postmodernity and neoliberal practices has, in part, sustained a long "tradition" of communication, the sharing of similar (forced) experiences of racism and exclusion, between black communities around the Atlantic. However, Gilroy warns against the impulse to engage in backward and static notions via such tradition. Instead, tradition must be (re)conceptualized in order to embrace the hybridity and plural nature of diasporic communities and experiences. Thus a history and tradition of change and intermixture should be embraced.

Taking from the conversation in chapter 1, we can further think of this tradition of diasporic communication through sport and bodily performance to the increased visibility of African American sports stars, "the black athlete," over the years. From Jack Johnson, Joe Louis, Jesse Owens, and Muhammad Ali to Michael Jordan, Kobe Bryant, and LeBron James (to name a few), the athletic performances and actions of black athletes have often carried a political and ethical critique of Western notions of right, justice, and democracy similar to the ways black musical and other art forms have throughout history.[5] In some respects those performances resonate with black (nonwhite) communities all over the world because of what they mean for the possibilities of black peoples and because of local and global forces that make the cultural spheres of sport and entertainment two of few "viable" ways out of abject poverty. Carrington, Andrews, Jackson, and Mazur extend this notion of diasporic communication to sport through their concept of the "sporting Black Atlantic." In essence, "the black athlete" is and has been a part of the cultural resources of black communities in forming resistive transnational identities. Until now, the focus on and prominence of the African American athlete to the black diaspora, and the research concerning it, had to do with how African Americans and Black British were some of the first athletes to transgress racial boundaries of their day and reach new levels of possibilities for black peoples. As they explain, "The sporting black Atlantic can be defined, on one level, as a complex cultural and political diasporic space, which transgresses the boundaries of nation-states, whereby the migrations and achievements of black athletes have come to assume a heightened political significance for the dispersed cultures and peoples of the black diaspora—the sports arena thus operates as an important symbolic space in the struggles of black peoples against the ideologies and practices of white supremacy."[6]

Carrington and his colleagues note that the insular nature of American popular culture makes the sporting black Atlantic more likely to be found in countries other than the United States. For example, residents of cities like London and Soweto may be more comfortable reaching beyond national boundaries for their sport heroines and heroes than those in Chicago or New York. However, different black communities in different locations will symbolically appropriate black athletes in different ways because of the ways race and racism are experienced in different contexts. So despite the transnational nature of the sporting black Atlantic, a significant part remains rooted in local contexts and particularities. Such relativity makes determining how black communities identify with certain black athletes rather unpredictable, but that does not rule out the existence of generalizable similarities.

While it remains too early to tell what the real impact of these processes will be for U.S. or European sport, it is clear that the increasing presence in sport of those from the global South is an unstoppable trend. The many peoples of the global South, all along the continuum of blackness, will maintain a presence in the global sphere of cultural production that is sport. With increased migration and recent technological advances compressing time and space even further, black African migrant athletes are continuously emerging in the diaspora and taking their place alongside African Americans—or perhaps, as with Latinos and baseball, potentially displacing them. Despite their representations in Western media, these athletes bring new meanings to the cultural resources of black groups in the diaspora, meanings that are not as incompatible with those of African Americans and native blacks as we are led to believe. It is my aim in this chapter to begin exploring in a meaningful way what these athletes may mean to different populations and communities, particularly those in the black African diaspora.

In "The Diasporic African American Athlete" I examine moments when the black African athletes in my study (and some they intersect with) expressed some measure of appreciation for athletes we would think of as important to the diaspora. Here I attempt to tease out the meaning these athletes, primarily African Americans, have for those in African countries. Next, in "The Black African Athlete and the Continent," I examine the popularity of black African migrant athletes in their home countries and, to some extent, the African continent. I find that these athletes have in some ways displaced or taken a place alongside the African American diasporic athlete for those communities. Finally, in "Black African Athletes and the Diaspora," I discuss and revisit some cracks in the representations of black African immigrant athletes where we can see their importance not only to black African immigrants and communities in the West but also to native black communities in the form of popular culture, primarily music.

The Diasporic African American Athlete

African American athletes have historically held a prominent place in the literature on sport and the black diaspora. The early movements and achievements of these athletes made them a focal point around which diasporic blacks and those in Africa could wrap meaning and see potential for their own lives.[7] Still today African Americans remain significant around the black Atlantic because of the possibilities they represent and the inherent critique of white supremacy they embody. I begin my analysis here with Dikembe Mutombo, who offers a good example of how African American athletes were looked at by a child growing up in what was then Zaire.

> One of [Muhammad Ali's] most famous fights took place in Zaire, now the Democratic Republic of the Congo, where he battled George Foreman in the "Rumble in the Jungle" in 1974. At the ceremony Thursday, Mutombo recalled the impression Ali's visit made on him as an 8-year-old growing up in that country. "He changed my life," said Mutombo. . . . "I can never forget how inspired I was to see a black athlete receive such respect and admiration. He changed how the people of Zaire saw themselves, and in turn how the world saw them." Since ending his boxing career in 1981, Ali has traveled extensively on international charitable missions and devoted his time to social causes.[8]

The 1974 title fight between Muhammad Ali and George Foreman was an important spectacle, marking the return of Ali to prominence, and is often mentioned among the greatest fights of all time. Of course, it was also important to Africans who were still emerging from formal colonialism and for the Congolese, who were nearly ten years into Mobuto's rule. According to the documentary film *When We Were Kings*, Ali was treated like a hero in Zaire and spoke publicly to groups about race and politics.[9] In that documentary we see footage of Ali talking to a group about the marginalization of blackness and drawing links between the experiences of African Americans with segregation and those of Africans under colonialism. Ali is certainly one of the most well-known and remembered athletes in the world today, and his political resistance during the 1960s and 1970s is the most important part of his legacy. While some of his political actions remain contradictory to how most remember him, Mutombo tells us that Ali provided an example of what a black man could do or become.[10] The example Ali set and the feeling it gave Mutombo resonates with my discussion about the importance of black athletes, and their successes, to black communities throughout the twentieth century. We can contrast this glimpse that Mutombo gives us with

Hakeem Olajuwon's "idolization" of NBA great Kareem Abdul-Jabbar. "The Lakers' great center, who makes his final All-Star appearance Sunday, was one of the few players Olajuwon knew of when he came to the United States from Nigeria nine years ago. The former soccer player from Lagos said he idolizes Abdul-Jabbar. That hasn't stopped Olajuwon from trying to run him into the ground in their on-court encounters, however. He hasn't been picking just on Kareem."[11]

The idea that these athletes look up to or idolize other athletes occurs frequently in media reports with little question of why those particular athletes are looked up to. In that kind of coverage, a response such as Mutombo's, quoted above, is actually very rare. As I have pointed out, individuals in the black diaspora and on the African continent tend to be aware of their tenuous subject position in relation to Western societies. In their shared or forced experiences of oppression and rejection under white supremacy, it should come as no surprise that some individuals model themselves after others with similar experiences as a way to struggle against the devaluation of blackness. For Mutombo, growing up in a country emerging from its colonial terror and resultant political crises, Muhammad Ali provided a radical departure from his everyday experiences, and those of many other Africans, even if he was only eight years old at the time. Diasporic athletes like Ali, in the tradition of Jack Johnson and others, pushed the possibilities of what black individuals could do in life through the status and success they were able to achieve.

However, instead of this kind of insight and awareness, we are often left with the assumption that it is self-evident why someone would idolize, for example, Kareem Abdul-Jabbar. Perhaps the logic is simply that Abdul-Jabbar is one of the greatest players ever to play basketball, and therefore he is looked up to. However, that assumption by the media is laced with racial and, at times, nationalist undertones. Mutombo obviously looked up to Ali for reasons besides his athletic prowess, and he explicitly speaks to the impact of Ali's blackness on himself and the population of then Zaire. The lack of a "why" question being posed to Olajuwon on Abdul-Jabbar keeps us from potentially knowing how black diasporic athletes are interpreted by those in African countries. Olajuwon's "idolization," a term used loosely in the media, of Abdul-Jabbar is further complicated because it may not rest on Abdul-Jabbar's blackness but could rest on his conversion to Islam and political involvement during his professional career. Abdul-Jabbar, along with Oscar Robertson, served as a "cultural ambassador" to Africa in 1971 (Olajuwon would have been eight years old) as part of the U.S. State Department's efforts during the Cold War to show African countries that American racism was not what they had heard it was. Abdul-Jabbar, who had converted to Islam and changed his name three years prior, toured different African cities, including Lagos, Nigeria, during the trip.[12] Though Olajuwon reportedly does not remember Abdul-Jabbar during that time, Abdul-Jabbar's presence in Lagos is still relevant because of its influence, to whatever degree, on the fledgling basketball culture in Nigeria in the 1970s.[13]

The rarity of a black African athlete expressing what, for example, an African American athlete means to him or her demonstrates the media's tendency to essentialize and naturalize identity. For example, the success of Didier Drogba fueled media efforts to find the "next" Drogba. Those individuals were usually black with ties to Ivory Coast or Francophone Africa. Romelu Lukaku, who is a second-generation Belgian of Congo descent, is one such athlete who also holds Drogba as a "hero."[14] Lukaku may very well feel some affinity toward Drogba based on their links to Africa, but the media takes this as a given, an essentialized form of identity based on an ahistorical, whitewashed blackness rather than the result of white supremacy and colonial histories. The same phenomenon happened with Olajuwon when the next recruit originating from Africa became well known. Thus athletes like Yinka Dare, Michael Olowokandi, and even Mutombo were the "next" Olajuwon at some point in their careers.

The media actively create and foster these identifications. The media is one avenue through which people come to understand their social realities and categorize the world. There is thus something of a feedback loop created. Invariably, youths watch and learn about star athletes through media outlets. With athletes categorized along racial, ethnic, and national lines, they are likely to identify with athletes who are presented as similar to them. This process is not a one-off event but rather a persistent, everyday process of defining who, what, and how an individual should behave. These definitions are then rewarded through social interaction, for example, as children pick out players to emulate on the playground. Picking the "right" player is casually accepted and thus encouraged, while choosing the "wrong" player could be met with jokes or ostracism. People are certainly free to choose whomever they wish to emulate, but those choices are often conditioned by the social world around us and the media images we have access to.[15]

I reiterate that these diasporic links between African Americans and Africans are often hidden from us. The paucity of examples like those of Mutombo and Olajuwon not only indicates as much but demonstrates that when they do emerge they are often terribly incomplete and lacking any notion of nuance. Particularly during the 1980s and 1990s, when Mutombo and Olajuwon emerged, there was a noticeable assumption among the media that they would have had no knowledge of American basketball stars, given their perceived lack of experience with basketball. To some degree this has changed with more recent athletes to the West, as with Drogba and, noticeably, Mwadi Mabika, who once discussed watching NBA games late at night and then trying to replicate the moves the next day.[16] Further, Mabika, in a "twenty questions with . . ." promotional effort for WNBA.com, lists among her "favorite" things primarily American (and African American) movies, actors, athletes, and musicians.[17] Though we should be skeptical of any promotional media, it nevertheless supports my point that how and why black African (im)migrants have come to enjoy or appreciate black American culture are uncritically ignored. Instead we are left either with the assumed cultural superiority of the West or some uncomplicated (essential) notion of black affinity.

The African Athlete and the Continent

In earlier chapters I have explored how Western media is quick to elevate the stature of black African immigrant athletes in their home countries. Filtered through the lens of a predominantly white media and intended for white audiences, this portrayal is problematic because it tends toward simplification and reduction of African politics and society. However, media articles are based on events that have actually happened; they are not fictional. Athletes who have emigrated from Africa to achieve success in Western sport are at times highly heralded and serve as examples of what is possible to achieve coming from Africa. Yet we can reread these events through a more critical lens, taking into account the full weight of contemporary and historical forces. Hence there are times where we are granted insight into which "African" athletes were important to immigrant athletes when they were growing up or training.

> Ilo had begun playing basketball at a local playground, where the participants were nicknamed "Dr. J" and "Kareem" after their favorite overseas stars. Among the court's regulars, only Ilo did not have a famous monicker. "I was just Ilo," he said. Yet he looked at his quickly growing brother [Mutombo], and he saw the next Akeem Olajuwon, the native of Nigeria who was by then adorning magazine covers in Zaire.[18]

> "I love to see my name go behind Hakeem Olajuwon, someone who inspired all of us to come from Africa and follow the dream of basketball," said Mutombo, who came to the United States from Zaire. "He opened the door to show you can come to this game and dominate. I'm going out to buy champagne and toast Hakeem Olajuwon for leading me and inspiring me."[19]

While these responses by Mutombo and his brother certainly could have been conditioned by the questions being asked, there is no reason to believe they would give a false answer in lieu of naming someone who actually did hold some kind of meaning. What I prefer to argue is that the first person to find success established a way to succeed that others then began working toward. At the same time, that "first" (but not necessarily) individual's success becomes what talent scouts, coaches, front office managers, and fans begin to look for. So the success of Olajuwon, Mutombo, Drogba, Loroupe, Ndereba, and others constructs the trope of "the black African athlete" in ways that are both similar to and different from "the black athlete" in the West, depending on which discourses are invoked. For example, we have already seen how Olajuwon and Mutombo were questioned as to whether they could be tough enough (physically strong enough) to play at the college or NBA level. As a contrast, Drogba's size and strength play to well-established notions of "the black athlete," which only contributes to teams wanting to find the "next" Drogba in "Africa." We can even consider that Drogba's success changes the representation, what was thought possible, of "the black African athlete" on the soccer pitch, as he becomes the standard by which other black (African) players are judged—such as Arouna Kone, Wilfried Bony, Christian Benteke, and Romelu Lukaku (who again was said to have "idolized" Drogba while growing up in Belgium). Yet ultimately we come full circle to see that all of the problems of "the black athlete" remain in place, even in the instances of Mutombo and Olajuwon.

From a broader viewpoint, we can see these athletes as meaning something not only to other African athletes but to their respective countries and Africa in general. For example, both Didier Drogba and Dikembe Mutombo receive a great deal of attention when they go to their home countries of Ivory Coast and the Democratic Republic of Congo, respectively. Their visits include fanfare, meetings with high-ranking state officials (including the president or head of state), and, more sobering, people sleeping outside of their hotels and residences. Hence these athletes transcend sport and mean something quite different, or greater, than just an athlete, even if it relates in large part to their assumed wealth.

> When Mutombo goes home, he hands out money to relatives and strangers. "He is a big, big man with a much bigger heart," Mitifu, the Congolese ambassador, said. During his visit to Kinshasa two years ago, hundreds of people camped outside the hotel. "They come to cheer him because they are so proud of him," she said. "They come so they can at least shake his hand. He has always tried to shake as many hands as he could."[20]

> The youth of Ivory Coast love Drogba. Every time he returns to Abidjan airport now, he is swamped by media and fans, top of the television news, feted wherever he goes. Drogbacité—or Drogbaness, in English—is a cultural phenomenon in music and dance that shows no signs of disappearing, even though the Elephants, the national team,

did not get past the first round in Germany 2006. He is a symbol of success in life, the first Ivorian pro footballer who has been talked of like this. There is so much publicity around him and his performances that influences the life of young people. There are songs in which they sing his name. The way he dresses—the young copy it.[21]

It is clear that these athletes mean something, a great deal perhaps, to the people of their respective countries and, in various ways, to the African continent at large. Künzler and Poli explain that watching Drogba's games is an intense, insatiable interest for poor youths in particular and fuels the desire for other Western products.[22] Yet as I have argued earlier, reporting on the interventions and activities of humanitarian athletes often falls in line with the White Savior Industrial Complex or the older concept of the "white man's burden." The inevitable political complexities that come with trying to deliver the kind of aid that Drogba and Mutombo are attempting go unreported. In the aforementioned presentation at the University of Georgia, Mutombo explained some of the unforeseen difficulties he encountered when trying to build his hospital. Despite getting the land, permits, and tax breaks from the government, he encountered problems with the government feeling "embarrassed" by Mutombo overshadowing them and paying doctors and nurses more than those in state hospitals.[23] Mutombo also explained how his efforts to build a well in order for the hospital to get away from paying the city (Kinshasa) for water resulted in the government demanding payment because the hospital was still using the resources of the state. Mutombo accused the state of trying to get his money because he was a famous basketball player while ignoring the fact that he was helping thousands of the state's people essentially for free. "Politically, it was a little bit difficult for people to accept it," he said. "A lot of people felt it was something behind the project. 'Why this young African want to do something that has never been done on the continent of Africa?' The question was why, why, why, why, why? There was concern that I was going to try to run for office. I am not in politics. 'President Mutombo?' No, no, no. There has never been a politician in my family, and I am not going to try to be the first one."[24]

It is unrealistic for the media to raise the question of black African migrant athletes running for office, assuming that because they have gained wealth in the West that they are somehow equipped to insert themselves into inevitably political projects or national politics in general. To some degree the athletes perhaps even convince themselves that it would be easy. The discourse of the White Savior Industrial Complex is pervasive when it comes to simplifying causes concerning African countries. In the cases of Mutombo and Drogba, they seem to get more accomplished because of their immense fame and because they are not overtly expressing political opinions on leadership or policy. If they were to enter the political process by running for office we might expect the state reception to their humanitarian activities to change.

Yet the flow of youth into sport as an opportunity for economic gain, as opposed to education, is not a positive development. If increased access to sport by African Americans, even at institutions of higher education, is any indication, then we can look forward to, and already experience, problems of exploitation. What we have seen since the years of colonialism across the African continent is a gradual decay of the school systems at every level and fewer jobs to accommodate those who do receive a college degree. Ali Mazrui notes that various dictators and their fears of academics can in part be blamed on the dismantling of African institutions of higher learning.[25] Of course there remains the problems of underdevelopment and the continuation of neocolonial policies that limit the sovereignty of the African nation-state. The concurrent devaluation of African education by Western institutions has a significant impact on the lives of recent African immigrants to the West. Hence, with limited economic opportunities because of these complex factors, we begin to see sport overtaking education in the minds of youths who want to succeed. Sport is nothing if not a low-cost entry into a hard manual labor lottery. Though the excitement and emphasis on education that accompanied the wave of African independence still exists, the results have more recently been underwhelming. What the immense popularity of the African athlete in Africa reflects is a grasp for meaning and self-value in a Western-oriented world that has otherwise ghettoized Africa and black peoples in general. The success of these athletes is thus symbolic of the desire to achieve, whether that be by braving the trip by sea to Mediterranean countries or migrating from the rural areas to the growing urban slums to try for a better life and opportunity.

Black African Athletes and the Diaspora

Despite the increasing presence of black African (im)migrant athletes in the West, their relationship and meaning to diasporic black African immigrant communities is rarely explored in the media. In this respect, they are often made to mean something only for their particular African country or the African continent as a whole, as the previous section indicated. However, we do know they mean *something* to diasporic communities, even if it is often hidden from us by neglect. Black Atlantic processes of cultural exchange are perhaps most evident in the realms of music and fashion, but those forms are not often given mainstream attention. As popular sport exists in spaces where other cultural forms are absent, we can read it for how these cultural exchanges are ignored and when they slip through the cracks of the dominant discourse. In this section I bring to the forefront moments when the media allows us to partially see how those in the diaspora make meaning out of the black African migrant athlete.

"I was never really into [watching the Ivory Coast] until Drogba came because he's at an amazing level at the world. He put the Ivory Coast on the map for soccer," said Bell, 17, a Grade 11 student at St. George's secondary school. . . . Bell was born in Ottawa but his mother comes from the Ivory Coast. . . . At age five Bell moved to Vancouver but still frequently visits Ivory Coast's capital Abidjan where he has family. . . . "It's pretty nice. It's not the common conception people have of Africa. It's very developed. You'll see parks and places with soccer fields [all over]," Bell said. . . . "The Ivory Coast was never really at that [elite] level of soccer before Drogba and Kalou. . . . Everyone in the Ivory Coast is really proud of them." . . . Bell said he's looking forward to trying out next year for his school's soccer team. And as a symbol of his roots he plans on sewing an Ivory Coast flag to his grad jacket next year.[26]

We can see that the (successful) migrant athlete has the potential to become a point of cultural attachment for youths in the diaspora. Despite this recognition of attachment, Bell remains problematically tied to his Ivory Coast "roots." The growing black African population in Ottawa—as in the United States and Canada more generally—goes unacknowledged. Bell and his family remain singular and separate from his location in the West, only to find attachment with Drogba—who is here again situated firmly in Ivory Coast ("Africa"). Hence the ongoing theme of "Africa for Africans" is reaffirmed even when we can read a different reality in the background. Full representation (visibility) thus remains elusive and we are left with a carefully managed (segregated) visibility.[27] In a similar fashion, Mutombo does not go unnoticed by black African immigrants when he plays in Philadelphia—a city with a very long and significant history of black immigration, both native and foreign. This history too goes unacknowledged throughout Mutombo's time spent in Philadelphia.

> "I would fight for Mutombo," declares Bokulaka, who directs the International Eteko Bonyoma, a Congolese dance company. "He is our star. We are family. Brother, sister, no difference." . . . Bokulaka is trying to explain why Mutombo is so revered among the Congolese above the pitch of a steel drum at the Third World nightclub in West Philly. A slender Ugandan man collects a cover charge, while a robust Liberian woman does brisk business selling pork kabobs well into the wee hours. It's a modest spot, a place where Mutombo could probably enjoy himself—if he had the time. . . . "Everything Mutombo do is for us," says Bokulaka. "When Mutombo do something, people say, 'Do you see your brother?'" . . . "It takes a very big person to admit that where they're from is not that great and they want to help improve it," notes John Idi, a businessman who emigrated from Nigeria 13 years ago. "A lot of Africans don't want to admit that or they're ambivalent about it."[28]

We can see that Mutombo elicits strong feelings and appears to encourage self-reflection among recent migrants to the Philadelphia area. These responses to Mutombo are particularly resonant with Mutombo's later feelings on the election of Barack Obama in 2008, when he stated that "we have the son of an African man, not from a second or third generation, from the first generation. . . . It means a lot for Africans. I've had deep conversations with many African friends and they are very, very proud to see this history."[29] Mutombo draws explicit attention to the fact that Obama is the son of a first-generation African immigrant and the meaning that has to his African friends. This intersection of being black and foreign in a country where blackness occupies such a marginalized position is not lost on Mutombo or the immigrants quoted above. For Mutombo, the generational status of Obama is what seems to mean the most as it regards the future possibilities for his children, indicating to him that the efforts of (im)migration were not in vain. While it remains possible to be skeptical of the material impact of Obama, the symbolic meaning of his election clearly resonated with both native and foreign black populations. This is another example of the second generation having the ability to pull together similar narratives of blackness in a moment of racial awareness. As we will see with Balotelli, Obama's multiple subject positions make him available to a wide range of peoples and backgrounds in order to make meaning, create identity, and practice resistance in their everyday lives.

These celebrity figures are important to the black African (im)migrant community and its great diversity. At the end of the long quote above we get a sense of the difficult relationship many African immigrants have with their countries of birth. While every individual is different—especially among the athletes in this study—many African immigrants feel ambivalent about their countries of birth because they know how Africa and Africans are represented in Western media. Much of this ambivalence is rooted in an internalized antiblack (post)colonial ideology, or the double consciousness that is required in the black African diaspora.[30] In trying to correct for that negative imagery African immigrants—especially those who represent unskilled or semiskilled labor—may seek to either distance themselves from or artificially elevate their native country and culture, depending on context. The effort to negotiate white supremacy and a foreign labor market requires a nuanced politics of identity.

Abdulrafi, a program analyst, keeps a picture of Hakeem in his office, and proudly displays it to co-workers. "In the picture he's wearing a kufi and his eyes are cast downward, very modestly. . . . He's been down a rocky road, but when he came back and recommitted himself to Islam, his game sharpened. When I show people the picture, I tell them, this is what Islam can do for a person." . . . Musab, 16, follows basketball religiously. "I am proud to be Muslim when I see him play." . . . "When you look at most role models, you like what they do, but when you meet them or find out about their personal lives, you realize they're different from you, and some things they do, you can't do," says Faraaz Ahmed, 12. "But if he's Muslim, it's just perfect." . . . Muslim kids have a lack of visible role models in this country, believes Abdulrafi, father of eight. "Now I can say to my kids, I don't mind if you become a basketball player, as long as you model yourself after him."[31]

As with Mutombo, we are told that Olajuwon acts as a meaningful figure for Muslims in America, particularly youths. While this is at least partially true, the dominance of Islam in his representation tends to cloud the possibility for other points of attachment concerning race and immigration status. The essentialized nature of identity is reinforced as Olajuwon's racial status as "black" gets displaced by "Islam." Any notion of the interplay between black Americans, native and foreign Muslims, black Americans, and basketball as a sport with appeal to economically marginalized communities goes unexplored. The narrative above also plays into Olajuwon's practice of Islam as good, correct, and proper while also keeping Islam foreign to the Western state. That foreign and native Muslims are drawn to Olajuwon as a role model perhaps says less about Olajuwon and more about the struggle to find a place for one's self in society. The racial discrimination and violence faced by Muslims in America, even after 9/11, goes unexplored in the representation of Olajuwon. That he is allowed to be a "positive" role model demonstrates the policing of the Muslim community in America in that they must be careful which figures they affiliate with out of fear of repercussions and social exclusion. This is demonstrated no better than in Olajuwon's intersection with Mahmoud Abdul-Rauf, whereby Rauf's anti-imperial views mark him as a "bad" Muslim and prompted some in the Muslim community to verbally distance themselves from him via respectability politics.[32]

Some caution, then, is required when trying to read what is happening in these representations. On one hand, I do not doubt that these athletes are looked up to in the diaspora, particularly because they are some of the first and most successful athletes to represent black Africans and Muslims in popular Western sport. As another example, NFL Films produced an episode of *A Football Life* that focused on the career of Christian Okoye.[33] At the end of the forty-five-minute production we are given around five minutes of generation 1.5–2.0 Nigerian and Nigerian American NFL players discussing how Okoye gave them someone to look up to throughout their football careers. The list includes Johnson Bademosi, Prince Amukamara, Emmanuel Acho, James Ihedigbo, Nnamdi Asomugha, Sam Acho, Amobi Okoye, Osi Umenyiora, Brian Orakpo, and Israel Idonije. Interviewed individually, they briefly mention various activities such as their parents looking up Nigerians when they started getting into football and becoming aware of Christian Okoye, finding the "Nigerian Nightmare" nickname cool, and, for example, making it part of their email address, finding pride in his accomplishments, seeing that someone from their background could make it to the NFL, and knowing that their names could indeed be pronounced properly. Their statements are again terribly partial—limited to sentence-long quips—and they raise many of the same critiques as above, but they do speak to processes of meaning making in the diaspora. On the other hand, there is a careful policing of these (athletic) figures as well, which makes their "choosing" by those in the diaspora at least partly conditioned by the terms set forth by white supremacy. The athletes who are "good role models" are those who are already acceptable or accepted by the West, yet they also represent—to (im)migrants—that it is possible to get along in a society structured by white supremacy and that individuals "like them" have indeed succeeded. Despite this unsaid intention of Western media to pin the foreign Other into certain modes of identification, the possibility always remains for more radical forms of attachment and resistance, as seen in case of Mario Balotelli.

Balotelli, of all the athletes in my study, has perhaps had the biggest impact on popular culture—if only for a short time. Though early on he actively disavowed his Ghanaian parentage, he later affirmed his pride in being black and supported efforts to end racism in football. He also openly gave his support to the first black minister in the Italian Parliament, Cecile Kyenge, who faced racist and misogynistic harassment following her election to office. At one point Balotelli went as far as saying that being racially abused could see him turn to violence in response. "If someone throws a banana at me in the street I will go to prison because I will kill him," Balotelli said, adding, "I'm black and proud to have African roots. I think I'm lucky to be black. People say about me that I'm a black boy who has fun, earns money and has girls. It's not like that. It's too easy to judge people through what you see."[34]

Balotelli has often gone away from the well-known "script" in sport, and very quickly he became a popular cultural icon. For Western media he represents a contradiction in that he is a poor sportsman ("bad black") and yet also an example of social change in Italy, an individual through which debates on immigration, nationalism, and racism can take place. In short, he becomes a means through which to shame "racists" and Italian, Southern, and Eastern European society for "being" racist. As noted in previous chapters, this labeling of Southern and Eastern Europe as racist by Western media is hypocritical in light of its own racist undertones in covering Balotelli. However, for those in the African diaspora, Balotelli's frequent confrontations with racism reflect a familiar social experience. We can look to Balotelli's inclusion in popular music forms as establishing his value as a point of identity formation. The song and music video by Tinchy Stryder and Ruff Sqwad titled "Why Always Me?" revolves around a T-shirt with that same question that Balotelli displayed under his uniform after scoring a goal against Manchester United in 2011. The chorus to the song goes as follows:

We mean no malice, we need a challenge
The media say we are savage and we are callous
When we go at it, leave it damaged, believe in magic

They hope we burn, the thought is tragic, the thought is tragic

Why always me? Why always me?
Why always me? Why always me?
I'm screaming why always me? Why always me?
Why always me? Why always me? Mario Balotelli[35]

Balotelli later explained that the T-shirt was a message to the media concerning his feeling that he was being treated unfairly by the English tabloids. The song makes the link between Balotelli's victimization and criminalization and that of black men in England generally. That the artists are, similar to Balotelli, predominantly second-generation Ghanaian and have a relatively good amount of popularity within British hip-hop/rap/grime culture demonstrates the recognition of a common struggle against media attention and representation. Whereas the other athletes in my analysis entered pop culture in various ways—many of the men have had their names invoked in hip-hop or rap songs, Mutombo and Olajuwon each had his own shoe in the 1990s (both of which have recently been reissued), and Lornah Kiplagat has recently launched a clothing line—Balotelli, more than any other, has found meaning among increasingly hybridized black artists and within popular black culture. Of course, with Balotelli being so heavily criticized and subject to a normalizing gaze, there was the inevitable backlash to a song focusing on Balotelli's actions in a positive light. As Balotelli's action in revealing his shirt was criminalized in the first place—a sign of his poor sportsmanship—there was a general sense of sarcasm and eye-rolling in the media concerning the Ruff Sqwad song. That Balotelli would be seen as cool or a popular icon—later linked with the American rapper Drake—is not in line with the media narrative that has invested in the representation of Balotelli as a figure worthy of our derision. Any effort to turn Balotelli into a symbolic figure reflecting the racial injustices of the West is treated with a distinct skepticism reflecting the color-blind norms of the day. Balotelli may reflect racial problems in Italy or elsewhere in Europe, but in the West, the United Kingdom specifically, there are no such problems and it is irrational to think that there are—or so we are told.

Another incident related to Balotelli concerns a trip with the Italian national team to Brazil a year before the 2014 World Cup. Balotelli took time one evening to visit some of the Brazilian children he was then sponsoring as part of a charity effort. What is compelling about Balotelli's visit to the children is that the rest of the Italian national team was, in essence, under curfew. Because of recent protests against Brazil's hosting of the 2014 World Cup and the social disruptions that inevitably occurred, the Italian team was not allowed out after nightfall. This applied to the entire team except Balotelli, who reportedly told the coach, Cesare Prandelli, that he would be okay in the Salvador region of Bahia in Brazil (a population with a large percentage of African ancestry) because he is black. "Mario told me: 'Being black, I'd like to go to see the children for a social project.' . . . Later, Balotelli wrote on his Twitter account: 'salvador!! i look like a person from Bahia!!! [sic].'"[36] Despite jokes made by Prandelli and the humorous way in which the events were reported, we can reread the incident and the salient racial understandings in another way. Never was it questioned why the (white) Italians would not be able to go out at night; there was an obvious assumption of danger given the recent protests—often labeled riots—but also the assumed racial and class composition of those protests. The latter is indicated by the commonsense idea that Balotelli would of course be fine among the populace because he is black, otherwise it would not make sense to bring his skin color into play. There is a criminalization of blackness as well as protest here, from which Balotelli is apparently immune. I would imagine that the white Italian players could have gone with Balotelli if they wished, but it was overdetermined as too dangerous.

Conversely, however, I would argue that Balotelli recognizes that he may very well be "safe" (though not from the police) not only because he is black but also because he stands for something else and is involved in Brazilian society through his charitable efforts. Balotelli exists as a diasporic athlete whose struggles and accomplishments are not likely lost on those of the black and African diaspora in Brazil who are fighting against white supremacy in a society that tells them race is unimportant. Thus Balotelli is safe at night in Brazil not necessarily because he is black, as Western media would lead us to believe, but rather because he is in part seen as a person who is similarly fighting racial oppression.

Coalition Building

It may be beneficial to try to think a little differently about black African migrant athletes in Western societies and their individual actions and impact. As athletic labor migration from African countries to the West will only continue, we would ideally like to see some development of community and coalition building between different black communities as well as white allies. Despite the often confusing and contradictory ways in which foreign and native black athletes are represented and separated, at certain moments we can see activity toward common goals that impact both groups. For example, Drogba is active in antiracism campaigns in soccer and has spoken out against racism not only on the field but in how Africans, and blacks generally, are paid less by their teams and endorsers. In his autobiography, Drogba discusses racism and the "immigrant experience" as he experienced them growing up in France, yet this topic receives only cursory attention in his wider media representation.[37] In this kind of activism he is often joined by other black players, both foreign and native (most notably, Lilian Thuram), who have experienced racism from the stands (terraces). Often this antiracist activity on the part of black players is a part of initiatives by European soccer leagues to "kick out" racism from stadiums. These initiatives tend to stress education and awareness. However, some black players have refused to take part in these "kick out" efforts because they are predictably ineffective and do not go far enough to address structural problems of racism in soccer. Often cited are the small amounts of fines that the Union of European Football Associations (UEFA) hands out for racism during matches compared to the much larger fines given for player actions that violate corporate sponsorship policies.[38]

Relatedly, Mutombo has been involved in getting African and African American NBA players to join him when he travels to the Democratic Republic of Congo or attends basketball camps sponsored by the NBA or the International Basketball Federation (FIBA) in different African countries. Players such as Shaquille O'Neil, Luc Mbah a

Moute, Tracy McGrady, Patrick Ewing, Alonzo Mourning, and others have joined Mutombo or traveled with similar programs. Many athletes of first- and second-generation African origin playing in the NBA also participate in such programs. Of course, what these activities mean or could mean goes unmentioned, and the institutions that contribute to African underdevelopment and black poverty in the West go unchallenged. Corporate concerns blunt any subversive potential of the athletes and programs through the commodification of black athletes. The NBA, FIBA, and other sports leagues, as well as a multitude of corporations, may donate millions to an athlete's charity or help set up camps, but they also expect to gain access to a new market and sell a lot of their product. When Mutombo lamented that he had not received many individual donations for his hospital he also noted that he had received donations from many corporations, like "Turner, Chevron, Mobil . . . they want to be represented. By contributing to this hospital they send the word to the rest of Africa."[39] And as previously mentioned, Drogba has benefited in his own efforts from companies like Coca-Cola, Samsung, and the cocoa industry.[40] Perhaps there is something to be said about working within the established system—indeed, my argument is not that these programs should rethink themselves to address global structural issues, because they were not designed to do so; instead they end up promoting a rhetoric that only maintains the current system—but we already know what kind of "development" will occur when the money being given is tied to the interests of corporate giants. That type of development is reflected in the poorly thought out emphasis on education that is ostensibly at the center of many of these programs, particularly those related to the NBA. Specifically, there are tensions between the establishment of NBA/FIBA basketball camps in Africa, their being "packaged" with educational and development programs (usually HIV/AIDS awareness), and the notion that basketball provides educational opportunities in the West, the United States in particular.

> The Africa 100 Camp is about more than basketball. In between individual drills in the morning and games in the evening, players will work with the American contingent on community service projects.

And seminars about life skills, staying away from drugs, and HIV/ AIDS prevention will be held. On Sept. 4, the N.B.A. will unveil its first Reading and Learning Center outside North America. . . . Desktop computers, printers, servers and other educational software will also be donated by Dell. . . . "The saying goes that in Africa, 'If you save one player, you save a thousand,' because he gives back so much," Bohuny said.[41]

I would question the efficacy of any "development" program putting the responsibility of thousands on one individual. Somewhat ironically, these articles often include "African" sayings or "proverbs" that, despite seeming timeless, are necessarily recent formulations that only further reduce and mystify "Africa." The language of saviordom and Africa's "need" for expertise are also apparent, which is a way of viewing those in need that strips them of their agency. We are also led to believe that the current state of "Africa" is African (black) degeneracy due to corruption, drug use, and sex. Thus we may wonder what, aside from increasing the popularity of the NBA, is the point of these camps in African countries. If education is ultimately the answer—(or *an* answer), as basketball will allow only a few athletes to, essentially, "escape" Africa or be "saved" from it—then perhaps the NBA should invest more in schools than basketball courts. If only a handful of these players even end up at American universities and colleges, then the notion that sport offers a "way out" is perhaps more misguided than we think.[42] After all, in the United States we are often told that sport represents an opportunity for African Americans to get out of the "ghetto," yet it offers dismal results. Despite Mutombo's participation in these camps and his predilection toward them, when questioned as to why he himself built a hospital instead of basketball courts, he responded that people cannot do anything without health.[43] The lottery ticket that basketball, and sport in general, represents for the lives of the poor all over the world should not overshadow the fact that basic human needs deserve our attention first and foremost. That sport is even considered a viable way out of poverty or means of getting an education is indicative of the current state of global inequality.

However, through these camps and the coverage they receive we get glimpses of the kind of connections that are being made between Africans and African Americans, as well as white Americans, through Americans' visits to African countries. For Alvin Gentry and Bob McAdoo, African American NBA coaches on a trip with Mutombo, the similarities between what native black South Africans were going through and what African Americans in the United States experienced were obvious.

> In South Africa, they saw townships where blacks are forced to live without electricity and running water. "The thing that was toughest for me was I met so many kids I thought had unlimited potential in a lot of areas," Alvin Gentry said. "Very bright, very talented, very personable kids, who I don't think will ever have a chance to succeed. In a way, it's the same thing I see in kids who hang outside the (Miami) Arena." . . . For McAdoo, 43, the racism brought back memories of growing up in Greensboro, N.C. . . . "I saw this in the United States. I lived through this."[44]

For the most part, comments such as the one above are not the focal point of the article from which they were pulled, as we might expect, but they point to the idea that if experiences are shared between different black populations and communities then we can begin to build some sense of shared understanding. This process, however, remains frustrated by the persistent lack of information coming from African countries and its perceived irrelevance to those in the West. In the end these camps are not designed to change the current political landscape at any level. While they may help some individuals find their way to a scholarship in America, the growing underside of African recruitment is exploitation and human trafficking. Those involved at both ends are increasingly interested in the economic payoff of finding a top recruit and hoping he makes it all the way to the NBA.[45] Hence it is difficult to argue that there is movement toward any kind of coherent social movement or awareness among those engaged in this diasporic activity—for example, despite Drogba's efforts on racism he, along with many other athletes, declined to sign on to a pro-Palestinian petition from Frédéric Kanouté (a fellow diasporic footballer) because he did not want to get involved in politics. So, regardless of the intermixture and cultural mixing that occurs throughout the African diaspora, we should expect the complexities of various African histories, individual experiences, and the racialization of different black subjects (and their associated identities formed in response) to impact the formation and awareness of "blackness" at every level—local, national, and global. We must also remain aware of the fact that the emphasis on unity and affinity in many diasporic texts does not necessarily reflect the contradictions and antagonisms within black diasporic populations (concerning origin, generation, gender, sexuality, etc.) at these different levels— particularly the local.[46]

Conclusion

In this chapter I have explored diasporic processes of meaning making, identity, and coalition building in the cracks within the discourses concerning the athletes in my study. It should be clear that these diasporic processes, their existence and complexities, are passively hidden from nonwhite Others because the discourses are not for "us." In thinking more on the theme of diaspora, if sport is to have antiracist humanist or radical democratic potential then those involved in sport must think beyond the nation-state and foster a notion of diasporic community based on common experiences of oppression as well as notions of hybridity and intermixture. This process is, obviously, no easy feat, as there are no permanent ways forward and many perils to avoid. As Gilroy identifies, the internalization of stereotypes, commodification of race consciousness, hierarchies of oppression, static conceptions of race, and claims of authenticity are all problems that have plagued the development of a coherent notion of and movement toward an antiracist humanism.[47] Western media's influence in creating and maintaining these perils cannot be overlooked. The representations I discuss throughout this book construct division and resentment between blacks and whites and among different black subjects. The representation of the successes of black African athletes despite their "primal" and "horrific" experiences in Africa creates hierarchies of oppression that make black diasporic coalition building more difficult. As I have argued, such constructions confuse and essentialize various elements of blackness and the black (immigrant) experience. Michelle Wright, discussing the creation of the black Other in Western philosophy, explains that while various Others can result from different forms of racism, such as "the Other-from-within" (native blacks) and "the Other-from-without" (foreign blacks), they are "conflated rather than discretely defined and, most importantly, . . . *one* racial group can have different types of alterity placed on it depending on which textual agenda locates it as Other."[48] The processes of reifying race are thus mutable over time yet accomplish the same end.

Wright goes on, similar to Gilroy, to denounce discourses of authenticity and homogeneity that often plague black diasporic identity, or nationalism, by explicitly denouncing the heteropatriarchal formations of these discourses while bringing issues of gender, sexuality, and class alongside those of race. In the end, blackness, or the black subject, cannot rely on exclusivity if it is to avoid the pitfalls of discourses that created black Otherness in the first place. If we are to establish meaningful ties and representation for all within the black diaspora then black discourse must recognize difference and reach beyond the limits of nation, gender, and sexuality in order to make links with black (and brown and other nonwhite) communities throughout the diaspora.

Concurrently, the lack of information coming from the African continent (not by "its" fault) is also problematic. While diasporic black leaders and celebrities, past and present, are often well known around the world and to those in African countries, the reverse cannot be said. Very few African leaders, entertainers, or athletes are well known to those in the diaspora—although perhaps athletes are better known than others. Though the one-way nature of this information flow is slowly changing, often virtually via web content, it has historically meant missed opportunities for understanding and coalition building in the black diaspora, meaning that the information is still not readily available to either diasporic communities or (non)whites in general.[49] These issues are further complicated when we consider that the issues confronting black communities and blackness are always worked out in the public sphere of popular culture and thus are subject to intervention and manipulation by white supremacist discourses. The public nature of these issues means that antiracist humanism and radical democracy consistently face the normalizing cultural and political pressures of the dominant neoliberal ruling order. These pressures have made deviant and irrational the historically black political tactics of protest and ideological resistance, particularly forms with socialist leanings—this is no better demonstrated than in the current (2014–16) white backlash against the #BlackLivesMatter movement, which has been labeled as a racist "hate group" by some U.S. media pundits. Though sport remains a contested terrain and often maintains racial stereotypes, it is one of the only avenues of cultural production and diasporic communication open to people of color.[50] Hence it retains a measure of potential for positive political transformation. As Howard Winant explains, the current political correctness of being color-blind is gradually becoming untenable as racial inequality persists and even worsens.[51]

7

The Sporting Migrant

Antiblack Racism and the Foreign Other

Paul Gilroy has continually tried to compel us to think "beyond" race, not because we are actually "beyond race" but because our conceptions of race are hurtful to our progress as human beings on this planet. His innovative work in *Against Race* implores us, in the end, to seriously consider those (Afro-futuristic) futures where our interactions with alien races truly make our present conceptions of race and racism obsolete. We should think about and figuratively "bring back" those futures to our present day in various forms to inform and educate "us" about our possibilities—in whatever forms we possibly can. At the local level he has argued for an "everydayness" to the multicultural experiences urban dwellers have within the global cities of the West. Gilroy's notion of "conviviality," scattered throughout his texts, compels us to recognize a comfortableness with change and the racial Other that is generally occurring within (post)colonial metropoles. While the forces of postcolonial melancholy resist the demographic changes brought by continual (im)migration and rest on nostalgic notions of the subservient colonial Other, it is an ongoing and necessary struggle to engage in antiracist, or "planetary humanism," practices even when they currently seem rather improbable—something that Stuart Hall has also noted.[1] Thus it is a requirement to recognize the processes of antiblack racism while acknowledging that a reliance on essentialized notions of race are difficult, ultimately, to work around in order to bring about social change. It is not that we should not recognize race or racism but that our end goal should be to eradicate race as the coherent subject it has often been taken as by successive generations throughout the world.

While in some ways African athletes give those in the diaspora more, or different, cultural resources, they do little if they are not moving us toward a better understanding of the marginality of blackness and, ideally, toward an antiracist humanism. A few of the athletes in my study move us toward the former, but it is difficult to say that any move us explicitly toward the latter. As mentioned earlier, Drogba speaks out on racism toward black athletes, but when asked by Frédéric Kanouté to sign a player petition against Israel's treatment of Palestinians he stated that he does not take political sides, even in his own country.[2] Mutombo is a great advocate for the Congo and Africa but yet, perhaps wisely, seems to realize that his efforts depend on certain discourses of Western charity that are often simplistic, stereotypical, and homogenizing and thus goes no further. Olajuwon frequently states that we are all equal and human, but he at times slips into a religious discourse that is inherently problematic, as with all religions, due to its demands based on scripture. Loroupe speaks out against African patriarchy in general, but neither she nor the other women (or men) in my study explicitly deal with the intersection of race, gender, and nation. Perhaps Balotelli gets us the closest by being such a focal point of racial animus through no fault of his own and because his being reflects back to the diaspora its own hybridization. Time will tell, although it appears his career is faltering. Yes, diasporic African athletes, by their mere presence, do work against nationalist understandings of spatial boundaries and rooted belonging, but the nature of sport, celebrity, and media often prevents athletes from being politically resistive figures.[3]

The celebrity-industrial complex that aims to routinize the process of producing celebrity athletes relies on narratives and storylines that audiences can interact with in various ways. Wrapping the celebrity athlete with Western cultural values represents a process of commodification that seeks a conservative durability and endless promotional opportunities. The celebrity athlete becomes a tool, or symbol, of the hegemonic neoliberal economic regime, a representation of consumer freedom and hyperindividualism primarily directed toward straight, middle-class white men. As creations of the West, the representations of African celebrity athletes in my study, through their stereotypical descriptors, reflect the bias of these (racialized) processes toward blackness, African peoples, and African countries.[4] My arguments throughout this book document a number of both subtle and overt ways in which foreign and native blacks are made different and similar depending on the situation. It becomes clear that native blacks represent "blackness" and that it is that "blackness" from which foreign blacks, black (im)migrants, attempt to distance themselves. Of course, they can never truly escape blackness because of the color of their skin and they come from geographic areas racially coded as "black." The reliance on easy narratives and single stories betrays the construction of celebrity athletes as serving the needs of Western corporate neoliberalism. These single stories celebrate the West and its individualist consumerism but also maintain the continued social exclusion of the (foreign) black Other. As mentioned near the beginning of the book, we can confidently extend this kind of research to include all marginalized and postcolonial peoples around the world, whether Maoris in New Zealand, Indigenous Australians in Australia, First Nations in Canada, Latinos in the United States, or Asians in Europe, while including a range of (more or less globalized) sports, such as baseball, basketball, soccer, rugby, distance running, and so on. These populations and their marginalized racial (foreign or native) statuses are variously articulated by global, local, and transnational processes of race, racism, and identity; (im)migration laws and citizenship; sport governing bodies; and capital markets and corporate media. In these ways the study of sport can at times allow us to see what is usually hidden from us on a daily basis: the inner workings of a globalized world.

With the West becoming more racially and ethnically diverse, investigating the processes by which blackness is remarginalized remains an imperative. If greater diversity can lead to better understanding and comfort with racial difference, then an antiracist humanism may very well be possible. African athletes are no longer the novelty they once were, and the second generation is clouding divisions that were once stark contrasts. Even within this study, however, the ability of white supremacist discourse to modify and place different modes of alterity on the foreign black Other should give us pause. Despite growing diversity within Western black populations, blackness continues to be constructed as a homogeneous whole. We also know that, because of colonialism, small numerical minorities of whites have maintained control over vast majorities of nonwhites. A numerical population shift in racial demographics as the twenty-first century advances may not mean greater access to power or racial awareness—or the destruction of various racisms—so long as the creation and distribution of what is accepted as "knowledge" or "news" remains in the hands of white elites. Thus the operation of antiblack racism and immigration fears within communities of color remains an obstacle to overcome. The legacies of slavery and colonialism and the current domination of global capitalism and neoliberalism have been neither properly addressed nor fully exhausted.

It can be difficult to know whether to have hope or to despair. Richard Iton explains that though work in the cultural spheres of production is often exploitative and devoid of ownership, these spheres are still important spaces that give minorities a voice of resistance they otherwise are prevented from having. In Western societies, the intrusion of white supremacist discourse into black and brown political efforts seeks to limit political action to those historical forms of protest that have been rendered obsolete.[5] At least that is what we are told by those very same discourses that decry public demonstrations and protests as harmful and counterproductive. Instead we are urged to wait (change takes time), be respectable (do not offend white liberals), and vote (where the energy of social movements goes to die). The nagging question, then, is whether giving marginalized peoples access to the cultural realm can and will be enough. In recent years we have seen something of a resurgence of political acts and statements by black athletes, women and men, protesting the continued violence visited upon black communities by the state, the police, and armed white men. Many of these examples of resistance within sport are tied to the now-global social justice movement #BlackLivesMatter, which has made gains in raising awareness of criminal justice abuses, developing potential political reforms, and pushing for the resignation of public officials or voting them out of office. In what has become a truly transnational movement we have seen #BlackLivesMatter protests bring attention to antiblack racism in Palestine, Israel, Canada, and South Africa and throughout European capitals. At the heart of this spread is the shared realization of oppression and circuits of familial migration throughout the black diaspora.

Such transnational movements remain crucial because throughout the twentieth century Western capitalist interests were highly effective in destroying the political left and rendering mute the political voice of the cultural sphere. Among efforts aimed at calls for black empowerment alone, artists, actors, musicians, and athletes were followed and harassed by the state—particularly the Federal Bureau of Investigation's Counter Intelligence Program (COINTELPRO)—at the least suspicion that they were engaging in antigovernment, socialist, or communist activities. As inequality has only grown in the twenty-first century, race has become an even more effective tool to pit poor, working-class, and middle-class whites—who have been marginalized in the global economy as well—against the ongoing struggles of black and brown minorities. While working-class and poor whites are critical of the "political correctness" and condescension of white elites, recent events have demonstrated that politicians "boldly" speaking their minds degrade the quality of political conversation on both the right and left. That protesting athletes or #BlackLivesMatter activists are routinely denounced by mainstream media pundits as the ones who are "really" being racist toward whites or hateful toward police only serves to maintain white supremacy. Such discourse gives life to the notion that whites are somehow the oppressed group and need to come together to "reclaim" what once was. The retreat into a mythological past by many whites is perhaps no more evident than in the backlash against efforts to remove the Confederate flag from public places after the white supremacist terrorist attack that claimed the lives of eight black individuals inside a South Carolina church in 2015. After the attack photos emerged of the shooter posing with Confederate flags and other racist paraphernalia. Not only did sales of Confederate flags skyrocket, but seemingly overnight flags better suited for flagpoles were attached to the back of trucks driving around my small town. To be clear, there is no place for black Americans within these romanticized Confederate dramas except as violent criminals, rapists of white women, and slaves. It is an old story that has proven remarkably stubborn in all of its varied forms. That white supremacy (under the guise of the "Alt-Right") has been mainstreamed by the Donald Trump presidential campaign (and his subsequent election) and by corporate media outlets eager to reap profits from his racist/sexist/xenophobic/ableist statements is, at first glance, dumbfounding, but it is understandable when we look at our history of racial politics and our inability to deal with, or even understand, white supremacy.

Across Europe, we see other evidence of the retrenchment of white supremacy and blatantly overt racist discourse, much as in the United States. Whether in the specific examples of the United Kingdom's exit from the European Union (Brexit), the continued presence and apparently growing popularity of the far-right National Front in France (and similar groups in other countries), or the more general fear of the nonwhite immigrant Other "overrunning" Europe, the situation appears to be reaching a head or at least moving toward a tipping point. How long can Western democracies increasingly militarize and erode civil rights in their own societies against the very threats and forms of unrest that both global and local militarization cause? Our current situation of neoliberal capitalism combined with imperial practices that only create new—always more threatening—enemies is only leading us down a road toward political disaster and, not to be forgotten, global environmental destruction.

The point that I have scattered throughout this book, and keep coming back to, is that we are not fighting for simple "equality" among races, genders, or sexualities; rather, we are trying to dismantle racism and heterosexism themselves. The categories that we hold to so dearly are socially constructed and keep us from our full human development. Hall argues that the approach of fighting political battles with identities that have essentially been forced upon us has outlived its usefulness and requires something new. Further, it does us little good when members of racial, gender, or sexual minorities achieve access to power if those individuals only perpetuate the neoliberal policies that came before them—an important criticism leveled at both Barack Obama and Hillary Clinton, among others. Edward Said explains that the theoretical projects of both Frantz Fanon and Aimé Césaire have not been fulfilled precisely because they realized that in order to be different and live different lives, postcolonials need to think differently, beyond nationalism, blackness, and any other fixed notions of identity and authenticity.[6] The desire to look backward and claim (create) some sort of pure, nostalgic, and untarnished "culture" or "history" is understandable among those who have been put in tenuous social positions for too long. These imagined histories give us stability, validate our suffering, make us feel safe, and very often give us a clear and understandable Other as the source of our problems. In the West, these Others are continually mutated to fit the desired end for the majority, whether it is immigrants, or communism, or Islam. At the same moment, those of us in the West are encouraged to remain ignorant about the imperial practices done in our name and to discount those who oppose "us" as unpatriotic or sympathetic to "terrorists"—which is always a vague and poorly understood term. Those impacted by (neo)colonial practices (internal colonial practices included) are expected to abide by the normative behavioral standards of Western imperialism—the docile and disciplined subject—their resistance only fueling further ethnocentrism and militarization in the West. Until we fully realize and resist the harmful effects of rooted and stable identities in nationalism, race, religion, gender, or sexuality, the current political structures will retain their shape and form.

Of course, many individuals have and continue to work on these problems in various ways. Hence there is little that I can offer as a solution that has not been stated elsewhere in some form or fashion. Certainly the problems of residential, occupational, and educational segregation must be meaningfully addressed. The endless wars, arms deals, military budgets, political interventions, and domestic and global militarization must end as well, because they do nothing to benefit the middle and working classes who face austerity measures aimed at welfare programs and crumbling infrastructures. Global institutions like the IMF and World Bank along with the global economy in general have made a mockery of the "independence" of colonized peoples and continue to do so when even their own reports admit that what they have done has been a failure.[7] Corporate multinational news media, which long ago stopped giving us news, instead providing entertainment, have only emboldened overtly racist politicians and pundits because they insist on seeing all speech as inherently equal, valid, and thus true. The political failure to address climate change and the role of media in allowing "skeptics" to continually state their falsities are now imperiling life on this planet. That social scientists and journalists have been talking about Western societies, the United States more specifically, being "post-truth" during the 2016 U.S. presidential election indicates the sad state of affairs.

I could go on and on. I think the importance of sport in these conversations is squarely rooted in the conflation of race, gender, culture, and nation. That global sport so often reinforces national boundaries in a way that no longer makes any sense to the transnationality of the teams only keeps race, gender, culture, and nation conflated in problematic ways. This kind of sport is also too often used by political leaders of every country in an attempt to gain public support. We need sport to remind us of our common humanity instead of consistently lending itself to jingoism. Romanticized views of certain playing styles and the physical capabilities of different peoples, genders, or races tied to distinct nations are horribly dated and ultimately unhelpful. A different education could be helpful here. I say "different" because while currently most people learn that they should not be racist or utter racial slurs in front of minorities, racial disparities persist. People are learning to be color-blind but are not receiving an education that displaces, or replaces, the white racial frame (to use Joe Feagin's term), that structures their interpretation of history and current events.[8] The white racial frame profoundly dehumanizes people of color by foreclosing empathy for their lives and disqualifying the knowledge they produce. Once we understand this it is not surprising that we keep returning to the same problems relating to white backlash (which always includes some people of color) against black protest.

To paraphrase James Baldwin, there is no question of whites liberating black people when they cannot liberate themselves—when they do not know their own history and thus do not know who they are. Without this knowledge there is a genuine ignorance of the realities, the physical and psychological violence, that nonwhites face around the world. Yet white Western societies continually place the burden of "proving" racism on those who directly experience its violence; too often, once the structural aspects of racism are proven the findings are systematically ignored. This problem is another aspect of power in general and white supremacy more specifically—the knowledge of nonwhites is not believed and the knowledge produced by white institutions is ignored. Hence blacks are blamed in various ways for the continuation of "race problems" or "race relations," when in reality the answers are not to be found in blackness or black peoples. The inflated value of whiteness under white supremacy puts the burden of becoming "equal" on black and brown communities, meaning that people of color are essentially being forced into becoming white. In other words, whiteness sees itself as something that black and brown people should *want* to become. Yet as Baldwin asks, "How can one respect, let alone adopt, the values of a people who do not, on any level whatever, live the way they say they do, or the way they say they should?" [9] Hence the fears, anxieties, and insecurities of whiteness have long been projected onto the nonwhite Other. Going forward, black and brown protest remains important in bringing awareness and visibility to the problems that exist—they will be messy and they will be imperfect, because there are no perfect social movements, and perfection is demanded only of blackness—but until those in power wish to live in an antiracist and antiheterosexist society I remain skeptical that such a thing is a possibility anytime soon. Contrary to the opinions of some, white supremacy is far from being on its deathbed, and it remains entrenched as a fundamental organizing principle that is irredeemable and harmful to the moral progress of a globalized world.

APPENDIX A

Methodology and Data-Gathering Procedures

Discourse analysis is a broad methodological approach to research, employing a variety of methods or techniques to analyze discourse, whether it is in conversational, textual, or any other form. Discourse refers to "a particular way of talking about or understanding the world (or an aspect of the world)."[1] The concept of discourse developed within linguistics and referred to interconnected writings and speech. However, it was the philosopher Michel Foucault who advanced the discourse concept to entail language *and* practice. Foucault saw discourse not only as a representation of knowledge but as the production of knowledge (meaning) through language. Since meaning influences individual practices, all social practices have a discursive aspect in that they help reinforce and create specific modes of thinking.[2] Because our access to and experience of reality is primarily mediated through language, the inherent creation of discourses through language results in both our creation and our understanding of the social world. Hence discourse influences our understanding and subsequent actions regarding race, gender, nationality, and other markers of social inequality. A further premise of this kind of research and analysis is that individual texts do not carry meaning on their own, as they draw upon, accumulate, and create meaning from a variety of other texts. The process of accumulating meaning or the selective use of familiar discourses across texts and reading within the context of other texts results in an intertextuality from which hegemonic—or dominant—discourse emerges. In this study, the hegemonic discourse around a specific athlete forms that athlete's "representation."[3]

In thinking about the impact of discourse on the individual, especially as it concerns mass media, Albert Bandura's theory of social learning remains useful. In the course of daily life we as individuals have direct contact with only a small portion of our environment. The lack of contact with other aspects of our (social) environment means that our perceptions of social reality largely depend on vicarious experiences, specifically what we see, hear, and read in popular media. The more our lives are intertwined with the symbolic environment of mass media the greater the social impact of media on "acceptable" behaviors and emotional responses. Bandura explains the importance of mass media being found in how we, as individuals, create and verify our conceptions of self based on the world around us.[4] According to Toby Miller, media—sport media in particular, with its emphasis on militarism and patriotism—provides a space where individuals can learn how to be (make themselves) citizens and actively perform citizenship. People conceive of themselves based on observations and regularities in the environment that give them knowledge about objects, relationships, and the likelihood of events.[5] Because the gaining of knowledge through mass media is a vicarious experience, it is also an inherently limited experience. This restricted range of access to the activities and experiences of others leads to biased observations and processes of overgeneralization, which in turn can result in people being less trustful of others and overestimating their chances of being victimized in general. The symbolic modeling of stereotypes cultivates and perpetuates misconceptions that people form regarding occupations, ethnic groups, social roles, and other aspects of social life.

Finally, this scholarship leans on "Reading Sport Critically," a methodology for interrogating power developed by Mary McDonald and Susan Birrell. They argue for a specific form of cultural criticism, "one that focuses analytical attention on specific sporting incidents and personalities and uses them to reveal a nexus of power that helps produce their meanings."[6] According to McDonald and Birrell, the tendency of some academics and mainstream media to focus on, or give primacy to, one relationship of power, such as race, simultaneously serves to ignore or erase others, such as gender, sexuality, and nationality. Reading sport critically seeks to avoid such erasures by uncovering and exploring multiple power relationships as they intersect around a particular incident or celebrity figure. McDonald and Birrell explain, "We find this move to read non-literary cultural forms as texts significant because it ties sport scholars to other critical scholars in terms of the theoretical and methodological choices we make as cultural critics. And we find the analyses themselves compelling because they concern the popular yet deceptively innocent cultural form of sport. Thus they offer insight into how to connect seemingly discrete incidents and events that are generated within the world of sport to the larger social world."[7]

Based on the legacy of British cultural studies, the methodology for reading sport critically is inherently "multi-interdisciplinary" in nature and thus blends multiple theoretical insights from Marxism, feminism, postmodernism and other intellectual movements.[8] The study and critique of cultural texts in the form of sport media can give us insight into broader social relations that have material consequences based on our understandings and subsequent actions regarding race, gender, sexuality, nationality, and other social categories. The methodology for reading sport critically achieves a theoretical and methodological foundation for the analysis and interrogation of power within sport. By outlining a critical strategy and establishing the ontological and epistemological bases from which to study sport celebrities, McDonald and Birrell show that the celebrity athlete as a text or collection of narratives can be read for the broader power relations that produce its meaning.[9]

David Andrews and Steven Jackson explain that sport has become a celebrity-focused form of entertainment, with narratives and storylines built around the personalities of celebrities whom audiences (fans) can relate to and virtually interact with. The corresponding industry that has built up around the celebrity athlete has routinized the production process regarding celebrity athletes. This process inherently requires essentializing and caricaturizing the celebrity individual. Because of these developments, Max Weber's concept of the charismatic prophet can be extended to the concept of celebrity in order to explain how, similar to the institution of the church, the culture industry seeks to give durability to the structure and meaning of celebrity through its routinization. Western cultural values, in particular the irrationality of excessive individualism, become rationalized as commodities for consumption through the routinization of the celebrity. With the ever-increasing blurring of institutional boundaries in postmodern societies, especially those between sport, entertainment, and politics, the celebrity athlete has become a "multi-textual and multi-platform promotional entity."[10]

P. David Marshall elaborates by claiming that celebrities represent a coming together of neoliberal democracy and consumer capitalism. As representatives of neoliberal democracies, celebrities stand for and reaffirm a political system built on notions of individualism, particularly as they concern individual achievement. Simultaneously, celebrities perpetuate the economic regime of neoliberal democracy, consumer capitalism, which also stresses individualism but through freedom of choice and individual identity—consumer freedom. Thus the dominant political and economic regimes benefit from the hyper-individualism of commercialized media programming. Though consumers may have a choice in their consumption, their choices are ultimately limited by the cultural products (celebrities) created by those who control the dominant modes of production.[11]

However, the nature of celebrities as carefully crafted cultural products does not mean that they are interpreted in a homogeneous manner, as audiences are themselves far from homogeneous. Celebrities can be interpreted in a variety of manners, sometimes in contested and sometimes in unintended ways. Yet because of the inability of the culture industry itself to perfectly predict how celebrities will be interpreted, care is often taken to surround celebrities with specific cultural modes of target audiences. These target audiences are usually a combination of those who control the dominant modes of cultural production and the actual audience, whose cultural sensibilities are targeted for reinforcement. As previously mentioned, this imagined audience for sport celebrities has historically been white, middle-class, heterosexual males. In this way, celebrities often become sources of cultural identification, drawing on widely held cultural beliefs regarding race, gender, class, sexuality, and nation. Commercial media or global sport media intentionally imbues celebrity athletes with cultural beliefs in order to build familiarity and interest among audiences. Although we are unlikely to meet celebrities, our virtual intimacy and daily saturation with them have implications for how individuals interpret and negotiate their everyday experiences. Thus celebrities are public entities around which meaning and ideology cohere and that serve as contextual roadmaps for how individuals make sense of the world.[12]

Hence I have chosen athletes who represent what Michael Patton calls "information-rich cases," as their celebrity status and exceptionality draw significant media attention and popular interest. This kind of sampling represents a mix between what Jennifer Mason calls "sampling strategically" and "sampling illustratively/evocatively" and is elsewhere comparatively referred to as criterion-based or purposive sampling. Sampling strategically and illustratively means that I have selected certain athletes not to represent the "wider universe," or *all* Africans in sport, but to capture a "relevant range" in relation to the wider universe. This richness of information allows for a deep understanding and the possibility for what Norman Denzin and Clifford Geertz call "thick" description. What I provide in this study, then, is a glimpse into one reality within the larger universe of Western sport media constructions of black African migrant athletes involved in professional sport leagues in the West.[13]

Though not uncomplicated, the "West" in this book refers to the dominant cultures and concentrated media structure of the United States and Western Europe. I admittedly use a nebulous metaconception of the West that adheres not so much to national borders as it does to primary locations of power and range of influence.[14] Through (post/neo)colonial discourses that frame and homogenize the perception of athletes from African countries as "Others," or non-Western, Western media inherently defines itself as Western. Where necessary, I draw attention to the media in specific countries. Similarly, I fully recognize the complexity of the African continent, and any references to Africa as a whole are made for the sake of readability. When talking about the West's version of Africa, I place the term in quotes: "Africa."[15]

The core of my data comes from major media outlets whose publications exist within the LexisNexis and, to a lesser extent, Factiva news databases. These databases were chosen because they contain news items from various U.S. and European media outlets and thus allowed for searching all available English-language news items. Through my searches I attained a variety of news items from Western media sources but also news from English outlets in Africa (Kenya, Ghana, Ivory Coast, Nigeria, South Africa), Asia (China and Japan), and the South Pacific (Australia and New Zealand). Additionally, the particularities of the sources for each athlete were dictated by where they competed, meaning that, for example, the *Houston Chronicle* was overrepresented during the time Hakeem Olajuwon and Dikembe Mutombo played for the Houston Rockets. The existence of both local and more global media sources in my dataset gives an added dimension to my study that will be relevant later, but for the most part there are no significant differences in how athletes are covered from one place to another—which, as I will discuss later, is indicative of a globalized and globalizing notion of industry standards or "best practices."

One immediate drawback of this study is the exclusive reliance on English-language news sources. However, English-language sources are not limited to predominantly English-speaking countries, as a number of news agencies provide English-language news services. For example, the Agence France Presse (France), the Deutsche Presse-Agentur (Germany), and the Agenzia Nazionale Stampa Associata ([ANSA] Italy) all provide English-language news. In addition, news agencies like the Associated Press and Reuters as well as the *New York Times* have offices in predominantly non-English-speaking European countries and provide English-language news from those sites. Where possible, I attempted to use online services to translate French-, German-, and Italian-language sources, yet given the embeddedness of media in these countries and the media's propensity to cover significant events, it quickly became apparent that little new knowledge was being produced. In the end, I am confident that any concerns about the "authenticity" of or missing viewpoints within English-language news from predominantly non-English-speaking countries are addressed by the use of the aforementioned sources, the pervasiveness of Western media in general, and Western media's tendencies toward industry norms of production.

To generate sources for each athlete separately, I set search terms to the athlete's whole name and last name using the Boolean search operator AND—for example, "Didier Drogba" AND "Drogba." This way of searching ensured that returned news items contained some reference to the athlete of interest. In terms of dates, I began with the earliest mention of each athlete in the database and ended the search in mid-2013. Around 1,000 articles were returned by the search for Loroupe, 14,000 for Olajuwon, 8,000 for Mutombo, 500 for Hali, 22,000 for Balotelli, 1,500 for Ndereba, 500 for Mabika, 1,000 for Dibaba, 500 for Okoye, and 19,000 for Drogba. From the outset it was clear just how devalued women are in terms of media attention in sport.

Once the datasets were constructed, I precoded the data and then proceeded to read each news article. Precoding, according to Johnny Saldaña, enables researchers to bring attention to potentially important quotes or passages by circling, highlighting, bolding, and underlining texts.[16] For my purposes, precoding consisted of bolding and coloring (1) the athlete's name, (2) the names of other athletes, (3) places and religions, and (4) various words relating to the representation of the athlete. While reading all of the articles was a daunting task, given the number of articles, we should remember a few things about collecting archival news media. First, repetition among articles is frequent—for example, Associated Press articles may be released in slightly different forms and then appear in multiple local news outlets—and the dataset included numerous long articles with irrelevant data (such as marathon race results with little to no commentary). Second, sports news articles are generally simple and banal. Most sports articles are not very long, often one page or shorter, and it is easy to understand their direction and purpose rather quickly. Finally, articles that take the time and space to explore, for example, the backgrounds of the athletes are relatively rare, given the size of my data. Such articles are important because their scarcity inherently privileges their discourse, and thus it is with these articles that I spent the most time during analysis.

Aside from precoding, I allowed my main codes and themes to emerge through a process of taking "field notes" combined with analytical memos. This approach borrows from discourse and narrative analysis. Discourse analysis often relies on the taking of detailed field notes and analytical memos that then become the basis for codes and themes. For my purposes, field notes can be thought of as a recording of "what happened," while analytical memos can be thought of as theoretical insights.[17] Hence my theme-building process consisted of a simultaneous process of taking field notes on the careers of the athletes and making links between those notes and my larger theoretical project. By using this method, I was able to see patterns and themes developing in the representation of athletes over time. As I discuss in the main text, some themes and subthemes are prevalent in the beginning of an athlete's career and then disappear, while others arise only in certain situations. In short, my approach allowed for variation over time.

Finally, the inclusion of other data sources—such as Internet videos, autobiographies and biographies, television documentaries, message boards, personal websites, and other online content—aids in what Denzin calls "data triangulation" and allowed me to address aspects of the athletes that I would not have had access to via archival news media databases alone.[18] Data triangulation refers to the use of multiple methodologies to study the same phenomena but also includes different forms of data, investigators, and theories. Triangulation is important when doing research because it lends greater validity, reduces bias, and increases the theoretical relevance of a project. In going beyond what is found in the media representation of athletes in a news database, I am able to give depth to our understanding of these athletes and to address issues such as immigrant reception, nationalism, identity, and meaning in the African diaspora. It is through data triangulation that I am able to explore the interactions and dependencies of the representation of the athletes in my study with representations of other athletes and nonathletes, white and black athletes, non-African migrant athletes, and sport and nonsport events, among other differences.

While the representation of each athlete is unique, I find that the emergent themes I discuss in this book are common and consistently appear in the representation of the athletes I research—as well as those they intersect with either directly or indirectly. These themes, and associated subthemes, appear in the titles for each of my chapters. Throughout this book I also draw links to similar phenomena in the experiences of athletes not strictly included in my research. As I have said before, my work here is about pulling together the different strings that give meaning to the transnational athlete at both the metaphysical and individual levels. My goal in conducting this qualitative inquiry is to construct a narrative that is an authentic, credible, and compelling representation of the "observations" made.[19]

APPENDIX B

Individuals in the Study

While the athletes I focus on are well accomplished in their respective sports, I am aware that not every reader may be familiar with them. Through the course of this research I have sometimes felt that I was reliving the career of each athlete, witnessing their highs and lows, all the while trying to read for how they were navigating not only their host societies but the media interactions as well. The ease of access to archival video online was one of the joys of the research, frequently invoking memories long forgotten or creating new ones. For example, being able to watch Olajuwon's team fall to North Carolina State in the NCAA finals, Mutombo tightly clutching the basketball after defeating the Seattle Supersonics in the 1994 playoffs, or Loroupe running marathons and Dibaba winning Olympic medals not only provided another form of analysis but also allowed me to see what is only described in text. The rest of this appendix will introduce the athletes who appear frequently in the book. I would encourage the reader to look up—watch and see—some of the events I discuss throughout this book.

Hakeem Olajuwon

In 1980 Hakeem Olajuwon first came to the United States from Lagos, Nigeria, his plane ticket bought by his family, to visit the University of Houston and potentially play collegiate basketball. According to his autobiography, though he had started playing basketball and had success in Nigeria, he did not arrive as a blue chip or highly touted prospect; rather, he was a walk-on to the University of Houston's basketball team. After two collegiate championship appearances with the University of Houston, Olajuwon would begin a Hall of Fame basketball career in the NBA after being selected number one overall in the 1984 NBA draft, ahead of Michael Jordan. He would win two NBA championships with the Houston Rockets and win a gold medal with "Dream Team II" during the Atlanta Olympics before being traded from Houston to Toronto, eventually retiring in 2002. History records Olajuwon among the greatest centers ever to play the game of basketball, often discussed alongside Hall of Famers such as "Magic" Johnson, Patrick Ewing, Larry Bird, and Michael Jordan. His creative and difficult to defend post moves around the basket are immortalized in NBA circles as the "Dream Shake."

The study of Olajuwon is significant not solely because he was a great basketball player. It is important because Olajuwon and the small group of Africans he played with during his career, notably Dikembe Mutombo and Manute Bol, were some of the *first* foreign players in the NBA, and many thought they represented the first of a coming "wave" of African talent. The combination of Olajuwon's success and the novelty of his situation makes the study of his representation of great academic interest. Olajuwon represents not only a black African foreigner in U.S. sport but a black African Muslim in a sport dominated by African Americans, who (along with the rest of the United States) tend to follow the Christian faith. In this way, Olajuwon serves as a triple minority in terms of being black, foreign, and Muslim. In previous work I have found that U.S. sport media constructed different representations of Olajuwon as his career progressed, and other academic work has found problems with Olajuwon's construction as a Muslim. Yet Olajuwon's career spanned more than two decades, meaning that further analyses will be able to go beyond a snapshot of his representation at a particular time and focus on a career's worth of discourse in the media.

Dikembe Mutombo

Dikembe Mutombo Mukamba Jean Jacque Wamutombo immigrated to the States in 1988 on a USAID scholarship to Georgetown University. Though initially focused on his studies to become a doctor (he instead graduated with a degree in linguistics and diplomacy), Mutombo was recruited by legendary Hoyas coach John Thompson to play basketball, and by his senior year he would win Big East Defensive Player of the Year and All–Big East First Team honors. He would go on to become a first-round pick (fourth overall) in the 1991 NBA draft, where over his career he would win NBA Defensive Player of the Year four times (1995, 1997, 1998, 2001), appear in eight NBA All-Star Games (1992, 1995, 1996, 1997, 1998, 2000, 2001, 2002), be named to the NBA All-Defensive First Team three times (1997, 1998, 2001), and end his career ranked second all-time in shots blocked, with 3,230.

Despite his success on the court, Mutombo is just as well known for his humanitarian efforts, particularly in the Democratic Republic of Congo, where he was born. His efforts have been focused through his Dikembe Mutombo Foundation, founded in 1997, which was created to help construct the Biamba Marie Mutombo Hospital and Research Center. Named after his mother, the hospital is part of a larger effort to help improve health, education, and quality of life in the Democratic Republic of Congo. Mutombo has received noticeable praise for his charitable contributions, including the President's Service Award in 1999, the NBA's J. Walter Kennedy Citizenship Award in 2001, and public acknowledgement by President George W. Bush in 2007 during the State of the Union Address.

Much more so than Olajuwon, Mutombo's actions and efforts have been aimed toward gaining attention to the problems of people in Africa. Combined with his participation in the NBA's Basketball without Borders program, among other, similar programs, we can see that Mutombo appears to have a deliberate transnationalism about his actions. His everyday involvement with issues all over the African continent begs for critical inquiry about how those efforts, along with other aspects of his blackness or "Africanness," are represented in Western media.

Tegla Loroupe

Tegla Chepkite Loroupe is from the West Pokot district in the Rift Valley province of northwestern Kenya. The Pokot are one of the ethnic groups that can be considered to make up the Kalenjin, the larger ethnic group to which many of Kenya's famous runners belong. The degree to which the Kalenjin have earned an international reputation as distance runners is important not only to Loroupe's framing as a runner but to the representation of the Kalenjin and Pokot as specific ethnic groups inside Kenya. In some ways the Kalenjin have become one of the most well-known aspects of Kenya, despite being only the third-largest ethnic group in that country. Loroupe's distinguished international career began with her victory at the New York City Marathon in 1994 and continues today through her work in her peace foundation. Loroupe's accomplishments include winning a number of major races: Goodwill Games 10K (1994 and 1998), IAAF World Championships 10K (third in 1995 and 1999), New York City Marathon (1994, 1995, and third in 1998), Rotterdam Marathon (three-time winner, 1997–99), Berlin Marathon (1999, second in 2001), Lisbon Half Marathon (six-time winner, 1994–97, 1999, 2000), London Marathon (2000), Cologne Marathon (2003), and Hong Kong Half Marathon (2006). Other successes include three consecutive world titles in the half marathon (1997–99), world records in the 20K, 25K, and 30K, past world record holder in the marathon, past world record for one-hour distance (18,340 meters), and finishing eighth in the New York City Marathon (2007).

Additionally, in 2006 Loroupe was named a United Nations Ambassador for Sport along with other prominent athletes such as Roger Federer, Elias Figueroa, and Katrina Webb. Loroupe holds a similar position, International Sports Ambassador, with the IAAF and UNICEF (United Nations Children's Fund). In 2003 Loroupe started the Tegla Loroupe Peace Foundation with the goal of curbing violence between pastoralist groups in the Rift Valley province of Kenya and bordering countries of Uganda and Sudan. The foundation holds peace marathons and has started the Tegla Loroupe Peace Academy, a school and orphanage, to help further that goal. Loroupe has transitioned from a respected runner to a successful humanitarian peace organizer. As one of the first African women to achieve great success and popularity on the international stage, she represents a "novel" celebrity entity around which to crystallize discourse and meaning.

Christian Okoye

Christian Emeka Okoye was a running back for the Kansas City Chiefs from 1987 to 1993. Prior to that Okoye played football at Azusa-Pacific University, where he first competed in track and field, amassing seven national titles in shot put, discus, and hammer throw as well as seventeen All-American honors in track and field. In fact, it was Okoye's success in track and field in Nigeria that led to his immigration from Nigeria to the United States. After being convinced to give football a try, Okoye showed enough impressive running ability, in only two college seasons, to be a high draft pick in the next NFL draft. Drafted in the second round of the 1987 NFL draft (thirty-fifth overall), Okoye played all his years for the Chiefs, totaling 4,897 rushing yards, a franchise record at the time. Though he was not the first athlete of African origin to play in the NFL, Okoye was one of the earliest athletes of African origin at a time when very few African immigrants were playing football. Even today, many NFL players of recent African descent are second-generation immigrants. The best years of Okoye's career were 1989 and 1991, when he rushed for 1,480 and 1,031 yards, respectively (the former being the NFL season high that year), and made the Pro Bowl both years. Though his career would be shortened by injury, Okoye's achievements would be enough to ensure his entrance into the Kansas City Chief's Hall of Fame, the thirtieth person to do so in the franchise's forty-five years. I have included him in this study because he was the first African immigrant to find success and become popular within the NFL. His nickname, the "Nigerian Nightmare," and his immortalization in the 1991 Tecmo Bowl video game as "untackleable" mean he is still remembered today by those who grew up playing such games.

Tamba Hali

Currently a defensive end/linebacker for the Kansas City Chiefs, Tamba Hali was drafted in 2006 with the twentieth overall pick. Hali immigrated to the United States when he was ten years old because of civil war and conflict in Liberia. Indeed, the stories of his "escape," or immigration, and the horrors he witnessed in Liberia are recurrent features concerning his success, from high school to college to the NFL. Hali began playing football in New Jersey, where he starred for his high school after being convinced to play because of his size. His performance would lead to him being recruited to play for the Penn State Nittany Lions, which at the time was a well-respected football program. During his senior year at Penn State he tallied eleven sacks and seventeen tackles for loss, garnering him All-American honors at his position on his way to being a first-round NFL draft pick. Contextually compared to the NFL Okoye played in, the current league that Hali plays in is one in which having an African background can almost go unnoticed due to the number of generation 1.5 and 2.0 athletes playing football in the college and professional ranks. Now in his seventh season in the NFL, Hali has been a Pro Bowler the last two seasons after reaching double-digit sacks. Generally recognized as an impact player, Hali has so far had a relatively successful playing career, even if he is not immediately recognized as being among the best at his position.

Catherine Ndereba

Catherine Nyambura Ndereba is a former distance runner from Kenya who grew up in Gatunganga, Nyeri District. She is interesting for the purposes of my study because, unlike many of Kenya's well-known runners, she does not come from the Kalenjin ethnic group but instead belongs to the Kikuyu ethnic group, the largest in Kenya. After competing in and dominating shorter distances, such as the 5K, 12K, 15K, and 10 mile, Ndereba moved to the marathon and continued her success. After winning thirteen U.S. road races in 1998, her first year back after giving birth to her daughter (her motherhood, in fact, often defines her as an athlete), Ndereba would win the Boston Marathon in 2000, the first of a record four wins, and gain the appropriate nickname "Catherine the Great." She would go on to represent Kenya internationally, claiming that, unlike others runners who now represent Western countries, she would never run for another country. Her silver medal in the marathon at the Athens Olympics would be the first Olympic marathon medal won by a Kenyan woman. At a time when Kenyan distance running was facing a crisis because of poor results at the Olympics and World Championships, Ndereba emerged as one of its greatest marathoners of all time.

Mwadi Mabika

Mwadi Mabika played in the Women's National Basketball Association (WNBA) for the Los Angeles Sparks most of her career, from 1997 to 2007. She grew up in Kinshasa, Democratic Republic of Congo (then Zaire), where she attended the well-known Masamba School and studied biology and chemistry. Considered too young to play basketball until she was thirteen, Mabika often shot around with older players and watched NBA highlights on television, copying the moves of Jordan and others and trying them for herself on the court. Once given the opportunity to play, Mabika flourished, becoming the Junior National Team captain at the age of fifteen. At nineteen, she scored twenty points against the U.S. National Team at the 1996 Atlanta Olympics and drew the attention of the WNBA. With the later help of Dikembe Mutombo, Tshitingo Mutombo (Dikembe's brother), and eventual WNBA vice president of player personnel Renee Brown, Mabika was able to attain a visa from authorities in the Congo in order to try out for the WNBA.

After winning a roster spot on the Los Angeles Sparks, Mabika would work to become an All-Star in the league, helping the Sparks to back-to-back championships in 2001 and 2002. Highly regarded as a player, at times she has been called the Michael Jordan of the WNBA and has become a popular figure, especially among young women, in the Congo. Of all the athletes in this study, Mabika had the fewest articles written about her, a trend that generally hampered the female athletes in this study. As such, she does not feature prominently in my analyses.

Tirunesh Dibaba

Starting her international career at fifteen years old, in 2001, Tirunesh Dibaba Kenene has so far had a stellar career and is the current world and Olympic champion in the 10K. Dibaba has won gold medals in cross country as well as at both the 5K and 10K at the Olympics, World Championships, World Cross Country Championships, and

African Championships. Originally from Ethiopia, Dibaba was born in the small town of Bokoji, which is in the Arsi zone (district) of Oromiya, a regional state. Though dominant in her own right, Dibaba represents a part of what has otherwise been a highly successful Ethiopian distance running program. Dibaba's family has links with this tradition, and though her parents were not athletes, she has received support from her family, and her sisters have often run with her during training. It is also worth noting that Ethiopia's running history is centered on Bokoji, where a number of runners have originated and still return to train. However, as with Mabika, the media coverage of Dibaba often leaves much to be desired and, while telling of the devaluation of women in sport, hurts the ability of this study to draw more meaningful conclusions about African female athletes.

Didier Drogba

Didier Yves Drogba Tébily made his professional soccer debut in France at the age of nineteen, secured his first full professional contract in France's Ligue 2 at age twenty-one (1999), and emerged as an elite player in France's first division, Ligue 1, at age twenty-four in 2002. After the 2003–4 season playing for Olympique de Marseille in France, which saw him score nineteen goals and lead the team to the 2004 UEFA Cup Final, Drogba moved to Chelsea in the English Premier League for a then-record £24 million fee. The move made Drogba one of the most expensive players in the world, and he proved to be one of the top players in the years following. During his time in the Premier League (arguably the top league in the world at the time) Drogba helped lead Chelsea to three Premier League wins (2005, 2006, 2010), three FA Cup victories (2007, 2009, 2010), two Carling Cup victories (2005, 2007), and one Champions League victory (2012). Individually, Drogba has won the Premier League Golden Boot twice as top goal scorer in the league (2007, 2010), won the CAF African Footballer of the Year award twice (2006, 2009), won European Player of the Year (Onze d'Or) once (2004), and scored one hundred career goals in the Premier League, ranking fourth all-time for Chelsea and the only African player to do so.

Drogba is also well known for his international soccer appearances for his native Ivory Coast. Despite having French citizenship—he moved to France to live with his uncle when he was four years old, technically making him a generation 1.75 immigrant—he has played for the Ivory Coast internationally since 2002, leading the team to the African Cup of Nations final in 2006 and semifinal in 2008. He also helped the team qualify for the World Cup in 2006 and 2010 and is the team's all-time leader in goals scored. Further, for his efforts in 2006 in helping bring a temporary peace to the civil war within Ivory Coast, Drogba was named by *Time* as one of the world's one hundred most influential people, joining the ranks of Muhammad Ali and Michael Jordan among the few sport icons to appear on the cover. Drogba's career on and off the field of play has reached heights only few have known, making him an ideal celebrity athlete to further examine through media discourse.

Mario Balotelli

Mario Barwuah Balotelli currently plays striker for Nice in the French League 1 and also plays internationally for the Italian national team. Balotelli began his professional career at the age of fifteen for AC Lumezzane in Italy, becoming the youngest player in history to do so. Later that same year he would sign a contract with FC Internazionale Milano (Inter) and play for their under-sixteen squad, leading that team to multiple youth tournament victories. In 2007, when he was seventeen, Balotelli made his debut for Inter with Serie A, the senior Italian league, quickly gaining regular playing time and making a name for himself with his play. Balotelli would have a stellar, if short, career with Inter, helping them to three straight championship seasons (2008–10) and a Champions League victory during the 2009–10 season.

In the summer of 2010 Balotelli would sign with Manchester City and promptly help them win the FA Cup, winning Man of the Match honors in the process. In his second season with Manchester, 2011–12, Balotelli would help the team win the English Premier League for the first time in forty-four years. After a great deal of controversy, however, Balotelli would be transferred back to Italy and Serie A, where he played for his favorite team growing up, AC Milan. Internationally, Balotelli made his Italian national team debut for the under-twenty-one squad in 2008 after his naturalization at the age of eighteen. In 2010, at nearly twenty years of age, he would debut for the senior national team, eventually headlining the team during the 2012 European Championships, where Italy would finish as the runner-up to Spain.

Despite his on-field success, Balotelli's personal story is what makes him a compelling celebrity athlete. Though naturalized in 2008, Balotelli was born in Palermo, Sicily, to Ghanaian parents, meaning that the Italian government considered him an immigrant. Because of his health problems as an infant his parents placed him in foster care in order to get proper treatment, and he eventually came to live permanently with the (white, Jewish Italian) Balotellis in Brescia, Italy. Even though he grew up as culturally "Italian," his inclusion into the Italian national team remains problematic because of how blackness is conceived in Italy. As one of few blacks to play for the national team, and the only one in recent memory, Balotelli has become a lightning rod for racial issues both within Italy and within European soccer generally. Combine this with his celebrity off the field of play, as evidenced by his common presence in the tabloids, for better or worse, and Balotelli is quite possibly the most popular athlete in my study at the moment. Thus I have included Balotelli because, as the lone second-generation immigrant in this study, his representation may give us a further glimpse into the complexities and politics of blackness, citizenship, and identity.

NOTES

Introduction

1. Gilroy, *Black Atlantic*; L. Gordon, *Bad Faith and Antiblack Racism*, 96; Mills, *Blackness Visible*.

2. For examples (in order), see Alvito, "Our Piece of the Pie," 524; Bains and Patel, *Asians Can't Play Football*; L. Dubois, *Soccer Empire*; Lanfranchi and Taylor, *Moving with the Ball*; Bamblett, "Straight-Line Stories," 5; Donaghue and Walker, "Contact Sports," 771; McNeill, "Black Magic," 22; Grainger, "From Immigrant to Overstayer," 45; Grainger, "Rugby, Pacific Peoples," 2335; Burdsey, "'If I Ever Play Football,'" 11; Burdsey, "Role with the Punches," 611; Burdsey, "That Joke Isn't Funny Anymore," 261; James, *Beyond a Boundary*; Marquesse, "In Search of the Unequivocal Englishman," 121; Burgos, *Playing America's Game*; Burgos, "Left Out," 37; Klein, "Chain Reaction," 27; Farred, *Phantom Calls*.

3. Small, "Introduction," xxiii; Arthur, *Invisible Sojourners*; Arthur, *African Diaspora*; Waters, *Black Identities*.

4. Bashi, "Globalized Anti-blackness," 584.

5. Gilroy, *Black Atlantic*; Thornton, *Africa and Africans*.

6. A. Gordon, "New Diaspora," 79.

7. Arthur, *Invisible Sojourners*; Bryce-Laporte, "Black Immigrants," 29; A. Gordon, "New Diaspora," 79; Bashi, "Globalized Anti-blackness," 584; Shaw-Taylor and Tuch, *Other African Americans*.

8. Arthur, *Invisible Sojourners*; A. Gordon, "New Diaspora," 79; Bashi, "Globalized Anti-blackness," 584; Shaw-Taylor and Tuch, *Other African Americans*.

9. Arthur, *Invisible Sojourners*; Johnson, "What, then, is the African American?," 77; Osirim, "African Women," 367; U.S. Department of Homeland Security, *2009 Yearbook of Immigration Statistics*; Alex-Assensoh, "African Immigrants and African-Americans," 89; Logan, "Who Are the Other African Americans?," 49.

10. Summerfield, "Patterns of Adaptation," 83; El-Tayeb, "Colored Germans"; Wright, *Becoming Black*; Vasili, *Colouring over the White Line*; Boittin, "Militant Black Men," 221; Chessum, *From Immigrants to Ethnic Minority*.

11. Keaton, Sharpley-Whiting, and Stovall, "Blackness Matters," 1; Constant, "Talking Race"; El-Tayeb, "Colored Germans."

12. Vasili, *Colouring over the White Line*; Boittin, "Militant Black Men," 221; Chessum, *From Immigrants to Ethnic Minority*.

13. Solomos, Findlay, Jones, and Gilroy, "Organic Crisis," 9; Vasili, *over the White Line*; Summerfield, "Patterns of Adaptation," 83; Evans, "Immigration Act of 1971," 508; Gilroy, *There Ain't No Black in the Union Jack*; Gilroy, *Postcolonial Melancholia*.

14. Wright, "Pale by Comparison," 260; Arthur, *African Diaspora*; Solomos, Findlay, Jones, and Gilroy, "Organic Crisis," 9; Blakely, "Emergence of Afro-Europe," 3.

15. Blakely, "Emergence of Afro-Europe," 3; Freedman, "Feminization of Asylum Migration," 209; Nimako and Small, "Theorizing Black Europe," 212; Small, "Introduction," xxiii; Human Rights Watch, *Everyday Intolerance*; Stovall, "No Green Pastures," 180; Thomas, *Black France*.

16. Balibar and Wallerstein, *Race, Nation, Class*, 43.

17. Balibar and Wallerstein, *Race, Nation, Class*; Bazenguissa-Ganga, "How Africans and Afro-Caribbeans became 'Black,'" 145; Diouf, "Lost Territories," 32.

18. Arthur, *African Diaspora*; Jacqueline Brown, *Dropping Anchor, Setting Sail*; Nimako and Small, "Theorizing Black Europe," 212; Stovall, "No Green Pastures," 180.

19. Blakely, "Emergence of Afro-Europe"; Jacqueline Brown, *Dropping Anchor, Setting Sail*; Di Maio, "Black Italia," 119; Nimako and Small, "Theorizing Black Europe," 212; Thomas, *Black France*; Wright, *Becoming Black*.

20. Bale and Maguire, *Global Sports Arena*; Bale, *Brawn Drain*; Maguire and Falcous, *Sport and Migration*; Miller, Lawrence, McKay, and Rowe, *Globalization and Sport*.

21. Bale and Maguire, *Global Sports Arena*; Bale, *Brawn Drain*; Maguire and Falcous, *Sport and Migration*, 6; Miller, Lawrence, McKay, and Rowe, *Globalization and Sport*.

22. Armstrong and Giulianotti, *Football in Africa*; Vasili, *Colouring over the White Line*; Bale and Sang, *Kenyan Running*; Mangan, "Ethics and Ethnocentricity," 362.

23. Vasili, *Colouring over the White Line*; Darby, "African Football Labour Migration," 495; Lanfranchi and Taylor, *Moving with the Ball*.

24. Bale, "Nyandika Maiyoro and Kipchoge Keino," 218; Bale, *Running Cultures*.

25. For examples, see Armstrong and Giulianotti, *Football in Africa*; Bale, "Three Geographies"; Darby, *Africa, Football and FIFA*; Darby, "African Football Labour Migration," 495; Darby, "Out of Africa," 245; Darby and Solberg, "Differing Trajectories," 118; Lanfranchi and Taylor, *Moving with the Ball*; Poli, "Migrations and Trade," 393; Poli, "Understanding Globalization through Football," 491; Vasili, *Colouring over the White Line*.

26. Poli, "Migrations and Trade," 393; CIES Football Observatory, *Annual Review*.

27. Bale, "Three Geographies"; Darby, *Africa, Football and FIFA*; Darby, "Out of Africa," 245; Darby and Solberg, "Differing Trajectories," 118; Poli, "Migrations and Trade," 393.

28. Darby and Solberg, "Differing Trajectories," 118; Maguire and Falcous, *Sport and Migration*; Darby, "Out of Africa," 245; Carter, *In Foreign Fields*.

29. Armstrong and Giulianotti, *Football in Africa*; Darby and Solberg, "Differing Trajectories," 118; Mangan, "Ethics and Ethnocentricity," 362.

30. Fanon, *Wretched of the Earth*.

31. Bale, "Three Geographies"; Darby and Solberg, "Differing Trajectories," 118; Poli, "Migrations and Trade," 393.

32. Lanfranchi and Taylor, *Moving with the Ball*.

33. Poli, "Migrations and Trade," 393.

34. Agergaard and Botelho, "Female Football Migration," 157.

35. Bale, *Brawn Drain*; Bale and Sang, "Out of Africa."

36. Bale, *Brawn Drain*; Bale and Sang, "Out of Africa."

37. Bale, *Brawn Drain*; Bale and Sang, "Out of Africa"; Bale, "Nyandika Maiyoro and Kipchoge Keino," 218; Bale, *Running Cultures*; Walton and Butryn, "Policing the Race," 1.

38. Jordan Conn, "Started from Yaoundé, Now He's Here," *Grantland*, June 27, 2014, http://grantland.com/features/joel-embiid-nba-draft-philadelphia-76ers-kansas-jayhawks/; Dana O'Neil, "Kansas' Joel Embiid a Secret No More," ESPN, January 20, 2014, http://espn.go.com/mens-college-basketball/story/_/id/10320046/kansas-joel-embiid-come-nowhere-become-perhaps-nation-best-freshman; Alexandra Starr, "Trafficked to Play, Then Forgotten," WNYC News, March 17, 2015, http://www.wnyc.org/story/basketball-trafficker/.

39. Ralph, "Prototype," 238.

40. Monica Anderson, "African Immigrant Population in U.S. Steadily Climbs," Pew Research Center, November 2, 2015, http://www.pewresearch.org/fact-tank/2015/11/02/african-immigrant-population-in-u-s-steadily-climbs/; "Foreign Players in America," Eurobasket, July 6, 2016, http://www.usbasket.com/Foreign-Players-in-America.asp?Country=AUS.

41. "Foreign Players in America," Eurobasket, July 6, 2016, http://www.usbasket.com/Foreign-Players-in-America.asp?Country=AUS.

42. Chepyator-Tomson, "African Women Run for Change," 239; Bale, *Brawn Drain*; Bale and Sang, *Kenyan Running*.

43. Besson, Poli, and Ravenel, *Demographic Study*; FIFA, "Regulations on the Status and Transfer of Players," http://www.fifa.com/mm/document/affederation/administration/regulations_on_the_status_and_transfer_of_players_en_33410.pdf.

44. "Mission & History," African Services Committee, http://www.africanservices.org/about-us/mission-history; "Our Achievements," Foot Solidaire, http://www.footsolidaire.org/actions-foot-solidaire/realisations-foot-solidaire-soutien-jeune-footballeur/; Alexandra Starr, "Trafficked to Play, Then Forgotten," WNYC News, March 17, 2015, http://www.wnyc.org/story/basketball-trafficker/.

1. Race and Sport

1. Carrington, *Race, Sport and Politics*.

2. Carrington, *Race, Sport and Politics*; Runstedtler, *Jack Johnson, Rebel Sojourner*.

3. Carrington, *Race, Sport and Politics*, 48.

4. Carrington, *Race, Sport and Politics*; Mills, *Racial Contract*, 21 (emphasis in original).

5. Mangan, *"Manufactured" Masculinity*.

6. Mangan, *"Manufactured" Masculinity*.

7. Blaut, *Colonizer's Model of the World*; Carrington, *Race, Sport and Politics*.

8. Carrington, *Race, Sport and Politics*, 45 (emphasis in original).

9. Carrington, *Race, Sport and Politics*.

10. Carrington, *Race, Sport and Politics*, 66.

11. Omi and Winant, *Racial Formation*, 55–56 (emphasis in original)

12. McClintock, *Imperial Leather*; Carrington, *Race, Sport and Politics*, 72.

13. Carrington, *Race, Sport and Politics*, 20 (emphasis in original).

14. Runstedtler, *Jack Johnson, Rebel Sojourner*.

15. Runstedtler, *Jack Johnson, Rebel Sojourner*.

16. Runstedtler, *Jack Johnson, Rebel Sojourner*.

17. Carrington, *Race, Sport and Politics*; Runstedtler, *Jack Johnson, Rebel Sojourner*.

18. Carrington, *Race, Sport and Politics*.

19. Carrington, *Race, Sport and Politics*, 80 (emphasis in original).

20. Carrington, *Race, Sport and Politics*, 81 (emphasis in original).

21. Carrington, *Race, Sport and Politics*.

22. Carrington, *Race, Sport and Politics*; Festle, "'Jackie Robinson without the Charm,'" 187; Grundy, "Ora Washington," 79; Liberti and Smith, *(Re)Presenting Wilma Rudolph*; Runstedtler, *Jack Johnson, Rebel Sojourner*; Wilson, "Wilma Rudolph," 207.

23. Hoberman, *Darwin's Athletes*.

24. Hoberman, *Darwin's Athletes*.

25. Hoberman, *Darwin's Athletes*.

26. Hoberman, *Darwin's Athletes*, 119.

27. Runstedtler, *Jack Johnson, Rebel Sojourner*.

28. Bale, "Nyandika Maiyoro and Kipchoge Keino," 218; Hoberman, *Darwin's Athletes*; Hoberman, "Price of 'Black Dominance.'"

29. Bale, "Nyandika Maiyoro and Kipchoge Keino," 226.

30. Nauright and Magdalinski, "Hapless Attempt at Swimming," 106.

31. Nauright and Magdalinski, "Hapless Attempt at Swimming," 106.

32. Kusz, "Much Adu about Nothing?," 147.

33. Denison and Markula, "Press Conference as a Performance," 311.

34. Denison and Markula, "Press Conference as a Performance," 332.

35. Jung, *Beneath the Surface*; Sewell, "Theory of Structure," 1.

36. Jung, *Beneath the Surface*, 36; all quotes are from the same page.

37. Jung, *Beneath the Surface*, 35.

38. Mills, *Racial Contract*, 1, 20.

39. Jung, *Beneath the Surface*, 35.

2. Everyday Othering

1. Said, "Problem of Textuality," 673.

2. Small, "Introduction," xxiii.

3. H. Araton, "Mutombo Making N.B.A. Feel His Presence," *New York Times*, November 15, 1991.

4. W. Wallace, "253 Pounds of Trouble for Jets," *New York Times*, November 13, 1987.

5. Salzmann, *Language, Culture and Society*, 175.

6. Hall, "Foucault," 41; Phillips and Jørgensen, *Discourse Analysis*.

7. "Inter Milan Spoil Genoa's Unbeaten Home Record," Deutsche Presse-Agentur, March 7, 2009.

8. A. Cagliano, "Balotelli Dumps Fuel Row with Mourinho," Deutsche Presse-Agentur, 2010.

9. Curry Kirkpatrick, "The Liege Lord of Noxzema," *Sports Illustrated*, November 28, 1983, http://www.si.com/vault/1983/11/28/627321/the-liege-lord-of-noxzema.

10. Curry Kirkpatrick, "The Liege Lord of Noxzema," *Sports Illustrated*, November 28, 1983, http://www.si.com/vault/1983/11/28/627321/the-liege-lord-of-noxzema.

11. J. Flores, "Sparks Fly as Mabika Polishes Her Offense," *USA Today*, July 7, 2000.

12. L. Robbins, "Lions' Hali Has Learned to be Strong," *New York Post*, November 16, 2005.

13. "Didier Drogba in China: Some Immigrants Are Better Than Others," *International Business Times News*, June 21, 2012.

14. Wright, *Physics of Blackness*, 34.

15. Hall, "Spectacle of the "Other," 324.

16. "Chiefs' Okoye Starts to Bloom as Player," *St. Louis Post-Dispatch*, October 15, 1989.

17. "Broncos Aim to Halt Chiefs' 'Nigerian Nightmare,'" *St. Louis Post-Dispatch*, September 17, 1990.

18. L. Gordon, *Bad Faith and Antiblack Racism*; L. Gordon, *Her Majesty's Other Children*.

19. Bale, *Brawn Drain*; Mills, *Blackness Visible*.

20. Adam Century, "Drogba Draws Crowds and Controversy in China," *International Herald Tribune*, September 7, 2012.

21. R. Johnson, "Olajuwon Charms and Dominates," *New York Times*, March 29, 1983.

22. M. Martinez, "Rocket's Olajuwon Finds Shortest Path to Stardom," *New York Times*, February 3, 1986.

23. Crenshaw, "Demarginalizing the Intersection of Race and Sex," 139.

24. Collins, *Black Feminist Thought*, 7.

25. Collins, *Black Feminist Thought*, 11.

26. Vertinsky and Captain, "More Myth than History," 532; Liberti and Smith, *(Re)Presenting Wilma Rudolph*; Collins, *Black Feminist Thought*; Collins, *Black Sexual Politics*.

27. Mwaniki, "Reading the Career," 446.

28. D. Patrick, "Loroupe, Recovered from Food Poisoning, Set for New York," *USA Today*, November 3, 2000; S. Roberts, "Loroupe Hoping to Forget Sydney Disappointment," *New York Times*, November 2, 2000; N. Woods, "Majestic O'Sullivan Storms Castle to Capture Roads Crown at Balmoral," *Sunday Times*, April 23, 2000; D. Gillon, "Science Counts in Long Run," *Herald*, April 22, 2000.

29. Reuters News, "Champions Both Repeat at New York City Marathon," November 12, 1995; E. Royte, "To the Victor—9 Cattle, 16 Sheep and Dignity," *New York Times*, June 23, 1996; R. Thomas Jr., "Loroupe Fades Near the End," *New York Times*, November 4, 1996; D. Mackay, "Loroupe Mixes It with the Big Boys," *Observer*, April 25, 1999; S. Mott, "London Marathon Baby Who Was Born to Run," *Daily Telegraph*, April 21, 2001.

30. D. Lewis, "Tegla—I Am All Woman," *Mirror*, April 17, 2000.

31. J. Gettleman, "A Kenyan Runner Seeks Peace for Her Corner of the World," *New York Times*, November 18, 2006.

32. J. Longman, "Trying to Fulfill Sister's Last Wish," *New York Times*, November 8, 1995.

33. M. Noden, "Nothing Stops Diminutive Loroupe," *Globe and Mail*, October 31, 1998.

34. P. Minshull, "African Women to Dominate Marathon," Reuters News, April 20, 1998; S. Mott, "London Marathon Baby Who Was Born to Run," *Daily Telegraph*, April 21, 2001.

35. A. Bloom and C. Herrman, "Interview with Lornah Kiplagat: Training for Change," *Frontline World*, PBS, http://www.pbs.org/frontlineworld/stories/kenya/kiplagat.html.

36. D. Mackay, "Ndereba Hits Out at Use of Pacemakers," *Guardian*, April 10, 2003.

37. M. Lowe, "Defending Champ Balances Family, Racing," *Portland Press Herald*, August 1, 1999.

3. Model Minorities

1. Said, *Orientalism*.

2. Kim, *Bitter Fruit*, 20.

3. Kalman-Lamb, "Athlete as Model Minority," 238; Kim, *Bitter Fruit*; Ong, *Spirits of Resistance*; Park, "Continuing Significance," 134.

4. J. Longman, "A Runner's Victory Is Cultural as Well," *New York Times*, April 16, 1995.

5. J. Moore, "Mutombo Gleams as Nugget in Rough," *Seattle Post-Intelligencer*, December 19, 1991.

6. Said, "Problem of Textuality," 673.

7. T. Kington, "Young, Black, Italian . . . and Abused," *Observer*, December 13, 2009.

8. Gates, *Tradition and the Black Atlantic*; Gilroy, *Black Atlantic*; Gilroy, *Against Race*; Waters, *Black Identities*.

9. M. Kreidler, "Chiefs' Backfield Is Big Enough for Two Stars," *San Diego Union-Tribune*, September 25, 1991.

10. E. Gustkey, "KC's Okoye Has Come a Long Way in a Short Time," *St. Louis Post-Dispatch*, September 16, 1990.

11. M. Beech, "Happy Landing Sender Defensive End Tamba Hali Had to Flee War-Torn Liberia, but He's Found a Home at Penn State," *Sports Illustrated*, November 14, 2005.

12. Trujillo, "Machines, Missiles, and Men," 403; Montez de Oca, *Discipline and Indulgence*.

13. J. Denberg, "Akeem Has Been 'The Dream' Come True for Rockets," *Atlanta Journal and Constitution*, May 29, 1986.

14. Dodoo, "Assimilation Differences," 527; Logan, "Who Are the Other African Americans?," 49; de Haas, "Myth of Invasion," 1305.

15. Goffman, *Presentation of Self*.

16. M. Maske, "For Mutombo, Sky's No Limit," *Washington Post*, January 17, 1991.

17. R. Johnson, "Olajuwon Charms and Dominates," *New York Times*, March 29, 1983.

18. Runstedtler, *Jack Johnson, Rebel Sojourner*; Collins, *Black Sexual Politics*.

19. B. Miklasz, "After a Long Climb, Olajuwon Is at a Peak," *St. Louis Post-Dispatch*, June 5, 1995.

20. Osirim, "African Women," 367; Vickerman, *Crosscurrents*; Waters, *Black Identities*.

21. L. Gordon, *Bad Faith and Antiblack Racism*; L. Gordon, *Her Majesty's Other Children*; Mills, *Racial Contract*; Mills, *Blackness Visible*; Pieterse, "Savages, Animals, Heathens, Races," 30.

22. Glennie, *Trouble with Aid*.

23. Künzler and Poli, "African Footballer," 207; Rowe, *Global Media Sport*.

24. S. Stammers, "Drogba 'Saved His Country from War,'" *Sunday Mirror*, August 5, 2007.

25. M. Delaney, "Disgraceful Didier Drogba," *Sunday Tribune*, September 20, 2009; A. Hayes, "How Drogba United the Ivory Coast," *Daily Telegraph*, August 8, 2007; B. Oliver, "The OSM Interview: Didier Drogba," *Observer*, February 4, 2007.

26. Jordan Conn, "The Legend of Les Elephants," *Grantland*, June 11, 2014, http://grant land.com/features/world-cup-ivory-coast-dider-drogba-yaya-toure-civil-war-legend/.

27. J. White, "Drogba? He's More Powerful Than the President," *Daily Telegraph*, February 16, 2012.

28. Teju Cole, "The White-Savior Industrial Complex," *Atlantic*, March 21, 2012, http://www.theatlantic.com/international/archive/2012/03/the-white-savior-industrial -complex/254843/.

29. Teju Cole, "The White-Savior Industrial Complex," *Atlantic*, March 21, 2012, http://www.theatlantic.com/international/archive/2012/03/the-white-savior-industrial -complex/254843/.

30. Bill Osinski, "Mutombo Asks Help to Rescue Homeland," *Atlanta Journal-Constitution*, August 13, 2005.

31. P. Jasner, "Mutombo Wants to Build a Legacy of Hope in His Homeland," *Philadelphia Daily News*, February 8, 2002.

32. Pablo S. Torre, "There's a Difference Between Broke and Bankrupt for Ex-NFL Players," *FiveThirtyEight*, May 4, 2015, http://fivethirtyeight.com/features/theres -a-difference-between-broke-and-bankrupt-for-ex-nfl-players/.

33. Arthur, *Invisible Sojourners*; Arthur, *African Diaspora*; Waters, *Black Identities*.

34. Denison and Markula, "Press Conference as Performance," 311.

35. Marshall, *Celebrity and Power*.

36. Jung, *Beneath the Surface*, 143.

37. Jung, *Beneath the Surface*.

4. "Bad" Blacks

1. Gilroy, *Against Race*, 173.

2. Arthur, *Invisible Sojourners*; Arthur, *African Diaspora*; Darby, "Out of Africa," 245; Künzler and Poli, "African Footballer," 207; Logan, "Who Are the Other African Americans?," 49.

3. Shaw-Taylor and Tuch, *Other African Americans*; Blakely, "Emergence of Afro-Europe," 3; Portes and Rumbaut, *Legacies*.

4. Dodoo, "Assimilation Differences," 527; Logan, "Who Are the Other African Americans?," 49; Mazrui, "Pan-Africanism and the Intellectuals," 56; Shaw-Taylor and Tuch, *Other African Americans*.

5. Boyd, *Young, Black, Rich and Famous*.

6. Michael Wilbon, "Akeem Lets Off Steam after End of Title Dream," *Washington Post*, April 3 1984; emphasis mine.

7. P. Alfano, "Houston's Players Blame Each Other," *New York Times*, April 3, 1984; B. Center, "Akeem's Dream Ends Same Way—With Loss," *San Diego Union-Tribune*, April 3, 1984; Michael Wilbon, "Akeem Lets Off Steam after End of Title Dream," *Washington Post*, April 3 1984.

8. F. Blinebury, "NBA Could Hit Akeem with a Fine," *Houston Chronicle*, May 1, 1985.

9. F. Blinebury, "Akeem Fined $1,500 for Hitting Paultz," *Houston Chronicle*, May 1, 1985.

10. J. Denberg, "Akeem Has Been 'The Dream' Come True for Rockets," *Atlanta Journal and Constitution*, May 29, 1986.

11. A. Truex, "Akeem Follows NBA's Advice, Won't Take Test," *Houston Chronicle*, December 11, 1987.

12. C. Johnson, "Rockets' Olajuwon Lashes Out at Coach," *USA Today*, March 24, 1988.

13. F. Blinebury, "Dr. Jekyll and Mr. Olajuwon," *Houston Chronicle*, September 3, 1988.

14. Boyd, *Young, Black, Rich and Famous*.

15. Olajuwon and Knobler, *Living the Dream*.

16. Jackie MacMullan, "Dream Season: Politics Aside, Houston Center Hakeem Olajuwon Is Playing Like a World-Beater and Looking Like an MVP," *Boston Globe*, January 12, 1994.

17. Jackson, "Twist of Race," 21.

18. M. Kiszla, "This Whine Has a Decent Bouquet Mutombo Is Not Nuggets' Problem," *Denver Post*, February 6, 1995.

19. F. Kerber, "Mutombo Slaps Critics on Wrist," *New York Post*, December 13, 2002.

20. Arthur, *African Diaspora*.

21. Mitch Albom, "Shaq-Dikembe Feud Has Making of a Hit," *Detroit Free Press*, June 13, 2001.

22. A. Maykuth, "Mutombo the Man," *Philadelphia Inquirer*, February 10, 2002.

23. S. Tongue, "Drogba Keeping His Feet on the Ground," *Sunday Tribune*, July 25, 2004.

24. I. Chadband, "Why Drogba Must Stand and Deliver," *Evening Standard*, May 21, 2008.

25. O. Holt, "Drogba Is a Pain Who Can Take Tantrums to Spain," *Mirror*, April 30, 2008.

26. G. Birtles, "He Is No Super Mario for Me," *Nottingham Evening Post*, January 31, 2013.

27. "Barmy Balo to Super Mario All in Good Time," *Manchester Evening News*, March 21, 2011.

28. W. Du Bois, *Souls of Black Folk*.

29. L. Gordon, *Bad Faith and Antiblack Racism*; Fanon, *Black Skin, White Masks*.

30. Jung, *Beneath the Surface*, 143.

31. D. Jones, "I Can't Bear Baloo-telli Baiting, so Mario's Right to Escape the Jungle," *Evening Standard*, January 31, 2013.

32. G. Marcotti, "Balotelli in Thick of the Action and Inaccuracy," *Times*, June 25, 2012.

33. Douglas, "Venus, Serena, and the Women's Tennis Association," 256; Shultz, "Reading the Catsuit," 338.

34. S. Findlay, "Olympics Struggle with 'Policing Femininity,'" *Star*, June 8, 2012, http://www.thestar.com/sports/london2012/article/1205025—olympics-struggle-with-policing-femininity.

35. S. Shapiro, "Caught in the Middle: A Failed Gender Test Crushed Santhi Soundarajan's Olympic Dreams," *ESPN: The Magazine*, August 1, 2012, http://espn.go.com/olympics/story/_/id/8192977/failed-gender-test-forces-olympian-redefine-athletic-career-espn-magazine.

36. Shultz, "Caster Semenya," 228; J. Ellison, "Caster Semenya and the IOC's Olympics Gender Bender," *Daily Beast*, July 26, 2012, http://www.thedailybeast.com/.

37. Samantha Michaels, "The Biggest Issue in Women's Sports Is About to Come to a Head," *Mother Jones*, August 10, 2016, http://m.motherjones.com/politics/2016/08/rio-olympics-caster-semenya-how-does-testosterone-affect-athletic-performance; Katrina Karkazis and Rebecca Jordan-Young, "The Trouble with Too Much T," *New York Times*, April 10, 2014, http://www.nytimes.com/2014/04/11/opinion/the-trouble-with-too-much-t.html?_r=0.

38. ESPN, *Too Fast to Be a Woman? The Story of Caste Semenya*, 2013, http://wn.com/Caster_Semenya_ESPN_Documentary.

39. Shultz, "Caster Semenya," 228.

40. Shultz, "Caster Semenya," 228.

41. Shultz, "Caster Semenya," 228; Vertinsky and Captain, "More Myth Than History," 532.

42. B. Floyd, "Every Time Brittney Griner Is on TV, This Happens," *SBNation*, July 11, 2012, http://www.sbnation.com/ncaa-basketball/2012/7/11/3153845/brittney-griner-espys-tweets.

43. S. Findlay, "Olympics Struggle with 'Policing Femininity,'" *Star*, June 8, 2012, http://www.thestar.com/sports/london2012/article/1205025—olympics-struggle-with-policing-femininity; Sean Ingle, "Caster Semenya's Comeback Puts Her on Course of Rio Gold—and Controversy," *Guardian*, April 17, 2016, https://www.theguardian.com/sport/2016/apr/17/caster-semenya-comeback-rio-olympics-gold.

44. S. Findlay, "Olympics Struggle with 'Policing Femininity,'" *Star*, June 8, 2012, http://www.thestar.com/sports/london2012/article/1205025—olympics-struggle-with-policing-femininity.

45. Walton and Butryn, " Policing the Race," 1.

46. D. Martin, "Loroupe Out to Silence Critics," *Scotsman*, October 16, 1998.

47. T. Knight, "Loroupe Angered by London," *Daily Telegraph*, March 27, 2003.

48. D. Mackay, "Marathon Incentive for Women to Discard Male Pacemakers," *Guardian*, December 18, 1998.

49. A. Campbell, "A Pace Odyssey: They May Not Always Have Been a Welcome Presence but Pacemakers Have Been Instrumental in Some of the Greatest Achievements in Athletics History," *Sunday Herald*, October 20, 2002.

50. Ayo Coly, "Why Obama Blundered by Speaking Out on LGBTQ Rights in Kenya," *Africa Is a Country*, August 2, 2015, http://africasacountry.com/2015/08/why-obama-blundered-by-speaking-out-on-lgbtq-rights-in-kenya/.

51. Iton, *In Search of the Black Fantastic*; Wright, *Becoming Black*.

52. Fanon, *Black Skin, White Masks*; Fanon, *Wretched of the Earth*; L. Gordon, *Bad Faith and Antiblack Racism*; L. Gordon, *Her Majesty's Other Children*.

5. Immigrant Reception

1. Arthur, *African Diaspora*; Portes and Rumbaut, *Legacies*; Waters, *Black Identities*.

2. Ong, *Flexible Citizenship*, 112.

3. Carter, *In Foreign Fields*; Ong, *Flexible Citizenship*.

4. Back, Crabbe, and Solomos, *Changing Face of Football*; Gilroy, *Postcolonial Melancholia*; Markovits and Rensmann, *Gaming the World*.

5. R. Telander, "World Class: Dikembe Mutombo, the Outgoing Nugget Center, Makes a Big Impression in the Paint and in Faraway Lands," *Sports Illustrated*, November 7, 1994, http://www.si.com/vault/1994/11/07/132489/world-class-dikembe -mutombo-the-cerebral-nugget-center-makes-a-big-impression-in-the-paint-and-in -faraway-lands.

6. George, *Elevating the Game*, 212.

7. "Georgetown's Dikembe Mutombo: Basketball Ambassador from Zaire," *St. Louis Post-Dispatch*, February 11, 1990.

8. O. Youngmisuk, "The Last Hoya Standing," *New York Daily News*, October 30, 2002.

9. "To Hakeem, a Dream; To Dikembe, a Puzzle," *Atlanta Journal and Constitution*, July 11, 1996.

10. M. Fine, "Mutombo Has Tons of Worry," *Patriot Ledger*, April 15, 1999.

11. Appiah, *In My Father's House*, 76.

12. Hall, "Old and New Identities," 52.

13. "Heard This One?," *San Jose Mercury News*, March 12, 2006.

14. Associated Press, "Dikembe Mutombo to Become American Citizen," March 9, 2006; emphasis mine.

15. Terry College of Business, University of Georgia, "Dikembe Mutombo—'Make a Life, Make a Living, Make a Difference,'" January 20, 2011, http://www.youtube.com /watch?v=Jk5N5hkRPqs.

16. M. Fine, "Mutombo Has Tons of Worry," *Patriot Ledger*, April 15, 1999.

17. Teju Cole, "The White-Savior Industrial Complex," *Atlantic*, March 21, 2012, http://www.theatlantic.com/international/archive/2012/03/the-white-savior-industrial -complex/254843/.

18. "KC Fans Will Love DE Hali," *Topeka Capital-Journal*, May 2, 2006.

19. R. Patton, "3 NBA Centers Heroes to Fellow Africans," *Pittsburgh Post-Gazette*, December 9, 1993.

20. Künzler and Poli, "African Footballer," 207.

21. Kasinitz, Mollenkopf, Waters, and Holdaway, *Inheriting the City*; Vickerman, *Crosscurrents*.

22. Gilroy, *Darker Than Blue*.

23. Schneider, Chavez, DeSipio, and Waters, "Belonging," 206.

24. Drogba and Penot, *Didier Drogba*.

25. Drogba and Penot, *Didier Drogba*.

26. N. McLeman, "Drogba Rap for Racism in Europe," *Mirror*, January 19, 2008.

27. G. Hunter, "Racists Are Victimising Africans, Says Angry Drogba," *Evening Standard*, January 30, 2008.

28. A. Thomas, "Assou-Ekotto: I Say What I Think . . . If You Don't Like it, I Don't Care," CNN, January 23, 2013, http://www.cnn.com/2013/01/23/sport/football/benoit-assou-ekotto-cameroon/index.html?iid=article_sidebar.

29. Anderson, *Imagined Communities*.

30. "I'm Italian, Not Ghanaian, Says Inter Star Balotelli," Agence France Presse, February 29, 2008.

31. S. Stone, "Players Need to Be Keen on England," PA *Newswire: Sports News*, November 13, 2012.

32. Kasinitz, Mollenkopf, Waters, and Holdaway, *Inheriting the City*; Portes and Rumbaut, *Legacies*; Waters, *Black Identities*; Vickerman, *Crosscurrents*.

33. L. Dubois, *Soccer Empire*; also see Dubois, "Louisa Necib, Algeria, and the Redemption of French Football," *Soccer Politics*, July 1, 2011, https://sites.duke.edu/wcwp/2011/07/01/louisa-necib-algeria-and-the-redemption-of-french-football/.

34. Gilroy, *Black Atlantic*; Gilroy, *Postcolonial Melancholia*.

35. Burdsey, "If I Ever Play Football," 11; Fanon, *Black Skin, White Masks*.

36. Reid, *Negro Immigrant*; Vickerman, *Crosscurrents*.

37. Olajuwon and Knobler, *Living the Dream*, 95.

38. Grewal, *Islam Is a Foreign Country*.

39. R. Reilly, "Patriot Games: Mahmoud Abdul-Rauf Caused an Uproar When He Sat Out the National Anthem," *Sports Illustrated*, March 25, 1996; Fran Blinebury, "US Citizenship Provides Passport to Dream Team," *Houston Chronicle*, July 14, 1996; R. Marquand, "A Real Gentleman on and off the Court, Hakeem Olajuwon's Islamic Faith Keeps Him on the High Road," *Dayton Daily News*, February 8, 1997; Olajuwon and Knobler, *Living the Dream*.

40. Grewal, "Lights, Camera, Suspension," 109.

41. T. Blount, "Dream Come True," *Houston Chronicle*, May 22, 1994.

42. V. Gregorian, "Hakeem's Dream; Olajuwon Savors His Olympic Experience," *St. Louis Post-Dispatch*, July 25, 1996.

43. Olajuwon and Knobler, *Living the Dream*.

44. J. Denberg, "Mutombo Yearns to Change Rockets' Olajuwon on Issue of Charity to Their Homeland," *Atlanta Journal-Constitution*, February 17, 1997.

45. M. Murphy, "Olajuwon Sets Record Straight," *Houston Chronicle*, February 25, 1997.

46. Said, *Orientalism*; Said, *Covering Islam*.

47. Olajuwon and Knobler, *Living the Dream*, 242.

48. Grewal, " Lights, Camera, Suspension," 109.

49. M. Hedges, "In '95 Olajuwon Said America Had 'No Morals,'" *Houston Chronicle*, February 20, 2005.

50. Hall, "New Ethnicities," 440; Gilroy, *Postcolonial Melancholia*.

51. Gilroy, *Postcolonial Melancholia*; Hall, "What Is This 'Black,'" 465; Hall, "Spectacle of the 'Other,'" 324.

52. Hall, "Old and New Identities," 52.

53. Hall, "New Ethnicities," 444.

6. The Diasporic Athlete

1. Gilroy, *Black Atlantic*; Gilroy, *Postcolonial Melancholia*; Carrington, *Race, Sport and Politics*.

2. Appiah, *In My Father's House*; Mills, *Racial Contract*; Mills, *Blackness Visible*; L. Gordon, *Bad Faith and Antiblack Racism*; L. Gordon, *Her Majesty's Other Children*; L. Gordon, "Thinking through Identities," 69; Gilroy, *There Ain't No Black in the Union Jack*; Gilroy, *Black Atlantic*; Gilroy, "Diaspora," 207; Gilroy, *Against Race*; Gilroy, *Postcolonial Melancholia*; Gilroy, *Darker Than Blue*; Wright, *Becoming Black*; Said, *Orientalism*; Said, "Representing the Colonized," 205; Hall, "New Ethnicities," 440; Hall, "Old and New Identities," 41.

3. Gilroy, *Against Race*.

4. L. Gordon, *Bad Faith and Antiblack Racism*; Gilroy, *Black Atlantic*; Said, *Orientalism*; Wright, *Becoming Black*; Mazrui, "Islam and the Black Diaspora," 344.

5. Carrington, *Race, Sport and Politics*; Gilroy, *Black Atlantic*; Iton, *In Search of the Black Fantastic*.

6. Carrington, Andrews, Jackson and Mazur, "Global Jordanscape," 204–5.

7. Carrington, *Race, Sport and Politics*; Runstedtler, *Jack Johnson, Rebel Sojourner*.

8. K. Matheson, "For Muhammad Ali, a Liberty Medal in Philly," Associated Press, September 14, 2012.

9. Gast, *When We Were Kings*.

10. As a good example of the contradictory politics of Ali, see Sean Jacobs, "What Muhammad Ali Believed," *Jacobin*, June 18, 2016, https://www.jacobinmag.com/2016/06/muhammad-ali-mobutu-sese-seko-congo-zaire-reagan-noi-palestine/. The article describes how Ali said nothing about Mobutu's abuses in office, was a puppet for U.S. international relations, and helped Ronald Reagan during his presidential run, among other things.

11. E. Bloom, "Akeem Takes Center Stage before Hometown Fans," *Orange County Register*, February 11, 1989.

12. Witherspoon, "Going 'to the Fountainhead,'" 1508.

13. C. Kirkpatrick, "The Liege Lord of Noxzema: Houston's Akeem Olajuwon Came Out of Nigeria to Give New Meaning to the Term 'Faze Jhob,'" *Sports Illustrated*, November 28, 1983, http://www.si.com/vault/1983/11/28/627321/the-liege-lord-of-noxzema.

14. "The Boy They Call the New Drogba," *Daily Mail*, December 1, 2009.

15. Bandura, *Social Learning Theory*.

16. K. Anderson, "Out of Africa: Stellar Sparks Guard Mwadi Mabika Is Living the Girlhood Dream She Had in Zaire," *Sports Illustrated*, June 11, 2001, http://www

.si.com/vault/2001/06/11/305052/out-of-africa-stellar-sparks-guard-mwadi-mabika-is
-living-the-girlhood-dream-she-had-in-zaire.

17. "20 Questions with . . . Mwadi Mabika," WNBA.com, June 4, 2014, http://www
.wnba.com/features/20questions_mabika.html.

18. M. Maske, "For Mutombo, Sky's No Limit," *Washington Post*, January 17, 1991.

19. J. Juliano, "Mutombo Rejuvenated," *Philadelphia Inquirer*, January 14, 2007.

20. L. Robbins, "Mutombo Works to Build Legacy off Court," *New York Times*,
December 25, 2002.

21. B. Oliver, "The OSM Interview: Didier Drogba," *Observer*, February 4, 2007.

22. Künzler and Poli, "African Footballer," 207.

23. Terry College of Business, University of Georgia, "Dikembe Mutombo—
'Make a Life, Make a Living, Make a Difference,'" January 20, 2011, http://www.you
tube.com/watch?v=Jk5N5hkRPqs.

24. R. Nance, "For Congo, a Big Step Forward," *USA Today*, August 15, 2006.

25. Mazrui, "Pan-Africanism and the Intellectuals," 56.

26. G. Wood, "Ivory Coast World Cup Soccer Fans," *Vancouver Sun*, May 28, 2010.

27. Hall, "New Ethnicities," 440.

28. A. John-Hall, "The Power to Do Good," *Philadelphia Inquirer*, May 8, 2001.

29. J. Feigen, "Mutombo to Attend Obama Inauguration," *Houston Chronicle*,
January 17, 2009.

30. W. Du Bois, *Souls of Black Folk*; Fanon, *Black Skin, White Masks*; Gilroy,
Black Atlantic.

31. R. Yaqub, "Hakeem Nets Praise as Muslim Followers See Man Who Prays,"
St. Louis Post-Dispatch, June 16, 1995.

32. Grewal, "Lights, Camera, Suspension," 109.

33. Gehring and Weiner, "Christian Okoye."

34. M. Ogden, "Mario Balotelli Says He Will Walk off the Pitch If He Is Racially
Abused in Poland and Ukraine," *Telegraph*, May 29, 2012.

35. Kwasi Danquah III, Slix Fleeingham, David Nkrumah, and Prince Rapid,
"Mario Balotelli," produced by Prince Rapid, Takeover Entertainment, London, 2011.
The video to the song is available online, and a search for the lyrics produces a num-
ber of sites where they have been edited to make fun of Balotelli.

36. "Italy Not Leaving Brazil, Says Prandelli," Agence France Presse, June 21, 2013.

37. Drogba and Penot, *Didier Drogba*.

38. D. Conn, "The Moral Compass Goes Awry When Stars Are Guilty of Racism," *Guardian*, December 11, 2012.

39. J. Denberg, "Hawks' Mutombo a Happy Man," Cox News Service, October
9, 1999.

40. Künzler and Poli, "African Footballer," 207.

41. Chris Broussard, "Talent Search Focuses on Africa," *New York Times*, August
24, 2003.

42. Isaac Mahlangu, "Shooting for the Stars," *Sunday Times*, August 22, 2004.

43. "Clinton Praises Mutombo Hospital in Kinshasa," Voice of America News, August 17, 2009.

44. T. D'Angelo, "NBA Tour to Africa Touches Heat Assistant Gentry, Wife," *Palm Beach Post*, October 26, 1993.

45. Alexandra Starr, "Trafficked to Play, Then Forgotten," WNYC News, March 17, 2015, http://www.wnyc.org/story/basketball-trafficker/.

46. Jacqueline Brown, *Dropping Anchor, Setting Sail*.

47. Gilroy, *Black Atlantic*; Gilroy, *Against Race*.

48. Wright, *Becoming Black*, 31; emphasis in original.

49. Reynolds, "Toward Understanding a Culture," 270, Mazrui, "Pan-Africanism and the Intellectuals," 56.

50. Iton, *In Search of the Black Fantastic*; Carrington, *Race, Sport and Politics*.

51. Winant, *The World Is a Ghetto*.

7. The Sporting Migrant

1. These ideas appear throughout the work of Gilroy and Hall, as I have noted throughout this book and chapter.

2. "Drogba Denies Backing Pro-Palestinian Petition," Agence France Presse, December 4, 2012.

3. Carrington, Andrews, Jackson, and Mazur, "Global Jordanscape," 177; Gilroy, *Black Atlantic*; Gilroy, *Against Race*; Hall, "New Ethnicities," 440.

4. Andrews and Jackson, "Introduction," 1; Marshall, *Celebrity and Power*; Montez de Oca, *Discipline and Indulgence*; Smart, *Sport Star*.

5. Iton, *In Search of the Black Fantastic*.

6. Said, "Representing the Colonized," 205.

7. Dabla-Norris, Kochhar, Suphaphiphat, Ricka, and Tsounta, *Causes and Consequence of Income Inequality*.

8. Feagin, *White Racial Frame*.

9. James Baldwin, "National Press Club Speech 1986," December 10, 1986, https://www.youtube.com/watch?v=CTjY4rZFY5c; also see Baldwin, *The Fire Next Time*, 108–18.

Appendix A

1. Phillips and Jørgensen, *Discourse Analysis*, 1.

2. Foucault, *Archeology of Knowledge*; Hall, "Foucault," 72.

3. Phillips and Jørgensen, *Discourse Analysis*, 1; Hall, "Spectacle of the 'Other,'" 324; Wood and Kroger, *Doing Discourse Analysis*.

4. Bandura, *Social Learning Theory*.

5. Miller, *Technologies of Truth*.

6. McDonald and Birrell, "Reading Sport Critically," 283–84.

7. McDonald and Birrell, "Reading Sport Critically," 283.

8. McDonald and Birrell, "Reading Sport Critically," 285.

9. McDonald and Birrell, "Reading Sport Critically," 283; Birrell and McDonald, *Reading Sport*.

10. Andrews and Jackson, "Introduction," 7; Marshall, *Celebrity and Power*; Smart, *Sport Star*.

11. Marshall, *Celebrity and Power*; Smart, *Sport Star*.

12. Marshall, *Celebrity and Power*; Montez de Oca, *Discipline and Indulgence*; Andrews and Jackson, "Introduction," 1; Whannel, *Media Sport Stars*.

13. Patton, *Qualitative Research and Evaluation Methods*, 230; Mason, *Qualitative Researching*; Denzin, *Interpretive Interactionism*; Geertz, *Interpretation of Cultures*.

14. Andrews, "Speaking the 'Universal Language of Entertainment,'" 99; Miller, Lawrence, McKay, and Rowe, *Globalization and Sport*; Rowe, *Global Media Sport*; Hardt and Negri, *Empire*.

15. Said, *Orientalism*; Said, *Covering Islam*.

16. Saldaña, *Coding Manual*.

17. Saldaña, *Coding Manual*; Boyatzis, *Transforming Qualitative Information*.

18. Denzin, *Research Act*, 297.

19. Denzin, *Research Act*; Mason, *Qualitative Researching*; Denzin, *Interpretive Interactionism*; Schram, *Conceptualizing and Proposing Qualitative Research*; Shank, *Qualitative Research*.

BIBLIOGRAPHY

Agergaard, S., and V. Botelho. "Female Football Migration: Motivational Factors for Early Migratory Processes." In *Sport and Migration: Borders, Boundaries and Crossings*, edited by J. Maguire and M. Falcous, 157–72. New York: Routledge, 2011.

Alex-Assensoh, Y. "African Immigrants and African-Americans: An Analysis of Voluntary African Immigration and the Evolution of Black Ethnic Politics in America." *African & Asian Studies* 8, no. 1/2 (2009): 89–124.

Alvito, M. "Our Piece of the Pie: Brazilian Football and Globalization." *Soccer & Society* 8, no. 4 (2007): 524–44.

Anderson, B. *Imagined Communities*. 2nd ed. New York: Verso, 1991.

Andrews, D. "Speaking the 'Universal Language of Entertainment': News Corporation, Culture and the Global Sport Media Economy." In *Critical Readings: Sport, Culture and the Media*, edited by David Rowe, 99–128. Buckingham, UK: Open University Press, 2004.

Andrews, D., and S. Jackson. "Introduction: Sport Celebrities, Public Culture, and Private Experience." In *Sport Stars: The Cultural Politics of Sporting Celebrity*, edited by David Andrews and S. Jackson, 1–19. New York: Routledge, 2001.

Appiah, A. *In My Father's House: Africa in the Philosophy of Culture*. New York: Oxford University Press, 1992.

Armstrong, G., and R. Giulianotti. *Football in Africa: Conflict, Conciliation and Community*. New York: Palgrave MacMillan, 2004.

Arthur, J. *The African Diaspora in the United States and Europe: The Ghanaian Experience*. Burlington VT: Ashgate, 2008.

——— . *Invisible Sojourners: African Immigrant Diaspora in the United States*. Westport CT: Praeger, 2000.

Back, L., T. Crabbe, and J. Solomos. *The Changing Face of Football: Racism, Identity, and Multiculture in the English Game*. New York: Berg, 2001.

Bains, J., and R. Patel. *Asians Can't Play Football*. Birmingham, UK: D-zine, 1996.

Baldwin, James. *The Fire Next Time*. New York: Dial Press, 1963.

Bale, J. *The Brawn Drain: Foreign Student-Athletes in American Universities*. Champaign: University of Illinois Press, 1991.

———. "Nyandika Maiyoro and Kipchoge Keino: Transgression, Colonial Rhetoric and the Postcolonial Athlete." In *Sport Stars: The Cultural Politics of Sporting Celebrity*, edited by David Andrews and Stephen Jackson, 218–30. New York: Routledge, 2001.

———. *Running Cultures: Racing in Time and Space*. London: Routledge, 2004.

———. "Three Geographies of African Footballer Migration: Patterns, Problems and Postcoloniality." In *Football in Africa: Conflict, Conciliation and Community*, edited by Gary Armstrong and Richard Giulianotti, 229–46. New York: Palgrave MacMillan, 2004.

Bale, J., and J. Maguire, eds. *The Global Sports Arena: Athletic Talent Migration in an Interdependent World*. London: Frank Cass, 1994.

Bale, J., and J. Sang. *Kenyan Running: Movement Culture, Geography, and Global Change*. London: Frank Cass, 1996.

———. "Out of Africa: The 'Development' of Kenyan Athletics, Talent Migration and the Global Sports Arena." In *The Global Sports Arena: Athletic Talent Migration in an Interdependent World*, edited by J. Bale and J. Sang, 206–25. London: Frank Cass, 1994.

Balibar, E., and I. Wallerstein. *Race, Nation, Class: Ambiguous Identities*. London: Verso, 1991.

Bamblett, L. "Straight-Line Stories: Representations and Indigenous Australian Identities in Sports Discourses." *Australian Aboriginal Studies*, no. 2 (2011): 5–20.

Bandura, A. *Social Learning Theory*. Englewood Cliffs NJ: Prentice-Hall, 1977.

Bashi, V. "Globalized Anti-blackness: Transnationalizing Western Immigration Law, Policy, and Practice." *Ethnic and Racial Studies* 27, no. 4 (2004): 584–606.

Bazenguissa-Ganga, R. "How Africans and Afro-Caribbeans Became 'Black' in France." In *Black France/France Noire: The History and Politics of Blackness*, edited by T. Keaton, T. Sharpley-Whiting, and T. Stovall, 145–72. Durham NC: Duke University Press, 2012.

Besson, Roger, Raffaele Poli, and Loïc Ravenel. *Demographic Study of Footballeurs in Europe*. Neuchâtel, Switzerland: CIES Football Observatory, 2010.

Birrell, S., and Mary McDonald. *Reading Sport: Critical Essays on Power and Representation*. Boston: Northeastern University Press, 2000.

Blakely, A. "The Emergence of Afro-Europe: A Preliminary Sketch." In *Black Europe and the African Diaspora*, edited by D. Hine, T. Keaton, and S. Small, 3–28. Urbana: University of Illinois Press, 2009.

Blaut, J. M. *The Colonizer's Model of the World: Geographical Diffusionism and Eurocentric History*. New York: Guilford Press, 1993.

Boittin, J. "The Militant Black Men of Marseille and Paris, 1927–1937." In *Black France/France Noire: The History and Politics of Blackness*, edited by T. Keaton, T. Sharpley-Whiting, and T. Stovall, 221–46. Durham NC: Duke University Press, 2012.

Boyatzis, R. E. *Transforming Qualitative Information: Thematic Analysis and Code Development*. Thousand Oaks CA: Sage, 1998.

Boyd, T. *Young, Black, Rich and Famous*. New York: Doubleday, 2003.

Brown, J. "Black Europe and the African Diaspora: A Discourse on Location." In *Black Europe and the African Diaspora*, edited by D. Hine, T. Keaton, and S. Small, 201–11. Urbana: University of Illinois Press, 2009.

Brown, Jacqueline Nassy. *Dropping Anchor, Setting Sail: Geographies of Race in Black Liverpool*. Princeton NJ: Princeton University Press, 2005.

Bryce-Laporte, R. "Black Immigrants: The Experience of Invisibility and Inequality." *Journal of Black Studies* 3, no. 29 (1972): 29–56.

Burdsey, D. "'If I Ever Play Football, Dad, Can I Play for England or India?' British Asians, Sport and Diasporic National Identities." *Sociology* 40, no. 1 (2006): 11–28.

——— . "Role with the Punches: The Construction and Representation of Amir Khan as a Role Model for Multiethnic Britain." *Sociological Review* 55, no. 3 (2007): 611–31.

——— . "That Joke Isn't Funny Anymore: Racial Microaggressions, Color-Blind Ideology and the Mitigation of Racism in English Men's First-Class Cricket." *Sociology of Sport Journal* 28, no. 3 (2011): 261–83.

Burgos, A, Jr. "Left Out: Afro-Latinos, Black Baseball, and the Revision of Baseball's Racial History." *Social Text* 27, no. 1 (2009): 37–58.

——— . *Playing America's Game: Baseball, Latinos, and the Color Line*. Berkeley: University of California Press, 2007.

Carrington, B., D. Andrews, S. Jackson, and C. Mazur. "The Global Jordanscape." In *Michael Jordan Inc.: Corporate Sport, Media Culture, and Late Modern America*, edited by David Andrews, 177–216. Albany: State University of New York Press, 2001.

Carrington, Ben. *Race, Sport and Politics: The Sporting Black Diaspora*. London: Sage, 2010.

Carter, Thomas F. *In Foreign Fields: The Politics and Experiences of Transnational Sport Migration*. London: Pluto Press, 2011.

Chepyator-Tomson, J. A. "African Women Run for Change: Challenges and Achievements in Sports." In *African Women and Globalization*, edited by J. A. Chepyator-Thomson, 239–57. Trenton NJ: Africa World Press, 2005.

Chessum, L. *From Immigrants to Ethnic Minority: Making Black Community in Britain*. Burlington VT: Ashgate, 2000.

CIES Football Observatory. *Annual Review of the European Football Players' Labour Market*. Neuchâtel, Switzerland: CIES Football Observatory, 2010.

Collins, Patricia Hill. *Black Feminist Thought: Knowledge, Consciousness, and the Politics of Empowerment*. New York: Routledge Classics, 2009.

———. *Black Sexual Politics: African Americans, Gender, and the New Racism*. New York: Routledge, 2004.

Constant, F. "Talking Race in Color-Blind France: Equality Denied, 'Blackness' Reclaimed." In *Black Europe and the African Diaspora*, edited by D. Hine, T. Keaton, and S. Small, 145–60. Urbana: University of Illinois Press, 2009.

Crenshaw, Kimberlé. "Demarginalizing the Intersection of Race and Sex: A Black Feminist Critique of Antidiscrimination Doctrine, Feminism Theory and Anti-racist Politics." *University of Chicago Legal Forum*, no. 1 (1989): 139–67.

Dabla-Norris, Era, Kalpana Kochhar, Nujin Suphaphiphat, Frantisek Ricka, and Evridiki Tsounta. *Causes and Consequence of Income Inequality: A Global Perspective*. International Monetary Fund, June 2015. http://www.imf.org/external/pubs/ft/sdn/2015/sdn1513.pdf.

Darby, P. *Africa, Football and FIFA: Politics, Colonialism and Resistance*. London: Frank Cass, 2002.

———. "African Football Labour Migration to Portugal: Colonial and Neo-colonial Resource." *Soccer & Society* 8, no. 4 (2007): 495–509.

———. "Out of Africa: The Exodus of Elite African Football Talent to Europe." In *Sport and Migration: Borders, Boundaries and Crossings*, edited by J. Maguire and M. Falcous, 245–58. New York: Routledge, 2011.

Darby, P., and E. Solberg. "Differing Trajectories: Football Development and Patterns of Player Migration in South Africa and Ghana." *Soccer & Society* 11, no. 1–2 (2010): 118–30.

De Haas, Hein. "The Myth of Invasion: The Inconvenient Realities of African Migration to Europe." *Third World Quarterly* 29, no. 7 (2008): 1305–22.

Denison, J., and Pirrko Markula. "The Press Conference as a Performance: Representing Haile Gebrselassie." *Sociology of Sport Journal* 22, no. 3 (2005): 311–35.

Denzin, N. *Interpretive Interactionism*. 2nd ed. Thousand Oaks CA: Sage, 2001.

———. *The Research Act: A Theoretical Introduction to Sociological Methods*. Chicago: Aldine, 1970.

Di Maio, A. "Black Italia: Contemporary Migrant Writers from Africa." In *Black Europe and the African Diaspora*, edited by D. Hine, T. Keaton, and S. Small, 119–44. Urbana: University of Illinois Press, 2009.

Diouf, M. "The Lost Territories of the Republic: Historical Narratives and the Recomposition of French Citizenship." In *Black France/France Noire: The History and Politics of Blackness*, edited by T. Keaton, T. Sharpley-Whiting, and T. Stovall, 32–56. Durham NC: Duke University Press, 2012.

Dodoo, F. "Assimilation Differences among Africans in America." *Social Forces* 76, no. 2 (1997): 527–46.

Donaghue, N., and I. Walker. "Contact Sports: Judgements of Aboriginal and Non-Aboriginal Australian Football League Players' Performance." *South African Journal of Psychology* 37, no. 4 (2007): 771–82.

Douglas, D. "Venus, Serena, and the Women's Tennis Association: When and Where 'Race' Enters." *Sociology of Sport Journal* 22, no. 3 (2005): 256–82.

Drogba, D., and H. Penot. *Didier Drogba: The Autobiography*. Translated by Paul Morris. London: Aurum Press, 2008.

Dubois, L. *Soccer Empire: The World Cup and the Future of France*. Berkeley: University of California Press, 2010.

Du Bois, W. E. B. *The Souls of Black Folk*. New York: Pocket Books, 2005.

El-Tayeb, F. "'Colored Germans There Will Never Be': Colonialism and Citizenship in Modern Germany." In *Extending the Diaspora: New Histories of Black People*, edited by D. Curry, E. Duke, and M. Smith, 225–44. Urbana: University of Illinois Press, 2009.

Evans, J. M. "Immigration Act of 1971." *Modern Law Review* 35, no. 5 (1972): 508–24.

Fanon, F. *Black Skin, White Masks*. Translated by J. Sartre. New York: Grove Press, 1967.

———. *The Wretched of the Earth*. Translated by Richard Philcox. New York: Grove Press, 2004.

Farred, G. *Phantom Calls: Race and the Globalization of the NBA*. Chicago: Prickly Paradigm Press, 2006.

Feagin, Joe. *The White Racial Frame: Centuries of Racial Framing and Counter-Framing*. 2nd ed. New York: Routledge, 2009.

Festle, Mary Jo. "'Jackie Robinson without the Charm': The Challenges of Being Althea Gibson." In *Out of the Shadows: A Biographical History of African American Athletes*, edited by David K. Wiggins, 187–206. Fayetteville: University of Arkansas Press, 2006.

Foucault, Michel. *The Archeology of Knowledge and the Discourse on Language*. New York: Pantheon Books, 1972.

Freedman, Jane. "The Feminization of Asylum Migration from Africa: Problems and Perspectives." In *African Migrations: Patterns and Perspectives*, edited by A. Kane and T. H. Leedy, 209–29. Bloomington: Indiana University Press, 2013.

Gast, L., dir. *When We Were Kings: The Untold Story of the Rumble in the Jungle*. DVD. United States: Gramercy Pictures, 1996.

Gates, Henry Louis, Jr. *Tradition and the Black Atlantic: Critical Theory in the African Diaspora*. New York: BasicCivitas, 2010.

Geertz, C. *The Interpretation of Cultures: Selected Essays*. New York: Basic Books, 1973.

Gehring, R., and James Weiner. "Christian Okoye." *A Football Life*. DVD. United States: NFL Films, 2015.

George, Nelson. *Elevating the Game: Black Men & Basketball*. Lincoln: University of Nebraska Press, 1999.

Gilroy, P. *Against Race: Imagining Political Culture Beyond the Color Line*. Cambridge MA: Belknap Press of Harvard University Press, 2000.

———. *The Black Atlantic*. Cambridge MA: Harvard University Press, 1993.

———. *Darker Than Blue: On the Moral Economies of Black Culture*. W. E. B. Du Bois Lectures. Cambridge MA: Belknap Press of Harvard University Press, 2010.

——— . "Diaspora." *Paragraph* 17, no. 3 (1996): 207–12.

——— . *Postcolonial Melancholia*. New York: Columbia University Press, 2005.

——— . *There Ain't No Black in the Union Jack: The Cultural Politics of Race and Nation*. Chicago: University of Chicago Press, 1987.

Glennie, Jonathon. *The Trouble with Aid: Why Less Could Mean More for Africa*. London: Zed Books, 2008.

Goffman, E. *The Presentation of Self in Everyday Life*. New York: Doubleday, 1959.

Gordon, A. "The New Diaspora: African Immigration to the United States." *Journal of Third World Studies* 15, no. 1 (1998): 79–103.

Gordon, L. *Bad Faith and Antiblack Racism*. Atlantic Highlands NJ: Humanities Press International, 1995.

——— . *Her Majesty's Other Children: Sketches of Racism from a Neocolonial Age*. Oxford: Rowman and Littlefield, 1997.

——— . "Thinking through Identities: Black Peoples, Race Labels, and Ethnic Consciousness." In *The Other African Americans: Contemporary African and Caribbean Immigrants in the United States*, edited by Y. Shaw-Taylor and S. Tuch, 69–92. Plymouth, UK: Rowman & Littlefield, 2007.

Grainger, A. "From Immigrant to Overstayer: Samoan Identity, Rugby, and Cultural Politics of Race and Nation in Aotearoa/New Zealand." *Journal of Sport & Social Issues* 30, no. 1 (2006): 45–61.

——— . "Rugby, Pacific Peoples, and the Cultural Politics of National Identity in New Zealand." *International Journal of the History of Sport* 26, no. 16 (2009): 2335–57.

Grewal, Z. "Lights, Camera, Suspension: Freezing the Frame on the Mahmoud Abdul-Rauf-Anthem Controversy." *Souls* 9, no. 2 (2007): 109–22.

Grewal, Zareena. *Islam Is a Foreign Country: American Muslims and the Global Crisis of Authority*. New York: New York University Press, 2014.

Grundy, Pamela. "Ora Washington: The First Black Female Athletic Star." In *Out of the Shadows: A Biographical History of African American Athletes*, edited by David K. Wiggins, 79–92. Fayetteville: University of Arkansas Press, 2006.

Hall, Stuart. "Foucault: Power, Knowledge, and Discourse." In *Discourse Theory and Practice: A Reader*, edited by M. Wetherell, S. Taylor, and S. J. Yates, 72–81. Los Angeles: Sage, in association with the Open University, 2007.

——— . "New Ethnicities." In *Stuart Hall: Critical Dialogues in Cultural Studies*, edited by David Morley and Kuan-Hsing Chen, 440–49. New York: Routledge, 1996.

——— . "Old and New Identities, Old and New Ethnicities." In *Culture, Globalization, and the World-System: Contemporary Conditions for the Representation of Identity*, edited by Anthony D. King, 41–68. Minneapolis: University of Minnesota Press, 1997.

——— . "The Spectacle of the 'Other.'" In *Discourse Theory and Practice: A Reader*, edited by M. Wetherell, S. Taylor, and S. J. Yates, 324–43. Los Angeles: Sage, in association with the Open University, 2007.

———. "What Is This 'Black' in Black Popular Culture?" *Social Justice* 20, no. 1–2 (1993): 104–15.

Hardt, M., and A. Negri. *Empire.* Cambridge MA: Harvard University Press, 2000.

Hoberman, J. *Darwin's Athletes: How Sport Has Damaged Black America and Preserved the Myth of Race.* New York: Houghton Mifflin, 1997.

———. "The Price of 'Black Dominance.'" *Society* 37, no. 3 (March/April 2000): 49–56.

Human Rights Watch. *Everyday Intolerance: Racist and Xenophobic Violence in Italy.* New York: Human Rights Watch, March 21, 2011. https://www.hrw.org /report/2011/03/21/everyday-intolerance/racist-and-xenophobic-violence-italy.

Iton, R. *In Search of the Black Fantastic: Politics and Popular Culture in the Post–Civil Rights Era.* New York: Oxford University Press, 2008.

Jackson, S. "A Twist of Race: Ben Johnson and the Canadian Crisis of Racial and National Identity." *Sociology of Sport Journal* 15, no. 1 (1998): 21–40.

James, C. L. R. *Beyond a Boundary.* London: Hutchinson, 1963.

Johnson, V. "'What, then, is the African American?' African and Afro-Caribbean Identities in Black America." *Journal of American Ethnic History* 28, no. 1 (2008): 77–103.

Jung, Moon-Kie. *Beneath the Surface of White Supremacy: Denaturalizing U.S. Racisms Past and Present.* Stanford CA: Stanford University Press, 2015.

Kalman-Lamb, N. "The Athlete as Model Minority Subject: Jose Bautista and Canadian Multiculturalism." *Social Identities* 19, no. 2 (2013): 238–53.

Kasinitz, P., J. Mollenkopf, M. Waters, and J. Holdaway. *Inheriting the City: The Children of Immigrants Come of Age.* Cambridge MA: Harvard University Press, 2008.

Keaton, T., T. Sharpley-Whiting, and T. Stovall. "Blackness Matters, Blackness Made to Matter." In *Black France/France Noire: The History and Politics of Blackness,* edited by T. Keaton, T. Sharpley-Whiting, and T. Stovall, 1–16. Durham NC: Duke University Press, 2012.

Kim, Claire Jean. *Bitter Fruit: The Politics of Black-Korean Conflict in New York City.* New Haven CT: Yale University Press, 2000.

Klein, A. "Chain Reaction: Neoliberal Exceptions to Global Commodity Chains in Dominican Baseball." *International Review for the Sociology of Sport* 47, no. 1 (2012): 27–42.

Kunzler, D., and R. Poli. "The African Footballer as Visual Object and Figure of Success: Didier Drogba and Social Meaning." *Soccer & Society* 13, no. 2 (2012): 207–21.

Kusz, Kyle. "Much Adu about Nothing? Freddy Adu and Neoliberal Racism in New Millennium America." In *Commodified and Criminalized: New Racism and African Americans in Contemporary Sports,* edited by David J. Leonard and C. Richard King, 147–63. Plymouth, UK: Rowman & Littlefield, 2012.

Lanfranchi, P., and M. Taylor. *Moving with the Ball: The Migration of Professional Footballers.* New York: Berg, 2001.

Liberti, Rita, and Maureen M. Smith. *(Re)Presenting Wilma Rudolph.* Syracuse NY: Syracuse University Press, 2015.

Logan, J. "Who Are the Other African Americans? Contemporary African and Caribbean Immigrants in the United States." In *The Other African Americans: Contemporary African and Caribbean Immigrants in the United States*, edited by Y. Shaw-Taylor and S. Tuch, 49–68. Plymouth, UK: Rowman & Littlefield, 2007.

Maguire, J., and M. Falcous. *Sport and Migration: Borders, Boundaries and Crossings*. New York: Routledge, 2011.

Mangan, J. A. "Ethics and Ethnocentricity in British Tropical Africa." *Journal of the History of Sport* 27, no. 1 (2010): 362–88.

———. *"Manufactured" Masculinity: Making Imperial Manliness, Morality and Militarism*. New York: Taylor & Francis, 2012.

Markovits, A., and L. Rensmann. *Gaming the World: How Sports Are Reshaping Global Politics and Culture*. Princeton NJ: Princeton University Press, 2010.

Marquesse, M. "In Search of the Unequivocal Englishman: The Conundrum of Race and Nation in English Cricket." In *"Race," Sport and British Society*, edited by Ben Carrington and Ian McDonald, 121–32. London: Routledge, 2001.

Marshall, P. D. *Celebrity and Power: Fame in Contemporary Culture*. Minneapolis: University of Minnesota Press, 1997.

Mason, J. *Qualitative Researching*. London: Sage, 2002.

Mazrui, A. "Islam and the Black Diaspora: The Impact of Islamigration." In *The African Diaspora: African Origins and New World Identities*, edited by Isidore Okpewho, Carole Boyce Davies, and Ali A. Mazrui, 344–50. Bloomington: Indiana University Press, 1999.

———. "Pan-Africanism and the Intellectuals: Rise, Decline, and Revival." In *African Intellectuals: Rethinking Politics, Language, Gender and Development*, edited by Thandika Mkandawire, 56–77. New York: Zed Books, 2005.

McClintock, Anne. *Imperial Leather: Race, Gender and Sexuality in the Colonial Contest*. New York: Routledge, 1995.

McDonald, M. "The Marketing of the Women's National Basketball Association and the Making of Post-feminism." *International Review for the Sociology of Sport Journal* 35, no. 1 (2000): 35–47.

McDonald, M., and S. Birrell. "Reading Sport Critically: A Methodology for Interrogating Power." *Sociology of Sport Journal* 16, no. 4 (1999): 283–300.

McNeill, D. "'Black Magic,' Nationalism and Race in Australian Football." *Race & Class* 49, no. 4 (2008): 22–37.

Miller, T., G. Lawrence, J. McKay, and D. Rowe. *Globalization and Sport: Playing the World*. London: Sage, 2001.

Miller, Toby. *Technologies of Truth: Cultural Citizenship and the Popular Media*. Minneapolis: University of Minnesota Press, 1998.

Mills, C. *Blackness Visible*. Ithaca NY: Cornell University Press, 1998.

———. *The Racial Contract*. Ithaca NY: Cornell University Press, 1997.

Montez de Oca, Jeffrey. *Discipline and Indulgence: College Football, Media, and the American Way of Life during the Cold War*. New Brunswick NJ: Rutgers University Press, 2013.

Mwaniki, Munene Franjo. "Reading the Career of a Kenyan Runner: The Case of Tegla Loroupe." *International Review for the Sociology of Sport* 47, no. 4 (2012): 446–60.

Nauright, J., and T. Magdalinski. "'A Hapless Attempt at Swimming': Representations of Eric Moussambani." *Critical Arts* 17, no. 1/2 (2003): 106–22.

Nimako, K., and S. Small. "Theorizing Black Europe and African Diaspora: Implications for Citizenship, Nativism, and Xenophobia." In *Black Europe and the African Diaspora*, edited by D. Hine, T. Keaton, and S. Small, 212–37. Urbana: University of Illinois Press, 2009.

Olajuwon, H., and Peter Knobler. *Living the Dream: My Life and Basketball*. New York: Little, Brown, 1996.

Omi, M., and H. Winant. *Racial Formation in the United States from the 1960s to the 1990s*. New York: Routledge, 1994.

Ong, A. *Flexible Citizenship: The Cultural Logics of Transnationality*. Durham NC: Duke University Press, 1999.

———. *Spirits of Resistance and Capitalist Discipline*. Albany: State University of New York Press, 1987.

Osirim, M. "African Women in the New Diaspora: Transnationalism and the (Re)creation of Home." *African & Asian Studies* 7, no. 4 (2008): 367–94.

Park, Lisa Sun-Hee. "Continuing Significance of the Model Minority Myth: The Second Generation." *Social Justice* 35, no. 2 (2008): 134–44.

Patton, M. *Qualitative Research and Evaluation Methods*. London: Sage, 2002.

Phillips, L., and M. Jørgensen. *Discourse Analysis as Theory and Method*. Thousand Oaks CA: Sage, 2002.

Pieterse, Jan Nederveen. "Savages, Animals, Heathens, Races." In *White on Black: Images of Africa and Blacks in Western Popular Culture*, edited by Jan Nederveen Pieterse, 30–39. New Haven CT: Yale University Press, 1992.

Poli, R. "Migrations and Trade of African Football Players: Historic, Geographical and Cultural Aspects." *Africa Spectrum* 41, no. 3 (2006): 393–414.

———. "Understanding Globalization through Football: The New International Division of Labour, Migratory Channels and Transnational Trade Circuits." *International Review for the Sociology of Sport* 45, no. 4 (2010): 491–506.

Portes, A., and R. Rumbaut. *Legacies: The Story of the Immigrant Second Generation*. Berkeley: University of California Press, 2001.

Ralph, M. "Prototype: In Search of the Perfect Senegalese Basketball Physique." *International Journal of the History of Sport* 24, no. 2 (2007): 238–63.

Reid, I. *The Negro Immigrant: His Background, Characteristics and Social Adjustment, 1899–1937*. New York: Arno Press and the New York Times, 1969.

Reynolds, R. "Toward Understanding a Culture of Migration among 'Elite' African Youth: Educational Capital and the Future of the Igbo Diaspora." In *African Migrations: Patterns and Perspectives*, edited by A. Kane and T. H. Leedy, 270–86. Bloomington: Indiana University Press, 2013.

Rowe, D. *Global Media Sport: Flows, Forms and Futures*. New York: Bloomsbury Academic, 2011.

Runstedtler, Theresa. *Jack Johnson, Rebel Sojourner: Boxing in the Shadow of the Global Color Line*. Berkeley: University of California Press, 2012.

Said, E. *Covering Islam: How the Media and the Experts Determine How We See the Rest of the World*. New York: Vintage Books, 1997.

——. *Orientalism*. New York: Pantheon Books, 1978.

——. "The Problem of Textuality: Two Exemplary Positions." *Critical Inquiry* 4, no. 4 (1978): 673–714.

——. "Representing the Colonized: Anthropology's Interlocutors." *Critical Inquiry* 5, no. 2 (1989): 205–25.

Saldaña, J. *The Coding Manual for Qualitative Researchers*. Thousand Oaks CA: Sage, 2009.

Salzmann, Zdenek. *Language, Culture and Society: An Introduction to Linguistic Anthropology*. 4th ed. Oxford, UK: Westview Press, 2007.

Schneider, J., L. Chavez, L. DeSipio, and Mary Waters. "Belonging." In *The Changing Face of World Cities: Young Adult Children of Immigrants in Europe and the United States*, edited by M. Crul and J. Mollenkopf, 206–33. New York: Russell Sage Foundation, 2012.

Schram, T. H. *Conceptualizing and Proposing Qualitative Research*. 2nd ed. Upper Saddle River NJ: Pearson Prentice Hall, 2006.

Sewell, William H. "A Theory of Structure: Duality, Agency, and Transformation." *American Journal of Sociology* 98, no. 1 (1992): 1–29.

Shank, G. D. *Qualitative Research: A Person Skills Approach*. 2nd ed. Upper Saddle River NJ: Pearson Prentice Hall, 2006.

Shaw-Taylor, Y., and S. Tuch, eds. *The Other African Americans: Contemporary African and Caribbean Immigrants in the United States*. Plymouth, UK: Rowman & Littlefield, 2007.

Shultz, J. "Caster Semenya and the 'Question of Too': Sex Testing in Elite Women's Sport and the Issue of Advantage." *Quest* 63, no. 2 (2011): 228–43.

——. "Reading the Catsuit: Serena Williams and the Production of Blackness at the 2002 U.S. Open." *Journal of Sport & Social Issues* 29, no. 3 (2005): 338–57.

Small, S. "Introduction: The Empire Strikes Back." In *Black Europe and the African Diaspora*, edited by D. Hine, T. Keaton, and S. Small, xxiii–xxxviii. Urbana: University of Illinois Press, 2009.

Smart, B. *The Sport Star: Modern Sport and the Cultural Economy of Sporting Celebrity*. London: Sage, 2005.

Solomos, J., B. Findlay, S. Jones, and P. Gilroy. "The Organic Crisis of British Capitalism and Race: The Experiences of the Seventies." In *The Empire Strikes Back: Race and Racism in 70s Britain*, edited by Centre for Contemporary Cultural Studies, 9–46. London: Hutchinson, 1982.

Stovall, T. "No Green Pastures: The African Americanization of France." In *Black Europe and the African Diaspora*, edited by D. Hine, T. Keaton, and S. Small, 180–200. Urbana: University of Illinois Press, 2009.

Summerfield, Hazel. "Patterns of Adaptation: Somali and Bangladeshi Women in Britain." In *Migrant Women: Crossing Boundaries and Changing Identities*, edited by G. Buijs, 83–98. Oxford, UK: Berg, 1993.

Thomas, D. *Black France: Colonialism, Immigration, and Transnationalism*. Bloomington: Indiana University Press, 2007.

Thornton, J. *Africa and Africans in the Making of the Atlantic World, 1400–1800*. New York: Cambridge University Press, 1998.

Trujillo, Nick. "Machines, Missiles, and Men: Images of the Male Body on ABC's *Monday Night Football*." *Sociology of Sport Journal* 12, no. 4 (1995): 403–23.

U.S. Department of Homeland Security, Office of Immigration Statistics. *2009 Yearbook of Immigration Statistics*. August 2010. http://www.dhs.gov/xlibrary/assets/statistics/yearbook/2009/ois_yb_2009.pdf.

Vasili, P. *Colouring over the White Line: The History of Black Footballers in Britain*. Edinburgh, UK: Mainstream, 2000.

Vertinsky, P., and G. Captain. "More Myth Than History: American Culture and Representations of the Black Female's Athletic Ability." *Journal of Sport History* 25, no. 3 (1998): 532–61.

Vickerman, M. *Crosscurrents: West Indian Immigrants and Race*. New York: Oxford University Press, 1999.

Walton, Theresa, and Ted Butryn. "Policing the Race: U.S. Men's Distance Running and the Crisis of Whiteness." *Sociology of Sport Journal* 23, no. 1 (2006): 1–28.

Waters, M. *Black Identities: West Indian Immigrant Dreams and American Realities*. New York: Russell Sage, 1999.

Whannel, G. *Media Sport Stars: Masculinities and Moralities*. London: Routledge, 2002.

Wilson, Wayne. "Wilma Rudolph: The Making of an Olympic Icon." In *Out of the Shadows: A Biographical History of African American Athletes*, edited by David K. Wiggins, 207–22. Fayetteville: University of Arkansas Press, 2006.

Winant, H. *The World Is a Ghetto: Race and Democracy since World War II*. New York: Basic Books, 2001.

Witherspoon, K. B. "Going 'to the Fountainhead': Black American Athletes as Cultural Ambassadors in Africa, 1970–1971." *International Journal of the History of Sport* 30, no. 13 (2013): 1508–22.

Wood, L., and R. Kroger. *Doing Discourse Analysis: Methods for Studying Action in Talk and Text*. Thousand Oaks CA: Sage, 2000.

Wright, M. *Becoming Black: Creating Identity in the African Diaspora*. Durham NC: Duke University Press, 2004.

———. "Pale by Comparison: Black Liberal Humanism and the Postwar Era in the African Diaspora." In *Black Europe and the African Diaspora*, edited by D. Hine, T. Keaton, and S. Small, 260–76. Urbana: University of Illinois Press, 2009.

———. *Physics of Blackness: Beyond the Middle Passage Epistemology*. Minneapolis: University of Minnesota Press, 2015.

INDEX

abandonment discourse, 52
Abdul-Jabbar, Kareem, 85, 159–61
Abdul-Rauf, Mahmoud, 147, 148, 150, 151, 153, 170–71
ability, discourses of, 57–59
Adu, Freddy, 43
Africa: African migrant athlete meaning to, xiv, 158, 162–67; aid to, 44, 74, 87, 90, 94; as backward and static, 69; civilizations in, 38; conflict and normalization of, 54; cultures of, 44; devaluation of, 75; development in, 41; dialects of, 75–76; diaspora of, 198; education decline in, 166; emigration from, 2; exoticism of, 60; as fixed in past, 154; identity of, 77, 130, 149, 154; independence movements in, 14; male-female relations in, 24, 67–69, 70–71; narratives about, 133–34; patriarchy in, 67, 69; problem-oriented focus on, 86–87, 96; references to, 195–96; remarginalization of, 61; representations of, 71, 132, 169, 177; slave trade participation of, 4; stereotypes of, xiii, 38, 44–45, 49, 52–53, 55, 58, 62, 71, 79–80, 145; underdevelopment in, 54–55, 74, 166; urban, 53, 54, 80; U.S. policy toward, 132–33; wars and warfare in, 78, 79; Western understandings of, 37, 48, 74, 94
"Africa for Africans" theme, 168
African American athletes: African athlete competition with, 158; attitude of,

toward Africans, 145; challenges of, 82–83; construction of, 27; diasporic, 158–62; exploitation of, 166; visibility of, 156, 157
African Americans: African admirers of, 22; African immigrants compared to, 3, 72, 80, 93; African migrant athletes compared to, 81, 82–83, 85, 86, 92, 93–94, 102, 145, 158; critique of, 72, 73; culture and cultural identity of, 4–5, 83; deaths of, 54; gender/sexuality politics and, 63; as internal blacks, 37; marginalization of, 117; and racism, 178; representation of, 86; status of, 33; successes of, 22, 43; as World War II veterans, 8
African American women, representations of, 63
African athletes, black, 39, 93, 95, 163–64
African athletes, black migrant: abuse and exploitation of, 15–16, 17, 19–21, 24–25, 97, 139, 166, 178; admirers of, 163–64; African Americans admired by, 158–62; African Americans compared to, 81, 82–83, 85, 86, 92, 93–94, 102, 145, 158; African athletes admired by, 163–64; attitudes toward, xiii, 40; backgrounds of, xiii, 74–78, 197–98; basketball camps backed by, 176; challenges and opportunities of, 15–18; at colleges and universities, 19–21; from colonies, 13–14; competition from, 158; conditional acceptance of, 96, 97, 103, 119; construction of, 51, 55; cultural resources

African athletes, black migrant (*cont.*)
provided by, 183; and diaspora, 167–79;
foreign status of, xii–xiii; history of struggle of, 72; humanitarian activities of, xiii,
165, 166; labeling of, 48, 49–52; marginalization of, 138; as "model minorities," 96;
national identities chosen by, 137–43, 144;
novelty reduced for, 184; political careers
rejected by, 165–66; in popular culture,
172–73; popularity of, 158; and racism, 138–
39; reception of, 124–25; recruitment of,
24; representations of, 1, 2, 3, 49–52, 54, 57,
73, 119–20, 153, 155, 158, 179–80, 184, 198–
99; research on, 27, 37; self-presentation of,
73, 81; sources on, 197; stereotypes about,
40, 44–45; transnational activities of, xi;
U.S. media coverage of, x–xi; war experiences of, 79
African countries: collapse of, 6; democracy in, 87; migrant athletes representing,
140–41; post-independence, 6, 93; processes toward, 184; representation of, xiii,
52–53; root causes of suffering in, 91–92;
underdeveloped, 6, 17; Western relationships with, 2, 15
African immigrants: African Americans
compared to, 3, 72, 80, 93; citizenship for,
6; definition of, 6–7; European communities of, 9–10; national identities chosen by, 137–43; nonathlete, 55, 94, 120,
166, 167–70; other immigrants compared
to, 81; visibility of, 27–28; Western relationships with, 2; white racist sentiments
toward, 103
African immigration to Europe, 3, 5, 7, 8–9,
11, 13–18, 97–98
African immigration to United States, 5,
6–7, 18–24
African immigration to West, xii, 3–11
African men, 24, 67, 69
Africans, black: bodies of, 40, 41, 44; civilizing missions aimed at, 13, 14, 16–17; construction of, 133; marginalization of, 117;
processes toward, 184; as refugees and
asylum seekers, 6, 10, 20, 86; representa-

tion of, 169, 177; self-help of, 45, 90; sta-
tus of, 33
African Union, 76
African women, 63–70
African women athletes, black: challenges
and opportunities of, 23–24; men in lives
of, 68–69; nicknames of, 62–63; and rac-
ism, 112–16; representations of, 49, 64–67
Afrobasket.com, 22
Against Race (Gilroy), 182
Agergaard, Sine, 18
Ali, Muhammad, 156, 159, 160, 209
Al-Qaida, 151–52
"Alt-Right," 187
"Amazing Athlete" theme, 64, 65
American colonies, slavery in, 4
"American Dream" immigrant story, 43,
60, 61
analytical memos, 198
Andrews, David, 157, 193
Antetokounmpo, Giannis, 20
antiblack immigration, 19–20
antiblack racism: components of, 96; dis-
courses of, 98–99, 123; global, 197; in
media, 110; "model minorities" versus,
105; naturalizing, 54; overview of, 3–4;
processes and logics of, 2, 182
anti-immigrant sentiment, 98
antiracism, politics of, 156
antiracist humanism, 179, 181, 182, 183, 184
apartheid, 7
Appiah, Kwame Anthony, 129, 130, 155
appropriation, discourses of, 41
Arabs, 10, 71
Asia, emigration from, 2
Asian Americans, 71, 73
Asian immigrants, 6
Asian Indians, 71
Asians, 71, 96
Asian women, stereotypes of, 73
Assou-Ekotto, Benoit, 139–40, 141, 142, 143
asylum, U.S. policies on, 134–35
athletes: as neoliberalism tool, 183–84; political constraints on, 183; representation of,
192; retirement challenges of, 92

"athleticism," 30, 35, 38, 39, 65
athletic labor migration: to Europe, 13–18; historic overview of, 3, 11–12; nonwhite domination of, 1; sport globalization and, 12–13; transnational approach to, xii; to United States, 18–24
authenticity discourses, 179, 180
authority, respect for, 73

Baartman, Saartjie, 112
Baldwin, James, 189–90
Bale, John, 12, 19, 23, 24, 40–41, 58–59
Ballack, Michael, 108
Balotelli, Mario: athletic ability of, 58; background of, 51–52, 71, 76–77, 169, 209–10; humanitarian activities of, 87, 174–75; immigrant reception experience of, 124; mental state of, 98, 110–11; national identity chosen by, 141; news sources on, xi, 197; and racism, 57, 109–12, 120, 141, 171–75, 183; representation of, 85–86, 105, 108, 121; same-generation athletes compared to, 125; songs about, 172–73
Bandura, Albert, 192
Bannister, Roger, 118
baseball, 21, 29, 71, 158
basketball, 16, 71, 170, 176–77; camps, 20–21, 22, 175, 176–77, 178; lifestyles of players of, 144–45; migration, 22–23; players, African, 19, 20, 21–23
Basketball without Borders camp, 21
Basuto tribe, "Kaffirs" of, 14
Belgian colonies, 13–14
Biafra, republic of, 77–78
Biamba Marie Mutombo Hospital and Research Center, 203
biracial children, 8
Birrell, Susan, 192–93
birth parents, abandonment by, 52
Biyombo, Bismack, 20
black African intellectuals, 129–30
black African migrants in China, 55–56, 57
black American Muslims, 147–48, 152–53
black athlete(s): and communication with media, 43–44; criticism of, 103–4; as cultural resource, 156–57; expectations of, 123; explanations of failure of, 41–43; explanations of success of, 38, 41; "foreign black athlete" versus, 37; and foreign/native coalition building, 175–79; formation of, 27–37, 38; mental state of, 109; mistreatment of, 139; political involvement of, 185; as racial trope, 45; representation of, xii, 27; sexual activities of, 36, 109, 116, 121; stereotypes of, 71; Western perceptions of, 37–38
black athleticism, 35, 38, 39, 65
black Atlantic, 155–56
Black British athletes, 27, 157
black communities: African American athlete meaning to, 156–57; African migrant athlete meaning to, 155; black athlete identification in, 157; coalition building between, 175–79; crackdown on, 102; in Europe, 7, 8, 9–11; immigrant, xiv, 1, 10, 48, 120, 124, 140, 167, 168–69; native, xiii, xiv, 3, 37, 74, 94, 158; political viewpoints harmful to, 38; and racism, 156; and violence, 185–86
black counterculture, 34
black criminality and violence, 95
black Europeans, 10–11, 33
black femininity, 116
black immigrants in Western societies: African Americans compared to, 80, 122–23; attitudes toward, 105–6; black Europeans differing from, 10–11; distancing selves from blackness, 184; identity construction of, 124; making sense of, 28; position of, xiii; and power and transnationality, 153
black immigration, 3, 5, 6–7, 13–24
#BlackLivesMatter movement, 9, 181, 185–86
black migrant athletes. See African athletes, black migrant
blackness: colonial fantasies about, 36; comparison of, in United States and Europe, 5; construction of, 27, 47, 106, 185; criminalization of, 174; definition of, 36; essentializing and exoticizing, 123, 180; as foreign, 37; formation and awareness of, 179; and

blackness (cont.)
gender issues, 120; historical representations of, 63; in Italy, 210; manipulations of, 37; marginalization of, xi, 119, 184; native blacks as representatives of, 184; popular image of, 45; processes toward, 184; pushing boundaries of, 32; reification of, 122–23; scholarly conversation on, 2; stereotypes of, 86, 109; stigmatization of, 54, 98, 101–2; transnational construction of, 155; understandings of, 48, 62; as whiteness antithesis, 38; white racist sentiments toward, 103

black Other(ness), foreign. *See* foreign black Otherness

blacks: beliefs in inferiority of, 111–12; as childlike figures, 106, 110; death of, 54; discrimination against, 3–4; diversity among, 185; in entertainment, 9; exclusion of, from modernity, 39; foreign, 10, 51, 76, 92, 93–94, 122–23; indifference to suffering of, 54, 96, 110; intellectual and mental capabilities of, 35; as objects of entertainment, 105–6; and politics, 49; self-governing abilities of, 133; shared experiences of, 178; stereotypes of, 102; and violence, 10

black unemployment, 96

black unity, 10

black women: as athletes, 37, 66, 98, 112; bodies of, 66, 112, 115; challenges of, 36–37; physical capabilities of, 116, 119; stereotypes of, 64. *See also* African women athletes, black

Bol, Manute, 202

Bono, 89, 90

Boston Marathon, 206

Botelho, Vera, 18

boundary making, xii, 72

Bourdieu, Pierre, 95

boxing, 32–33, 35, 39–40

Boy Scouts, 34

"brawn drain," 12, 20

The Brawn Drain (Bale), 23, 58–59

Brazil, 4, 174–75

Britain. *See* United Kingdom

British colonies, 13

British Nationality Act (1948), 8

Bryant, Kobe, 56, 156

Burns, Tommy, 32, 34

Butryn, Ted, 117

Cameroon, 139–40, 142

Campbell, A., 118–19

capitalism, 77, 185, 186

Caribbean, 4

Carrington, Ben, 27, 28, 31–32, 34, 35–36, 155, 157

celebrity, concept of, 194

celebrity athletes, xi–xii, 184, 193

celebrity industrial complex, 183–84

Chand, Dutee, 113, 114

charismatic prophet, 193–94

charitable giving, industry of, 132, 133–34

Chepchumba, Joyce, 117, 119

Chepyator-Tomson, Jepkorir, 23–24

Cheruiyot, Robert Kipkoech, 63

child and teenage immigrants, 137, 171, 206, 209

China, 56–57

Christian versus heathen dichotomy, 29

citizenship: attaining, xiv; and civil rights, 11; crossing boundaries through, 149; discussion of, xiii; hierarchies of, 137; performing, 192; statistics on, 22–23; utility of, 125–37

civilized versus savage dichotomy, 29

civil rights movement, 4–6, 7, 8

civil wars, 6

class, 180

Clinton, Hillary, 188

coalition building, 175–79, 180–81

Cold War, 49, 56, 161

Cole, Joe, 108

Cole, Teju, 90

Collins, Patricia Hill, 63

colonial education, 30

colonialism: and African civilizations, 38; and African masculinity, 67; black African beneficiaries of, 6; and black African immigration, 5; "black athlete" roots in, xii; discourse of, 123; and education decline, 166; in Europe, 9; European language spread through, 50, 76; ideology of, 111; legacy of, 133; nonwhites controlled through, 185; and race, 4, 93; and sport, 13–14, 15, 17, 28, 30; and stereotypes, 45; and white supremacy, 40; whitewashing of, 71

colonial natives, social control of, 30

colonial subjects, 45, 47, 111, 144, 182

colonized peoples, independence of, 188–89

color-blindness ideology: in Europe, 7–8, 10; narrative of, 77; norms of, 173; and racism, 43, 95, 111–12, 116; in United States, 95, 96; untenable nature of, 181; with white racial frame, 189

Commonwealth Immigrants Act (1962), 8

communism, 56, 188

Confederate flag, 186–87

conflict, perpetuating, 67

consumer freedom, 184

consumerism, 184

"conversionist fantasy," 41

Cookie Monster, 105, 107

corporate concerns, 89, 91

corruption, 6

counter discourses, 79–80, 95, 107

Counter Intelligence Program (COINTEL-PRO), 186

counternarrative, constructing, 153, 155

courage, white notions of, 38

Court of Arbitration for Sport, 114

cricket, 2, 13, 14, 30, 71, 143

crime, racial geography of, 94

criminal justice abuses, awareness of, 185–86

cultural attachment, 167–68

cultural criticism, 192

cultural heritage, 130

cultural identification, 194–95

culture and environment, 75

Darby, Paul, 16

Dare, Yinka, 120, 161

data triangulation, 198–99

death, discourses of, 54

democracy, 93, 156

Democratic Republic of Congo (Zaire):
African Americans in, 159; discussions concerning, 127; hospitals in, 87, 90–91, 131, 165, 203; languages spoken in, 76; representation of, 52–53, 54

Denison, Jim, 43–44

dependency, perpetuating, 67

development, hegemonic neoliberal notions of, 74

dialects, 50, 75–76, 84

diaspora, black: activities and experience in, 11; African athletes and, 167–79; athlete role in, 47; coalition building in, 180–81; and community "imagining," 22; identity construction in, 140; issues of, xiv; meaning making in, 171; migration circuits throughout, 186; obstacles to development of, 2; overview of, 155–58; safety issues in, 174–75

diasporic communities, 156, 179

diasporic processes, 179

Dibaba, Tirunesh, xi, 62–63, 68, 197, 207–8

Dikembe Mutombo Foundation, 91, 203

Dindane, Aruna, 88

discipline, 73

discourse, xiii–xiv, 41, 48, 50–51, 94–95, 191–92

disease, discourses of, 54

distance runners, African, 14–15, 20, 40–41, 75, 119, 136–37

distance running, 16–17, 19–20, 117

Dream Team III, 135

Drogba, Didier: advertising and marketing activities of, 136, 176; American basketball knowledge of, 162; antiracism campaign involvement of, 175; athletic ability of, 58; background of, 71, 137–39, 208–9; humanitarian activities of, 88–90, 165, 166; immigrant reception experience of, 124; mental state of, 98; migration of, to China, 55, 56; national identity chosen by, 137–39, 140, 141, 142–43; news sources on, xi, 197; nickname of, 59; political involvement rejected by, 166, 178–79, 183; and racism, 137–38; representation of, 85–86, 87, 89, 108, 111; same-generation athletes compared to, 125; as success model, 17, 161, 163, 164–65, 167

drug abuse, 102
Dubois, Laurent, 143
Du Bois, W. E. B., 34, 110

Eastern Europe, 10, 15, 25
economically marginalized communities, 170
economic gain, sport for, 166
economic inequality, 9
economic recessions, 98
economics, 154
education, sport overtaking, 166, 177
Egypt, 5
Embiid, Joel, 21
empire-states, 96
England, 5, 7, 8, 173
English language, 93
English-language news sources, 196–97
entertainment, blacks in, 9
environmental destruction, 187
environment and culture, 75
Essien, Michael, 108, 139
Ethiopia, 70–71, 208
ethnic isolation, ix–x
ethnocentrism, 188
eugenics, 33
Euro-America, racial schemas in, 46
Eurobasket, 22–23
Europe, 28–31, 57, 187
Europeans, identity of, 28–29
European soccer leagues, 2
European Union, 11, 15, 187
European versus non-European dichotomy, 29
Ewing, Patrick, 121, 127, 128, 176, 202
"exteriorization of the interior," 10
Ezeli, Festus, 20

Falcous, Mark, 13
family reunification, 5–6, 7, 134–35
Fanon, Frantz, 17, 123, 188
Farrakhan, Louis, 147, 152, 153
Fashanu, Justin, 121–22
fatherhood, 70
Federal Bureau of Investigation, 186
Ferguson MO, 95

field notes, 198
Findlay, Stephanie, 116
first-generation immigrants, 125
Fitch, Bill, 101
fitness, obsession with, 29
flexible citizenship, 125–26
Flora London Marathon, 65
Floyd, Sleepy, 101
football, 19, 20, 29, 79, 172, 205
A Football Life, 171
Foot Solidaire, 25
"foreign black athlete," 37, 45
foreign black Otherness: acceptance of, xiii;
and African athletes, 86; and American
values, 60; and colonial thinking, 41–42;
construction of, 37–45; discourses related
to, 81–82, 84–85, 154; emphasizing aspects
of, 50; exclusion of, 184; and global white
supremacy, 3; marginalization of, 120–21;
and native black Other, 180; as outsider,
71; and religious identity, 147; and second-
generation athletes, 51–52; and society
navigation, 153; and white supremacist
discourses, 45, 185
foreign/native separation, 3, 37
Foreman, George, 159
Foucault, Michel, 48, 191
France, 5, 7, 8, 10, 93, 187
French colonialism, 40
French colonies, 13–14
"front" or "front stage," 81

Garner, Eric, 54
gay athletes, 121–22
Gebrselassie, Haile, 44, 45
gender: African immigrant representation
and, 49; inequality, 67; policing of, 66–67;
politics of, 63; race and, 180, 183; women
athletes and, 112–16
generation 1.5 and 1.75 immigrants, 125, 137,
171, 206, 209
Gentry, Alvin, 178
geographies of sport, 2
German colonies, 7
Germany, 7–8, 93
Gerrard, Steven, 62, 108

Ghana, 16

ghettoization, 10

Gibson, Althea, 37, 85

Gilroy, Paul, 4, 97, 137, 144, 155–56, 179, 180, 182–83

global color line, 32–33

global competitions, 12

global economic structures, 39

global economy, 188–89

Global Fund to Fight AIDS, Tuberculosis, and Malaria, 89

globalization, 6, 12–13, 22, 125

globalized world, workings of, 184

global South, 157–58

global sport, 1, 39, 189

global white supremacy. See white supremacy ideology

Goffman, Erving, 81

"good blacks," 94

"good black" versus "bad black" dichotomy, 83

"good" businessman, stereotype of, 44–45

"good" immigrant, 81–82, 92–93

good versus bad subject dichotomy, 37

Gordon, April, 5

Gordon, Lewis, 123, 155

"great white hope," 34, 62, 117–19

group identity, 129–30

Hali, Tamba: athletic ability of, 58; background of, 55, 76, 79, 205–6; news sources on, xi, 197; nickname of, 59; representation of, 81–82; U.S. citizenship of, 134, 135

Hall, Stuart, 130, 154, 155, 182

Hamas, 151–52

hard work, discourse of, 88, 93

"hard workers and friendly faces" theme, 80–86

Hart-Celler Immigration Act (1965), 5–6

heathens, civilizing, 30

Hedges, Michael, 151, 152

hegemonic discourses, 51, 191–92

hegemonic socio-political geographies, 49

hegemony, 96, 153

heteronormativity, 66, 112–13, 121

heterosexism, 187

High Altitude Training Centre (HATC), 68

higher education, African, 98

hip-hop culture, 83, 102, 173

Hitler, Adolf, 8

HIV/AIDS, 87, 89, 132, 176, 177

Hoberman, John, 38, 39, 40

home country, xiv, 158, 162–63, 165, 169

homosexuality, 121–22

host countries, 1, 97–98, 124–25, 136

Houston Rockets, 100, 131, 144, 196, 202

Hrabosky, Al, 61

human development, obstacles to, 187

humanitarian narratives, 73–74, 86–93, 96

humanity, 156, 189

human trafficking, 21, 25, 178

Hungarian immigrants to United States, 61–62

hyperindividualism, 184, 194

hypersexual criminal threat, trope of, 110

Ibaka, Serge, 20

idealization, discourses of, 41

identity formation, x, 140, 155

immigrants: distrust of, 143–44; identity construction of, 124, 125; national allegiance tests of, 143; reception of, xii, xiii, 124–25; sports participation by, 1; staying versus returning, 130

immigration, 3–4, 48, 153

Immigration Act (1990), 6

Immigration Act (United Kingdom, 1968), 8

Immigration Act (United Kingdom, 1971), 7, 8–9

immigration policies, Western, xii, 98

Immigration Reform and Control Act (1986), 6

imperialism, xii, 29, 30, 34, 71

Indigenous populations, Australian, 71

individualism, 184, 194

inherited traits, 46

innocence, trope of, 76

"interiorization of the exterior," 10

International Association of Athletics Federations (IAAF), 113, 114, 115

International Basketball Federation (FIBA), 175, 176

International Federation of Association Football (FIFA), 15, 16, 24–25, 57
International Monetary Fund (IMF), 87, 188–89
International Olympic Committee (IOC), 113, 115
international player transfers, 24–25
international sports organizations, 12
intersectionality, 63, 64
intersexuality, 113, 114, 115, 116
invisibility, 9, 10
Islam: beliefs concerning "proper," 146; conversion to, 161; foreign status of, 170; religious identity through, 125; representation of, 148, 151, 152; stereotypes of, 147, 151; terrorism associated with, 143, 151–52; translational character of, 135; white attitudes concerning, 152–53
"Islamic" terrorism, war against, 143
Islamophobia, 10
Italy, 76–77, 210
Iton, Richard, 185
Ivory Coast: athletes from, 141, 142, 208–9; civil war in, 87, 209; humanitarian activities in, 88; identification with, 137, 138, 139, 167–68; popular figures in, 88–89, 164–65; representation of, 52–53

Jackson, Steven, 103, 157, 193
Jackson County NC, ix
James, Lebron, 56, 156
Jeffries, Jim, 32, 34, 62
Jim Crow, 7, 32, 33, 36
jingoism, 33, 79, 189
Johnson, Ben, 103
Johnson, Jack, 32, 33, 34, 36, 39, 83, 156, 160
Johnson, "Magic," 202
Johnson, Weldon, 118–19
Jordan, Michael, 22, 83, 85, 104, 156, 202, 207, 209
Jozwik, Joanna, 115–16
Jung, Moon-Kie, 45, 46–47, 95–96
justice, Western notions of, 156

Kalenjin, 68, 203–4
Kalou, Solomon, 139, 167
Kanouté, Frédéric, 138, 178–79, 183

Kansas City Chiefs, 58, 205
Karkazis, Katrina, 114
Kastor, Deena, 117
Keino, Kipchoge, 14, 40–41
Kenya: aid to, 87; athlete underdevelopment in, 20; college and university athletes from, 19; distance runners from, 14, 16–17, 20, 203–4, 206–7; languages spoken in, 76; representation of, 52–53, 68–69; women athletes from, 23–24, 67–69, 203–4
Kikongo language, 76
Kikuyu, 206
Kim, Claire, 72–73
Kimondiu, Ben, 119
Kiplagat, Lornah, 68, 119, 137, 173
knowledge, production of, 191
Kone, Arouna, 90, 164
Kristiansen, Ingrid, 117–18
Künzler, Daniel, 88, 165
Kusz, Kyle, 43
Kyenge, Cecile, 172

labeling processes, 48, 49–52, 71
Lagos, Nigeria, 53, 55, 79
Lampard, Frank, 108, 109
Lanfranchi, Pierre, 17–18
language(s), 49, 50, 51, 75–76, 191
Latin America, 2, 21, 25
Latin Americans in soccer clubs, 15
Latinbasket.com, 22
Latino immigrants, 6
Latinos, 71, 96, 158
leisure, rise in, 29
Lewis, Guy, 99
Liberia, 6, 52–53, 55, 77, 78
Lingala language, 76
Logan, John, 6–7
London Marathon, 117–18
Loroupe, Tegla: African patriarchy opposed by, 183; background of, 74–75, 203–4; devaluing of accomplishments of, 119; and gender issues, 66–67, 112; humanitarian activities of, 87; news sources on, xi, 197; relationships of, with men, 68; representation of, 64–67, 85, 98; as success model, 163; world record set by, 117, 118, 119

Los Angeles Sparks, 207
Louis, Joe, 36, 83, 156
Luba-Kasai language, 76
Lukaku, Romelu, 161, 164

Mabika, Mwadi, xi, 54–55, 162, 197, 207, 208
MacMullan, Jackie, 102–3
Magdalinski, Tara, 41–42
Maguire, Joseph, 12, 13
Maina, Anthony, 69
Maiyoro, Nyandika, 14, 40–41
Makelele, Claude, 108
Malcolm X, 148
male supremacy, 114–15
Mangan, James, 29–30
marginalization, 9, 10
marginalized groups, 95
marginalized peoples, 184, 185
Markula, Pirrko, 43–44
Marshall, P. David, 194
masculinity: African, 67, 121, 122; black, 36, 37, 84, 122; global crisis of, 84; hegemonic, 121, 122; militant, 29–30, 33–34; white, 38
Mazur, C., 157
Mbah a Moute, Luc, 21, 175–76
M'Barick, Amadou "Battling Siki," 39–40
McAdoo, Bob, 178
McClintock, Anne, 31–32
McDonald, Mary, 192–93
media, social impact of, 192
media imagery, racist, 9
migration pipelines, 71
militarism, 29, 30, 188
Million Man March, 152
Mills, Charles, 29, 46, 59, 155
mind versus body dichotomy, 35
misogyny, 71, 121
"model minorities": antiblack cynicism toward, 105; athletes constructed as, 51, 54, 83, 96, 98; black African immigrants as, 97; fear of, 84; overview of, 72–74
"modernity" versus "tradition" dichotomy, 31
morality, 29, 135
motherhood, 69–70
Mourning, Alonzo, 126, 128, 176

Moussambani, Eric, 41–43
Mudiay, Emmanuel, 20
multiculturalism, 7, 182
muscular Christianity, 29, 33–34
music, sports themes in, 172–73
Muslim Arab Youth Association, 151
Muslims: black American, 147–48, 152–53; Hakeem Olajuwon's meaning to, 152; and power relations, 135; and racism and discrimination, 10; and role models, 170–71; stereotypes of, 147, 151; and violence, 152, 170
Mutombo, Dikembe: advertising and marketing activities of, 173; on Africa, 154, 183; age of, 106; athletic ability of, 58; background of, 202–3; coalition building activities of, 175; counterdiscourse of, 107; criticism of, 98, 103; and Hakeem Olajuwon, 149; humanitarian activities of, 90–93, 104, 128, 131–34, 149, 165, 166, 176, 177, 203; immigrant reception experience of, 124; language knowledge of, 49, 75, 93, 104–5, 107; mental ability and temperament of, 104–8; and Muhammad Ali, 159, 160, 162; name of, 49, 50, 106; news sources on, xi, 197; pan-African identity of, 128, 129; and Patrick Ewing, 128; political career rejected by, 165–66; representation of, 49, 62, 75, 81, 82, 83, 87, 92, 104–8; sexual activities of, 121; stereotypes of, 71; as success model, 162, 163–64, 168; travels of, 178; U.S. citizenship of, 128–29, 130–31; on U.S. foreign policy, 132–33
Mutombo, Ilo, 163

naiveté, 74–75, 76
narrative, constructing, 199
nation, race link to, 51–52, 183
National Basketball Association (NBA): Africans in, x, 85, 92; basketball camps sponsored by, 21, 175; education programs sponsored by, 177; historical context of, 101–2; products promoted by, 176; recruiting by, 20; as "too black," 99, 102; "trash talking" in, 144–45
national boundaries, 48, 137

National Collegiate Athletic Association (NCAA), 19–20, 21
national identity, 120, 129–30, 137–44
nationalism, xii, xiii, 46, 51, 143
nationality, 48, 49, 50
national origin, 120
national teams, African, 17, 20–21
national teams, European, 13–14
Nation of Islam (NOI), 146, 147–48, 152–53
nation-states, xii, 37, 49, 125, 157
native black athletes, 81, 82, 94
native blacks: blackness represented by, 185; foreign blacks distinguished from, 51, 76, 92, 93–94, 122–23; as Other, 180; politics of, 49; and racism and discrimination, 10, 11; stereotypes of, 86
native sport, destruction of, 12, 13
natural disasters, 6
naturalization, 130, 153
Nauright, John, 41–42
Ndereba, Catherine: abilities of, 119; background of, 74–75, 206–7; contemporaries of, 68; humanitarian activities of, 87; marriage and motherhood of, 69–70, 206; media focus on, 117; news sources on, xi, 197; nickname of, 62; religious identity of, 151; representation of, 98; as success model, 163
negation, discourses of, 41
Negritude, 34, 36
"negro problem," 110
neocolonialism, 9, 17, 40–41, 87, 188
neofascist organizations, 11
neoliberal order: antiracist humanism versus, 181; athletes serving needs of, 184; conflict perpetuated by, 67; dangers posed by, 187; development programs of, 98; domination of, 185; impacts of, 84; individual achievement in, 93; Islam and, 153; migrant reinforcement of, 136; need to combat, 91; practices of, 156; preservation of, 89; white supremacy link to, 77
New York City Marathon, 85, 204
nicknames, 48–49, 59–63
Nigeria: athletes from, 19, 23, 150, 171; and

gender issues, 116; post–civil war, 77–78; remarginalization of, 61; representation of, 52–53, 79–80
Nigerians, 53–54, 58, 59–60, 62, 102
Nimphius, Kurt, 100
Niyonsaba, Francine, 115
"noble savage," 42, 43, 51, 62, 76, 82
non-Europeans, 29, 30, 31
nonwhite Other, 33, 187, 190
nonwhites, 2–3, 34, 180, 185, 190

Oathkeepers, 95
Obama, Barack, 168–69, 188
Okoye, Christian: athletic ability of, 50, 58; background of, 77–78, 205, 206; films about, 171; news sources on, xi, 197; nickname of, 58, 59–60
Olajuwon, Hakeem: advertising and marketing activities of, 135, 136, 173; athletic ability of, 58; background of, 53–54, 75, 79–80, 81, 144–45, 201–2; humanitarian activities of, 87; on identity and belonging, 130; immigrant reception experience of, 124; interpersonal and legal troubles of, 98, 100–103, 146–47; and Kareem Abdul-Jabbar, 159–61, 162; language knowledge of, 84; as Muslim, 125, 135, 144, 146–48, 149–50, 151–52, 153, 170, 202; national identity chosen by, 145–46; news sources on, xi; nickname of, 59, 60–61; and racism, 146; recruitment of, 23; religious discourse of, 183; representation of, 62, 83, 84–85, 99; stereotypes of, 71; as success model, 161, 162, 163–64, 170–71; U.S. citizenship of, 60, 84, 128–29, 134, 135, 144, 148–49; and violence, 98, 99–100; worldview of, 135–36; and Yinka Dare, 120
Olympics, 12, 41, 42, 135
Omi, Michael, 31
O'Neal, Shaquille, 104, 106, 175
Ong, Aihwa, 125–26
oppression, 156, 179–80
Orientalism, discourse of, 48, 76
origin stories, 72, 74–80, 93
Other: civilizing needed by, 42; comfortableness with, 182; contempt for, 33; cre-

ation of, 180; diasporic processes hidden from, 179; inferiority association of, 2; nonpersonhood of, 29; problems blamed on, 188; representation of, xii

Othering: antiblack racism as, 96; duality of colonial, 152; examples of, 57; and foreign versus native blacks, 76; and gender differences, 64; intraethnic, 3, 10; kinds of, 49; norm violation resulting in, 108–9; and objects of entertainment, 106; processes of, xii, 49; stereotypical forms of, 72; by Western media, 71

Owens, Jesse, 83, 156

Owens, Terrell, 43

pacemakers, 117–19

Palestinian issues, 178–79, 183, 186

pan-Africanism, x, 129, 130, 149–50

Patton, Michael, 195

Paultz, Billy, 99–100

peoples of color, 156, 189

Philadelphia, 168

Philadelphia Seventy-Sixers, 21

planetary humanism, 182

"planetary humanity," 156

Pokot, 68, 203–4

Poli, Raffaele, 15, 88, 165

political conflict, discourses of, 54

political correctness, 186

political instability, 6

political left, 186

Portuguese colonies, 13–14

postmodernity, 156

postracial society, myth of, 43

"post-truth" era, 189

poverty, 5, 16, 22, 54, 67, 157, 177

Powell, Enoch, 8

power, nexus of, 192–93

power relations, xi–xii

race: antiracism politics and, 156; black athletes and, 86; colonialism and, 4, 93; concept of, 46, 179; consciousness of, 179; economic marginalization and, 186; in Europe and United States, 40; gender issues and, 115–16, 183; hegemonic notions

of, 143; immigrant identity and, 124; labeling and, 49; modern conceptions of, 27; mutated idea of, 4; nation link to, 51–52, 183; naturalizing and dehistoricizing of, 154; production and formation of, 47; rethinking of, 182–83; sport and, 1–2, 32; Western attitudes concerning, xi, 93, 94; Western military interventions and, 133

Race, Sport and Politics (Carrington), 28

racial awareness, 7–8

racial boundaries, 48, 157

racial demographic shift, 185

racial formation, theories of, 31

racial inequality, 96

racialization, 9–10

racialized religions, 156

racial project, 31

racial science, 35, 38

racial unity, 156

racism: discursive practices of, 1–2; dismantling of, 187; in Europe, 7–8, 9, 10, 40, 173; experiences of, xii, 91, 178; forms of, 95; immigrant identity and, 124; immigration policies and, xii, 5; at international level, 46–47; in Italy, 76–77; marginalized impact of, 76; mutations in, 4; nationalisms and, 135; neoliberal, 43, 45; perceived end of, xiv; production and formation of, 47; recognizing and resolving, 190; schemas of, 45–46; scientific, 31–32; sport and, 1–2, 32; struggle against, 11, 156; transnational nature of, 46–47; in United States, 127, 145, 178; Western military interventions and, 133. *See also* antiblack racism

Radcliffe, Paula, 70, 117, 118, 119

radicalization, 84

Ralph, Michael, 22

rap music, 173

"Reading Sport Critically" (McDonald and Birrell), 192–93

Reagan-era politics, 101–2

record keeping, 106–7

Refugee Act (1980), 6

refugees, 6, 10

Reid, Robert, 100

religious identity, 120, 125, 144–53
remarginalization process, 24, 60–61
representations, 124–25
Rice, Tamir, 54
right, Western notions of, 156
right-wing political movements, xiv, 187
Rodman, Dennis, 121, 150
role model policing, 170–71
Rudolph, Wilma, 37, 64
rugby, 29, 33, 71, 184
Runstedtler, Theresa, 32–33, 34, 39

Said, Edward, 48, 76, 155, 188
Salzmann, Zdenek, 50
sampling, 195
schemas, 45–46
scientific journalism, 40
scientific racism, 31–32
Scott, Walter, 54
second-generation athletes: African ath-
    letes admired by, 161, 171; basketball camps
    backed by, 176; and citizenship and integra-
    tion issues, 137, 210; divisions blurred by, 184–
    85; in football, 205; origin stories of, 76–77;
    reception of, 77, 125; representation of, 51–52
segregation: addressing problems of, 180;
    "black athlete" roots in, xii; crime geogra-
    phy and, 94; experiences of, 159; legal end
    of, 34; visibility and, 168; white suprem-
    acy and, 33
"selective breeding," 38
self-determination, 34
self-segregation, 138, 140, 146, 152
Semenya, Caster, 67, 112–13, 114, 115, 116
Senegal, 22
sexism, 24
sexuality, 63, 180
Sharp, Lynsey, 115–16
Shultz, Jaime, 115
slavery and slave trade, xii, 4, 6, 9, 27, 38, 185
soccer: academies, 16; basketball conditions
    compared to, 22; Chinese, 57; clubs, 15,
    17, 97, 139; dreams of, 16, 88; leagues, 13–
    14; players, African, 13–14, 15–18, 25; play-
    ers, South American, 71; teams, 143; U.S.
    media coverage of, x–xi

social change, 182
social Darwinism, 29, 33
social justice movement, 185–86
social learning theory, 192
social reality, 192
social welfare programs, 98, 102
society values, 48
Solberg, Eirik, 16
Soundarajan, Santhi, 113, 115
South Africa, 5, 7, 178
sport: African immigrant visibility through,
    27–28; African immigration for, xii; apo-
    litical ideology versus reality in, 1, 31;
    black participation in, ix–x, 9; capital-
    ist conception of, 17; celebrities in, 194–
    95; character-building in, 35; clubs and
    associations in, 12; context outside of, 71;
    corruption and exploitation in, 25; criti-
    cal reading of, 192–93; culture of, 28, 104;
    development of modern, 28, 29–31; glo-
    balization of, 12–13; immigrant recogni-
    tion in, 1; male domination in, 65
"sporting black Atlantic," 157
"sporting Black Diaspora," 155
sporting negritude, 36
Sports Illustrated, 53, 54
Sqwad, Ruff, 172
Starr, Alexandra, 21, 25
stereotyping. *See under specific subjects*
sterilization, forced, 33
Sterling, Scotty, 99–100
Stryder, Tinchy, 172
sub-Saharan Africa, 5, 6, 30
Sunni Islam, 144, 146
surveillance, discourses of, 41
Swahili language, 76
"symbolic coercion," 95

Takahashi, Naoko, 118
Tanzania, 76
Taylor, Matthew, 17–18
Tebbit, Norman, 143
technological advancement, 39, 42, 75, 84
Tegla Loroupe Peace Academy, 87, 204
Tergat, Paul, 119
terrorism, 143, 151–52

Terry, John, 108, 109
Thatcher, Margaret, 8
theme-building process, 198
"thick" description, 195
Third World countries, immigrants from, 56
Thompson, John, 82, 126, 128, 203
Touré, Kolo, 88
track and field athletes, African, 19, 20, 24, 113
transgressive politics, 154
transnational athletes, 13, 199
transnational blackness, xiv, 11
transnational corporations, 89
transnational identities, 29, 157
tribal languages, 49, 50
Trump, Donald, 187
Tulu, Derartu, 70–71
Tyson, Mike, 147

Uganda, 76
Union of European Football Associations (UEFA), 175
United Kingdom, 7, 8–9, 14, 93, 143, 173, 187
United States, 3, 5–6, 7, 61, 93, 132–35
"Untethered Mote" theme, 64, 65–66
USbasket.com, 22
U.S. goodwill tours, 85
U.S. national anthem, refusal to stand for, 147
U.S. presidential election (2016), 189

Walter-McCarran Immigration Act (1952), 5
Walton, Theresa, 117
Wambui, Margaret, 115
war, 77–78, 79, 154
Washington, Ora, 37
Weber, Max, 193–94
welfare fraud, 102, 106
West: African country relations with, 2, 15; African immigrant relationship with, 2, 91; African immigration to, 3, 4–11; African migrant athlete acceptance into, 72; African sentiments toward, xiv; as Africa's benefactor, xiii; charity discourses of, 183; China compared to, 56–57; critique of notions of, 156; cultural values of, 194;

definition of, 195; and economic inequality, 9; exceptionalism of, 24, 134; global conquest by, 45; hegemonic discourses of, 122; Italy compared to, 76; and loss through modernity, 42, 75; media of, 1, 28, 48, 55, 77–78, 79, 81, 93, 96, 169, 173; military interventions of, 133; nation-states of, 45; neoliberal democracy of, 88; and perceptions of Africa, 37; postfeminism of, 24, 67, 70; post-9/11 nationalist discourse of, 153–54; progress narrative of, 57, 59; race as seen by, xi; racial and ethnic diversity of, 184–85; racial inequality in, 96; racism in, xii, xiv; and religious identity, 150; right-wing political movements in, xiv; self-aggrandizement of, 94; supremacy of, 55, 130; as war-making power, 79
Western Africa, 4, 15–16
Western colonialism. See colonialism
Western Europe, 25
Westernization, lack of, 86
West Indies, 5
West versus Africa dichotomy, 42, 75, 85, 88
When We Were Kings, 159
white African immigration to United States, 5
white America, black critique of, 152–53
white athletes, 61–62, 90, 117–19, 123
white ethnic groups, 61–62
white European immigrants, 6
white humanitarian activities, 90
"white man's burden," 34, 52, 165
whiteness, 2, 32, 36, 38, 190
white press corps, 43–44
white race, 29, 33
whites, 10, 119, 186, 189–90
"White-Savior Industrial Complex," 52, 90, 91, 134, 165, 166
white supremacy ideology: blackness definition and, 36; colonialism and, 40; discourses of, 181, 185; in Europe, 33, 187; expectations and norms of, 45, 111; fight against, 32, 34–35, 157, 159, 174–75; global nature of, 46, 77; mainstreaming of, 187; maintaining, 186; male supremacy and, 33, 37, 38; "model minorities" and, 73; non

white supremacy ideology (*cont.*)
   white knowledge rejected by, 190; overview of, 27; processes and logics of, 2; role
   model policing in, 171; science as basis for,
   33; transnational development of, xii; U.S.
   goodwill tours and, 85; victories against,
   34; workings of, 3
white versus nonwhite dichotomy, 29
white women athletes, 66, 115–16
"Why Always Me?" (song), 172–73
Williams, Serena, 65, 112, 115
Williams, Venus, 112
Winant, Howard, 31, 181
"woman," definition of, 114, 115
women: as athletes, 18, 37, 63, 66, 98, 112,
   117–19; marginalization of sports of, 18;
   media attention paid to, 197; potential and

capabilities of, 67; sport labor migration
for, 23–24; world records of, 117
work ethic, 81–82, 88, 94
World Bank, 87, 188–89
World Cup, 12, 88–89, 136, 174, 209
World Junior Cross Country Champion-
ships, 24
World War I, 34, 39
World War II, 8, 87
Wright, Michelle, 57, 155, 180

Yeboah, Anthony, 40
young men, social control of, 30
Young Men's Christian Association (YMCA), 34

Zaha, Wilfried, 141, 142–43
Zaire. *See* Democratic Republic of Congo
(Zaire)

IN THE SPORTS, MEDIA, AND SOCIETY SERIES:

The Black Migrant Athlete: Media, Race, and the Diaspora in Sports
Munene Franjo Mwaniki

To order or obtain more information on these or other University of Nebraska Press
titles, visit nebraskapress.unl.edu.

www.ingramcontent.com/pod-product-compliance
Lightning Source LLC
Chambersburg PA
CBHW051723260326
41914CB00031B/1705/J